OXFORD MONOGRAPHS ON MUSIC

THE FINALE IN WESTERN INSTRUMENTAL MUSIC

# The Finale in Western Instrumental Music

*ন্ঠ ৪ঠ*

MICHAEL TALBOT

**OXFORD**

UNIVERSITY PRESS

# OXFORD

UNIVERSITY PRESS

Great Clarendon Street, Oxford OX2 6DP
Oxford University Press is a department of the University of Oxford.
It furthers the University's objective of excellence in research, scholarship,
and education by publishing worldwide in

Oxford New York

Athens Auckland Bangkok Bogotá Buenos Aires
Cape Town Chennai Dar es Salaam Delhi Florence Hong Kong Istanbul
Karachi Kolkata Kuala Lumpur Madrid Melbourne Mexico City Mumbai
Nairobi Paris São Paulo Shanghai Singapore Taipei Tokyo Toronto Warsaw

and associated companies in Berlin Ibadan

Oxford is a registered trade mark of Oxford University Press
in the UK and certain other countries

Published in the United States
by Oxford University Press Inc., New York

© Michael Talbot 2001

The moral rights of the author have been asserted
Database right Oxford University Press (maker)

First published 2001

British Library Cataloguing in Publication Data

Data available

Library of Congress Cataloging in Publication Data
Talbot, Michael.
The finale in western instrumental music / Michael Talbot.
p. cm.—(Oxford monographs on music)
Includes bibliographical references and indexes.
1. Finales (Music)—History and criticism. 2. Musical form. 3. Music—Philosophy and aesthetics.
I. Title. II. Series.
ML448 .T25 2001    784.18—dc21    2001016287
ISBN 0-19-816695-8

1 3 5 7 9 10 8 6 4 2

Typeset in Palatino by Kolam Information Services Pvt. Ltd,
Pondicherry, India
Printed in Great Britain
on acid-free paper by
Biddles Ltd., Guildford & King's Lynn

# PREFACE

As ONE grows older and one's academic routine, however frenetic, runs along familiar grooves, one hankers after small luxuries. In my own case, the luxury takes the form of a first opportunity to step outside the comfortable prison represented by the speciality within musicology for which I am best known: the music of the Italian Baroque.

German scholars usually have to work in at least two distinct areas before they are deemed fully qualified as musicologists. Oddly enough, we British, for all our reputation as all-rounders, do not. The result is that many of us find our one and only niche early on and remain buried in it until retirement.

I have been lucky to work in a university department of music, at Liverpool, where the subjects on offer and the colleagues who teach them are very diverse, and where, if only because of staff shortage, nearly all of us have to lecture or give classes 'out of area'. On the teaching front, at least, we are rarely allowed to forget our origin as generalists.

The present book is the fruit of thoughts that have built up over many years in the course of teaching the history of the music of many different periods. It would be untrue to say that my main speciality is entirely excluded from its content, but it remains at the margin, leaving other repertories and discourses to take centre-stage.

Naturally, an extraordinary (even if still inadequate) amount of preparatory reading and listening needs to be done before one is in a position to enter new territory, particularly when the subject is as unusually broad as the one I have chosen. I have been both lucky and unlucky in that the finale as a concept and practice in Western art music has, it seems, escaped earlier coverage in this amount of detail. Lucky, because it is easier to be original when one has few predecessors. Unlucky, because it is harder in those circumstances to winkle out the material forming the substructure of existing knowledge on which a musicologist always has to build. There always lurks an awareness, or at least a nagging suspicion, that round the corner there is a book or article that one ought to read but never will until it is too late. (This is an appropriate point at which to make apology to all those who have anticipated arguments that I shall innocently be advancing as original in these pages.)

My aim has been to write a book that is scholarly in the wider sense rather than academic in the narrower sense. I do not shirk footnotes, technical terms (in moderation, and explained where necessary), or the occasional foreign expression, but I have nevertheless done my best to produce a text that will be readable not only by other musicologists and their students but also by composers, performers, and music-lovers of all kinds. Unusually, perhaps, the tables will be as easy to comprehend as the surrounding words—at least, that is my intention. And there are plenty of music examples that, while not necessarily more eloquent than my words, make many of the same points in an alternative way that may sometimes prove more effective. I remain conscious that there is much more to say on the subject and apologize in advance to those whose favourite composers and works I fail to mention or to do full justice to.

This venture would have been impossible without taking time out from normal duties and activities. For the opportunity to do so, I have to thank the Arts and Humanities Research Board, whose Research Leave Scheme funded my study during the first semester of the session 1998–99, and the University of Liverpool for funding my leave during the second semester. Many distractions prevented this work from coming to fruition as soon as I would have liked, and I am especially grateful to my editor at Oxford University Press, Helen Peres da Costa, for her patience, interest, and technical advice.

Other people I have to thank are David Fanning, who read and commented on my last chapter, and my colleague John Williamson, for whose exceptionally wide and deep knowledge of the music of the nineteenth and twentieth centuries I have good reason to be thankful. Bonnie Blackburn gave me valuable advice on Renaissance music. I also thank the publishers whose names appear in the List of Musical Examples for their permission to reproduce extracts from music of which they hold the copyright.

I dedicate this book to the staff and students of the Department of Music at the University of Liverpool. Our long ride together has been more often smooth than bumpy, and so may it continue.

M.T.

*Liverpool*
*November 2000*

# CONTENTS

# LIST OF TABLES

# LIST OF MUSICAL EXAMPLES

# 1

# *First Thoughts*

IN HIS *School of Practical Composition* Carl Czerny endeavoured to demonstrate how the finale of a sonata might suitably differ from its first movement.[1] He begins with an affirmation that despite their possible similarity of tempo and temper, the character of their respective opening themes ought to be different.

We have already observed that the commencement of the *first* movement of a Sonata may be either energetic, or melodious; excited, or soft and tranquil. The same may be said of the Rondo or Finale; but there must be a palpable difference between the two, in regard to the description of the leading idea: for rarely would a suitable commencement for a first movement, serve also for the theme of a Finale.

'Palpable' the difference may indeed be, but for its elucidation Czerny trusts more to musical notes than to any prose description. He continues:

It is not easy to render this difference intelligible by words. In all cases the beginning of the first movement must possess a distinctive character, and be either broader, more noble, or more tranquil. As this can be explained most clearly by examples, we here place the themes of the first movements and of the Finales of several Sonatas opposite one another.

There follows, in a two-column arrangement, a procession of incipits of the first and last movements of twelve piano sonatas. Four are by Czerny's former teacher Beethoven (Op. 10 No. 1 in C minor, Op. 22 in B flat major, Op. 31 No. 3 in E flat major, and Op. 53 in C major), two by Mozart (K. 309/284b in C major and 310/300d in A minor), and one each by Haydn (Hob. XVI/52 in E flat major), Clementi (Op. 25 No. 4), Dussek (Op. 9 No. 3), Steibelt, Cramer (Op. 29 No. 1), and Hummel (Op. 81).[2]

Having, as he believes, made his point, Czerny concludes his introduction:

---

[1] Czerny's *School of Practical Composition or Complete Treatise on the Composition of All Kinds of Music both Vocal and Instrumental from the most simple Theme to the Grand Sonata and Symphony and from the shortest Song to the Opera, the Mass, and the Oratorio: together with a Treatise on Instrumentation* (at this point we will cut the title short) was published in three volumes c.1848 by Robert Cocks in London. It was translated from the German-language original by John Bishop. The extracts quoted here appear on pp. 67–9 of the first volume at the head of the tenth chapter, entitled: 'Of the Rondo or Finale as the Fourth Movement of the Sonata'.

[2] For a table listing and identifying the sonatas, see Malcolm Cole, 'Czerny's Illustrated Description of the Rondo or Finale', *Music Review*, 36 (1975), 5–16 at 7. Cole devotes most of his article to a study of the twelve rondo movements and their relevance as paradigmatic examples of the form.

Every one will perceive the great difference between the beginnings of these first movements and of the Finales; and as each young composer is doubtless acquainted with all the Sonatas of the masters here named—for who can expect to become a composer, without having studied all the good works of his predecessors?—he will find that the Finale, in its way, must be as strictly and carefully written, as the other movements of the Sonata, and that it is only in the construction and the ideas that a sensible difference lies.

Because the rondo is the form par excellence used for final movements, and because its typical character and structural properties accord perfectly with those thought desirable in a sonata finale of the early nineteenth century, Czerny comes close to equating the concepts 'rondo' and 'finale'.[3] But he is well aware that finale character can exist even when the same sonata form used for the first movement is adopted. Later in the chapter he remarks:

The proper Finale of a Sonata (and consequently of each similar work, such as a Trio, Quartett, Symphony &c.) is of precisely the same construction as the *first movement*, and differs only in containing more lively and animated, and less broad and noble ideas and passages. At all times it can be more sprightly and exciting, than the first movement.[4]

One sympathizes with Czerny's reluctance to go beyond broad generalities in his verbal descriptions. Finale character, which takes different forms in different ages (and sometimes also in the same age), is not so easy to pin down with precision. Part of the problem is that it is multifactorial: it depends on no single element considered in isolation. The main obstacle, however, is that it is something so traditional that it is largely unspoken, simply imprinted on the memory and consciousness of composers and listeners alike. And while it may be an exaggeration to claim that there is something instinctive in the common perception of finale character, the position of the finale, by definition, as the last part of a multimovement work to be heard before it ends inevitably shapes and circumscribes our response to it. (The 'we' of the last sentence naturally includes the composer, who, even as he writes the piece, becomes its first, and usually most discriminating, listener.)

Czerny's observation that first movements and finales ought to—and in practice actually do—proclaim their contrasted characters already in their opening themes will strike most musicians and music-lovers as well founded, even if the vocabulary used to describe the difference is inadequate. Let us take as a case study Beethoven's Op. 22 Piano Sonata, the tenth of Czerny's specimens. Its two incipits appear as Ex. 1.1(*a*) and (*b*).[5]

[3] This apparent equation is encouraged by the structure of the volume, in which the four movements of the post-Beethoven sonata are used as convenient 'pegs' on which to hang the musical forms especially associated with them.

[4] *School of Practical Composition*, i. 76.

[5] Czerny gives only two bars of the first movement and three bars of the last, but I have expanded both of them in order to make my arguments clearer.

But first, some general remarks. The first movement has the task of taking the music out of the void that makes up one side of the frame of silence enclosing the work. Its main function, and especially that of its opening, is expository, since there is nothing previously heard to develop. For a few notes or bars the music is totally unconstrained. One could liken the composer's situation to that of a stallholder setting out his wares on a table. The first few items can be placed with great freedom, but as the table fills up, both the choice of items to display and the manner of their arrangement become increasingly predetermined. The zone of choice open to a composer as he works on a piece never narrows right down to zero—I would agree with Edward Cone's statement that in music there is probably no such

Ex. 1.1.   Beethoven, Piano Sonata in B flat major, Op. 22: (*a*) first movement, bars 1–8; (*b*) last movement, bars 1–8

Ex. 1.1.   (*contd.*)

(*b*)

thing as 'true inevitability' (as opposed to composer's or commentator's impression, formed after the event, that a given passage could not have been other than it is).[6] Nevertheless, the more of a composition one has already completed (either before or after the passage to be written), the less freedom of action one still has.

Edward Said's comments (made apropos of literature but equally applicable to music) that a beginning is 'the point at which, in a given work, the writer departs from all other works' and 'the first step in the intentional production of meaning', to which we could juxtapose Kofi Agawu's description of a beginning as 'a detachable and internally complete abstraction, with a life of its own', lend support to the idea that in any artwork governed by temporal sequence, as when one reads or listens, the beginning performs a discrete, unique, and irreplaceable function.[7] This function is shared by the openings of all the movements in a multimovement cycle—but not equally. Only the first movement is bounded at its start by the frame

---

[6] Edward T. Cone, *Musical Form and Musical Performance* (New York, 1968), 55.

[7] Edward W. Said, *Beginnings: Intention and Method* (London, 1997[3]), 3 and 5; V. Kofi Agawu, *Playing with Signs: A Semiotic Interpretation of Classic Music* (Princeton, 1991), 62.

of silence. Carrying no baggage at the outset, it makes its first task to acquire some.

It is characteristic of first movements—at least, those of the eighteenth and nineteenth centuries, which form the core area of the present study—not to rush into acquiring and displaying their motivic material (that is, the corpus of melodic, figurational, and rhythmic ideas whose combined or separate repetition and development dominate its course). It arrives at a leisurely pace, often accompanied by caesuras, feigned hesitations, or play with contrasts that augment its expansiveness. This relative unhurriedness, the 'broad and noble' quality identified by Czerny, favours the cultivation of asymmetry in the phrase structure, since precisely symmetrical (quadratic) arrangements, often very coercive at the lower levels of rhythmic organiza-tion, become decreasingly so (probably because they are less easily percep-tible) at the middle and higher levels.[8] This asymmetry can be achieved by a variety of means that include pauses, repetitions, excisions, overlaps, and sequential *Fortspinnung*.

Example 1.1(*a*) is a case in point. Beethoven stabilizes his opening with an eight-bar pedal-point and retains tonic harmony over this for four bars.[9] Even after the advent of foreign harmony (chord IV) in bar 5, to which bars 1–4 act as a hugely extended upbeat, the harmonic rhythm (rate of chord change) remains slow, with no more than one change per bar. The rests occupying the third beats of bars 1 and 2 supply the element of hesitancy—the contrived interruption to the flow of information—to which reference was made in the last paragraph. (The prime purpose of such caesuras is of course to tease, and thereby sharpen, our expectancy.) At the point where our extract breaks off, four bars before the first strong cadence (a half-close on a tonicized F), the listener has been made familiar with the complex of motivic material that will supply not only the first movement but also, in varied guise, the remaining movements. It is a matter for debate whether, in a multimovement cycle, there is inherent virtue in making the material of the first movement serve, at least in part, for all the others. There is no doubt, however, that composers and theorists throughout the core period of our investigation (1700–1900) believed that there was, even if the means for achieving it—by instinct alone or with the help of rational planning—were left open.

Before we look at Ex. 1.1(*b*), we should consider the vastly different circumstances under which the last of four movements has to begin. It has been preceded by three substantial, self-contained movements together

[8] The idea that controlling factors relevant to one level of musical organization necessarily apply also to other levels, higher and lower, was resisted by Leonard Meyer, who called it the 'fallacy of hierarchic uniformity' (*Music, the Arts and Ideas: Patterns and Predictions in Twentieth-Century Culture* (Chicago, 1967), 96). Even in a piece of music as short as the 32-bar (with repetitions, 64–bar) 'Aria' used as the theme for J. S. Bach's 'Goldberg' Variations, it is improbable that most listeners actually take in the perfect quadraticism at the level of the whole movement.
[9] The B flat pedal continues implicitly even when interrupted by rests.

lasting eighteen or more minutes. Each has added its quota to the stockpile of memories and expectations, not only in narrowly thematic terms but also in respect of what Carl Dahlhaus liked to call 'tone'—the equivalent for the Classical and Romantic periods of what the Baroque period termed 'affect'. The finale comes laden with a charge that, at its end, when it delivers the work back into the void, it will have to discharge. Many modern writers on music use a tension/release model (paralleling the dissonance/consonance relationship in harmony, of which it is sometimes viewed as an extension) to describe the inner dynamics of both single movements and movement cycles. The model is very apt and useful provided that one accepts that, even if at some level it finds a correlate in human nervous activity, it is in the last analysis only a convenient metaphor. So a 'charge' is some force that has accumulated and needs to be dissipated in one way or another, leaving the movement 'discharged' and returning the listener to the starting point. Each of the three preceding movements has, in its own terms, been discharged to some extent, but not so completely (one hopes) as to give the listener the impression that the cycle is over. By virtue of abutting on the frame of silence that follows the work, the finale has the unique task of discharging completely not only itself but the whole backlog of musical energy that it carries over from the preceding movements.

The tension/release model, which could perhaps be represented more clearly as a three-stage progression from low tension to high and back to low, is valid only if the music is conceived as a rounded experience. To adopt another metaphor: the course of the music is a circular tour beginning and starting at the same point rather than a journey from A to B. Even if the movement or cycle begins with a whisper and ends with a roar, a satisfactory rounding may be achieved by other means, such as return to a home key or to an initial theme.[10]

This line of argument presupposes that roundedness, like thematic integration, is an inherent virtue in music. Once again, the theoretical premises are debatable, whereas the practical evidence is conclusive. It is true that overall tonal rounding (tonal 'concentricity') was abandoned very early on for cyclic works on the largest scale (operas and oratorios), although most of their individual numbers retained it.[11] Towards the beginning of the twentieth century, some symphonists (Mahler and Nielsen are the celebrated

[10] For 'tension' and 'release' the Finnish semiotician Eero Tarasti, following Algirdas Julien Greimas, substitutes the metaphors of *embrayage* and *débrayage*, which have more the sense of engagement and disengagement (as in the action of the clutch of a motor vehicle). Were these terms not French, they would add usefully to the everyday jargon of Anglo-Saxon musicology.

[11] Edward Cone (*Musical Form and Musical Performance*, 88) argues persuasively that in opera-length works 'synoptic' comprehension (i.e. comprehension of the work as a whole) is an impossibility, which would make overall tonal unity—at least in an architectonic rather than colouristic sense—a meaningless goal in purely practical terms. With Mahler's symphonies especially in mind, Dika Newlin coined the expression 'operatic tonality' to describe the free succession of tonalities characteristic of a complex work with a wide time-span (*Bruckner, Mahler, Schoenberg* (New York, 1947), 152).

examples) repudiated it, and their precedent has occasionally been followed in subsequent tonal music.[12] It is naturally legitimate to argue that rounding, being multifactorial, can be achieved in the absence of tonal unity by other means, thematic or textural. In that sense, Mahler's and Nielsen's symphonies are arguably also rounded. Or rather: they have it both ways, conforming simultaneously to the contrasted narratives (equally dear to late-Romantic thought) of the 'progress of the hero' and the 'return to the source'.[13]

However, there is no denying that in the major genres of instrumental music from Corelli to Bruckner (and in most cases, beyond) the tonal unity of the framing movements, leaving aside the major/minor antithesis, was an absolute requirement. This applies to sonatas, trios, quartets, symphonies, and concertos alike. In a Beethoven sonata one takes for granted the desire to achieve, at the end of the finale, a comprehensive closure that meets both formal and emotional expectations. The nature of such a closure is aptly captured by the literary theorist Barbara Herrnstein Smith, who observes: 'Closure allows the reader [for which substitute: "listener"] to be satisfied by the failure of continuation or, put another way, it creates in the reader the expectation of nothing.'[14] Or again: 'Closure occurs . . . by providing a point from which all the preceding elements may be viewed comprehensively and their relations grasped as part of a significant design.'[15] There is therefore an inevitable duality about the opening of a final movement.[16] It is the 'beginning of an end' and shows both aspects of its nature at once. It has first to expose its material, but since this material does not emerge *ex*

---

[12] There are a few much earlier works exemplifying progressive tonality—for instance, Berlioz's *Grande Symphonie funèbre et triomphale* (1840) and the four-movement 'Symphony' for solo piano comprising the fourth to seventh studies in Alkan's *Douze études dans les tons mineurs*, Op. 39 (1857). In the case of the Berlioz symphony, the contrast of key in the outer movements (F minor versus B flat major) reflects, in programmatic fashion, the extreme change of affect (comparable with that between a 'Crucifixus' and an 'Et resurrexit' in a Mass setting); in that of Alkan's work, the conventional tonal demands of a symphony are sacrificed to those of a twelve-movement cycle of studies in which each tonality appears only once. To borrow a term coined by Jonathan Dunsby (to whose idea we will return), Alkan's four movements can be viewed as a 'multi-piece within a multi-piece'. It is pertinent to observe that suites, from the 19th c. onwards, have never made tonal unity the absolute requirement that it has always been in the traditions of the sonata and symphony.

[13] If Natalie Bauer-Lechner's testimony is to be believed, Mahler confessed in 1899 that his progressive tonality (in his second and third symphonies) originated partly from a desire to be 'different' and that he intended to revert in future to more conventional tonal treatment. In the event, this promise was fulfilled only in Symphony No. 6. See Newlin, *Bruckner, Mahler, Schoenberg*, 173.

[14] Barbara Herrnstein Smith, *Poetic Closure: A Study of How Poems End* (Chicago, 1968), 34.

[15] Ibid. 36. Smith's formulation presupposes the feasibility of 'synoptic' comprehension as described by Edward Cone (see above, n. 11).

[16] William Newman has introduced (with particular reference to one-movement sonatas such as those of Liszt and Skryabin) the related notion of 'double-function design', in which a given section operates equally as an autonomous unit and as a subunit of a larger whole (*The Sonata since Beethoven* (New York and London, 1972²), 134–5 and 373–8). In theory, the possible number of different levels at which a given group of bars could be said to function is unlimited.

*novo*, as it did in the first movement, this can be done simply and quickly. Although the finale may be equal in 'weight' (we will examine this problematic concept later) to the first movement, it has to differentiate itself immediately and establish a separate identity. Traditionally, this is achieved by 'lightness' (another problematic and value-laden term) of one sort or another: by a quicker tempo (making the music 'more sprightly and exciting', as Czerny puts it); by a shorter metre (duple, triple, or compound, as opposed to quadruple); by a simpler texture; by a more quadratic, or at least more transparent, phrase structure; by a formal structure in which simple repetition is preferred to elaboration or complex development; by an effusion of virtuosic brilliance; by a humorous or quirky tone; and usually by several of these elements in combination. Even when, in accordance with a more recent vision of the finale's role, the last movement is designed to be weightier (instead of lighter) than the first, some of the same techniques, paradoxically, remain. For instance, the process for which Schoenberg coined the term 'liquidation'—the stripping down of thematic material into even more basic shapes, a kind of 'reverse' development—can be used to make the music either naive (as in the finale of Haydn's Symphony No. 104) or monumental (as in that of Nielsen's Symphony No. 3). Either way, a necessary contrast with the opening movement is obtained.

The 'allegretto' finale of Beethoven's Op. 22 (Ex. 1.1(*b*)) asserts its individuality vis-à-vis the 'allegro con brio' first movement immediately. We are plunged *in medias res*. The first eight bars exhibit a quadratic phrase structure: bars 1–2 are answered by bars 3–4 according to the classic pattern of closely matching antecedent and consequent; and this four-bar group is answered with perfect symmetry by a similar four-bar group running continuously. The half-close in bar 8 promises the modified repetition terminating in a full close that indeed materializes after a further eight bars; an ornamented restatement of the last two bars (15–16) prolongs the period for greater emphasis and, more important, to signal its end. The harmonic rhythm is mostly fast, and the repeated semiquavers forming part of the accompanimental background in bars 2 and 4 are a quasi-onomatopoeic device traditionally suggestive of chuckling—exactly the right affect for a rondo finale.[17]

To end our discussion of Op. 22, we will play a little game suggested by Hugo Leichtentritt's *Musikalische Formenlehre*. For the purpose of illustrating the difference between a theme used for variations and one used for the refrain of a rondo, the German scholar took the first eight bars of the opening movement of Beethoven's Piano Sonata in A flat major, Op. 26 (a set of variations), and those of the same rondo finale that we have been examining (in Op. 22), composing paraphrases of each that took over the distinguishing

---

[17] It is not the note repetitions *per se* that convey the chuckling effect but the quickness, evenness, and, above all, detached quality of the semiquavers. (On a keyboard instrument rapid repeated notes cannot but be staccato.)

characteristics of the other.[18] The result was a rondo theme in A flat major and a theme for variations in B flat major. We can do a similar thing here by concocting a 'typical' first movement opening using the thematic material of Ex. 1.1(b) and a 'typical' finale opening using that of Ex. 1.1(a). The products of this intermingling appear as Exs. 1.2(a) and (b).

Like Czerny, we hope that a few bars are worth a thousand words, but the calculations behind the transformations are these. In the conversion of the finale material, the harmonic rhythm has been slowed down to the point where, after bar 8, many possibilities exist for expansion and the use of 'delaying' devices as described earlier. The 'chuckles' have naturally been removed as inapposite. In the new finale, the harmonic rhythm has been speeded up and a more repetitive (as well as quadratic) rhythmic structure installed. The registral contrast between the first and second—likewise, the third and fourth—phrases introduces a mildly comic effect (one could imagine a dialogue between Harlequin and Columbine) appropriate for a finale.

Ex. 1.2. (a) imaginary opening of a first movement, using material from the last movement of Beethoven, Op. 22; (b) imaginary opening of a last movement, using material from the first movement of Beethoven, Op. 22

[18] Hugo Leichtentritt, *Musikalische Formenlehre* (Leipzig, 1952[5] [repr. in facsimile from the 3rd edn. of 1907]), 116–17.

Ex. 1.2.  (*contd.*)

Note that we have dealt here only with movement openings. As each type of movement progresses into the developmental or 'contrast' phase, further differentiation is encouraged, finales tending to be more clearly sectionalized and more hospitable to frankly episodic material. Likewise with codas: the first-movement coda has only its own movement to round off, whereas that of the finale sums up the entire work. (To simplify and generalize rather sweepingly, one might say that a first movement favours a drawn-out opening, while a finale favours a drawn-out close.)

Most of the arguments so far advanced are not new to musicology. The problem for whoever wishes to provide a reasonably full, reasonably wide-ranging, account of the finale as it has existed in the music of the last few centuries is that comments are dispersed in musical literature and take the form of passing *aperçus* rather than extended arguments employing a common technical terminology, even within the same language. Take, as an example of this style of treatment, the following remarks on the main theme of the finale of Mozart's Piano Concerto in E flat major, K. 271, made by Charles Rosen in *The Classical Style*. Rosen's insights, expressed with great elegance in a few sentences, are not developed further or repeated elsewhere in connection with other works. They form no part of a grand theory of 'the finale', and the context for which they are considered valid is not closely defined.

As the finale is itself a resolution of the entire work, and demands melodic material that will resist, rather than imply, development—in other words, a theme that gives the impression of squareness, regularity and completeness—antiphonal treatment both brings out this character most clearly and colors it most effectively... The thematic material of a finale is always rhythmically squarer than that of a first movement, the cadences heavily emphasized, the phrases well-defined, and the first theme completely rounded off before any harmonic movement can take place.[19]

Or take Hugo Leichtentritt's more pedagogically oriented characterization of the finale (perhaps written with Beethoven especially in mind): 'A finale does not favour the complex ramifications of a first movement. It prefers simple, straightforward structures that are less liable to be interrupted by digressions. It has to be imposing, a demand that does not exclude the most meticulous attention to detail.'[20]

There are perhaps only two leitmotifs concerning the finale (in instrumental music) that occur with any frequency in musicological literature and can therefore be claimed as frequent topics for discussion. The first is that of the finale 'problem'. Oddly enough, although the word 'problem' is standard—it translates without change into German, although the nuance is slightly altered there (in the German tradition a problem is more an interesting unanswered question than an irksome snag!)—the nature of this problem becomes all things to all people.

It stands to reason, of course, that a movement with a unique position in the cycle (and in a three-movement or four-movement cycle all positions are obviously of this kind) will have unique tasks and thus pose a potential problem to a composer who finds those specific tasks especially difficult to fulfil (or to a listener who finds their solution difficult to assimilate). But by no means all composers have found the finale the hardest movement to write. We learn that Weber (in the spirit of the small boy who empties his dinner plate of the most appetizing items first) made a regular habit of postponing the composition of a first movement until its sequels were written.[21] One must of course concede the reality of self-imposed 'problems' in finale-writing, particularly as regards those movements we shall later describe as 'summative'. If the finale is planned from the start to be the

[19] Charles Rosen, *The Classical Style: Haydn, Mozart, Beethoven* (London, 1971), 213 and 275.

[20] Leichtentritt, *Musikalische Formenlehre*, 169. All translations are the author's own, unless otherwise credited.

[21] See John Warrack, *Carl Maria von Weber* (London, 1968), esp. 119, 128, 134, and 172. The works to which the remark applies include Weber's Bassoon Concerto, his first two piano sonatas, and his Second Piano Concerto. Moscheles's Second Piano Concerto in E flat began, in similar fashion, with the composition of its concluding polonaise.

longest, most thickly scored, and thematically richest movement, the composer is almost inevitably going to encounter a greater measure of difficulty. The *Grosse Fuge* undoubtedly cost Beethoven more effort than the shorter and more conventional (but still hardly lightweight) movement that replaced it in his quartet Op. 130.

Sheltering in the tent of the 'global' finale problem are a host of individual finale problems of varied kinds. For Schubert, arguably, the problem was to prevent his finales from becoming over-long or over-discursive. For Mendelssohn, Schumann, Brahms, and many others, it was to make them sufficiently different in kind from their first movements while maintaining equivalent weight and thematic relevance. For Bruckner and Mahler, it was to make them truly climactic, even in the wake of three or more movements of exceptional scale. For Shostakovich, it was to steer them towards their (often) mandatorily optimistic conclusions without compromise of compositional standards. (We exclude Haydn, Mozart, and Beethoven from the list. As Hans Keller so provocatively but acutely put it, these three masters 'solved [the finale problem] at the time when they created it'.)[22]

Since the supposedly problematic nature of the finale has been a topos ever since the time of Beethoven, it is understandable that several composers have pronounced on the question. Wagner, doubtless with Beethoven's Ninth Symphony in mind, described finales as a precipice that he hoped to avoid by writing only one-movement symphonies.[23] Carl Nielsen remarked in 1922, after completing his Fifth Symphony, that (in the words of Robert Simpson) 'while most composers were successful enough in managing the first three movements of a normal symphony, many of them 'slipped' up...in the finale;...he himself often felt that this was a very real problem'.[24] Nielsen even had the bad grace to wonder whether Beethoven's introduction of voices into the last movement of his Ninth Symphony was not a decision born of desperation! So deeply entrenched among composers, music-lovers, and (dare I say it?) musicologists is the idea of a finale problem that it is probably routinely accepted by many who have never knowingly experienced, or witnessed the result of, any such thing.

The other constant motif is the view of the progress of the finale (especially in symphonies, but to a degree also in sonatas) from early-eighteenth-century lightness to late-nineteenth-century monumentality. This evolution has been regarded by mainstream German and German-influenced musicological thought as inevitable, aesthetically beneficial,

---

[22] Hans Keller, *The Great Haydn Quartets: Their Interpretation* (London, 1993[2]), 234.

[23] Cosima Wagner, *Die Tagebücher* (Munich, 1977), ii. 827. Wagner's original words, as reported by Cosima, ran: 'Die letzten Sätze sind die Klippe, ich werde mich hüten, ich schreibe nur einsätzige Symphonien.'

[24] Robert Simpson, *Carl Nielsen: Symphonist* (New York, 1979[2]), 92.

and historically important.[25] The expression 'Finalsymphonie' is widely used, and I have recently noticed 'Finalsonate', which must be a coinage by analogy.[26]

Where these authorities sometimes disagree is on how to apply the term. For Alfred Einstein, Mozart's Salzburg symphonies, K. 129, 130, 132, and 133, all from 1772, are already 'finale symphonies', since their finales rival their first movements in length and weight.[27] A more conventional view waits for the 'Jupiter' Symphony, K. 551, or at least the last three symphonies, before using this label for a Mozart work, while Alexander Ringer postpones it until Beethoven's 'Eroica' Symphony.[28] A German school of thought inaugurated by Paul Bekker in the earlier twentieth century, and later developed in different ways by Bernd Sponheuer and Karl Heinrich Wörner, betrays an astonishing fixation with 'finale character'. For Bekker, the rise of the finale begins modestly and inconsistently with Schubert, reaches a higher stage with Bruckner, and culminates with Mahler, whose First Symphony ranks as the earliest fully-fledged *Finalsymphonie*.[29] Sponheuer's prime concern is with balance. Whereas most other writers (including Wörner) conceive balance, in relation to finales, as a matter concerning primarily the two outer movements—they are, so to speak, the twin pillars of the musical edifice on which the middle movements rest—Sponheuer brings all the preceding movements into the equation: the finale 'balances out' rather than simply 'balances' by drawing into itself, and for the first time integrating, the significant content, thematic and hermeneutic, of the earlier movements.[30] Wörner, taking Bekker's approach a stage further, narrativizes the finale's significance. For him, *Finalcharakter* is equatable with the fate of a hero and exists in three variants: *Entwicklung* ([further] development), *Polarität* (polarity, or oscillation), and *Statik* (stasis).[31] So insistent is Wörner that the idea of a finale is bound up with *Erhöhung*

[25] In the words of Karl H. Wörner (*Das Zeitalter der thematischen Prozesse in der Geschichte der Musik* (Regensburg, 1969), 65: 'Without the awareness that the supreme value of the symphony as a cyclic work is brought about solely by the build-up to a climax in its finale; without this spiritual awareness, we would not possess the riches that we see, as we today look back over the history of the symphony.'

[26] In Udo Zilkens, *Beethovens Finalsätze in den Klaviersonaten: allgemeine Strukturen und individuelle Gestaltung* (Rodenkirchen, 1994), in reference to Beethoven's 'Hammerklavier' Sonata, Op. 106.

[27] As quoted in Neal Zaslaw, *Mozart's Symphonies: Context, Performance Practice, Reception* (Oxford, 1989), 517.

[28] Alexander Ringer, 'Clementi and the *Eroica*', *Musical Quarterly*, 47 (1961), 454–68 at 466.

[29] Paul Bekker, *Gustav Mahlers Sinfonien* (Berlin, 1921). Bekker opens his study with a long chapter entitled 'Der symphonische Stil' ('Symphonic Style', pp. 11–34), in which he identifies a specifically Austrian school of symphonists (different from the German) leading from Schubert via Bruckner to Mahler.

[30] Bernd Sponheuer, 'Haydns Arbeit am Finalproblem', *Archiv für Musikwissenschaft*, 34 (1977), 199–224 at 204.

[31] Wörner, *Das Zeitalter der thematischen Prozesse*, 4. It may be objected that the three categories inhabiting Wörner's typology are between them sufficiently broad to accommodate literally any finale, regardless of its nature and of the composer's intention.

(apotheosis) that he is reluctant to allow the very word to be used for a non-monumental last movement such as that of Bach's Fifth 'Brandenburg' Concerto.[32]

We will have many opportunities later to return to these themes. For now, one critical (in both senses) observation needs to be made. In the many discussions of the instrumental finale as a distinct musical 'species' the historical purview is rarely other than very restricted. We read of no 'finale character' in Bach, no 'finale problem' in Bartók. The concluding movements that existed for two hundred or more years in cyclic vocal compositions before they occurred in instrumental music (outside the realm of dance music, at least) are left out of the story, as if it were inconceivable that they exerted any relevant influence. The way in which some twentieth-century music has exemplified in a peculiarly clear and self-aware way the various subtypes of the finale is ignored. If one adopts a time perspective of five hundred rather than two hundred years (even though these two hundred years remain as the core area under investigation), the durability of certain techniques and characteristics that have attended final movements from the time of the Renaissance up to the present day becomes fully apparent. In truth, a genuinely 'new' kind of finale would by now be hard to invent. (Perhaps this is because whereas there are many modalities of being in the middle, there is only one modality of being at the end.)

As I attempt, in the chapters that follow, to draw together the existing threads and bind in a few more, I shall adopt an approach that is primarily historical, dealing as it does with continuities, ruptures, quantitative and qualitative changes, lines of influence, and singular events. Some of the discussion will qualify as analytical. I must stress, however, that of the two interfaces that analysis possesses—one with history and the other with theory—it is only the first that will concern me. All my analyses will be, to use the current term, informal. This is not out of principle but simply because I lack the competence and experience to do otherwise. For a similar reason, I will deal with music before 1700 and after 1900 much more selectively than that within the core area (except for a long excursus on Shostakovich's quartets in the last chapter), and I will be guided in my choice by its relevance to the main material under discussion.

When one deals with such a vast slice of music that embraces many genres over a very wide historical span, it is essential to preserve a balance between general statements, which run the risk of becoming mere catalogues and, worse, of lapsing into superficiality, and the detailed description of selected works, which may not be as truly representative of historical trends as one would like. What I have done is to punctuate my general survey with case studies of a few especially interesting works and movements and the occasional digression dealing with a point of special interest.

---

[32] Wörner, *Das Zeitalter der thematischen Prozesse*, 3.

The aim is to set up a kind of running counterpoint between the general and the particular.

It was gratifying for me to read, in an article from 1987 by Arnold Whittall which examined and compared the finales of Brahms's two Op. 51 quartets, that at least one other person considered 'the general issue of the character and function of finales' 'a subject well worth pursuing [in the future]'.[33] This is indeed my subject, and I will now pursue it.

[33] Arnold Whittall, 'Two of a Kind? Brahms's Op. 51 Finales', in Michael Musgrave (ed.), *Brahms 2: Biographical, Documentary and Analytical Studies* (Cambridge, 1987), 145–64 at 145.

# 2

# *The Idea of a Movement*

To have a last movement, one must first have a piece of music divided into separate movements. So much is obvious, but it is important to accept from the outset that the existence of a multi-movement (or cyclic) work is not an eternal 'given': it is one particular form of packaging music (among many) that has come into being at a specific point in history, initially only in certain genres, and even today enjoys only a provisional status. It is not hard to imagine a future situation in which, following the convergence of Western (but by then global) art music and commercial popular music, nearly all musical compositions became single movements that one could couple freely with others in the fashion of a modern concert programme, recorded album, or live 'set'.

The word 'movement' itself has come to be applied to what we today understand it to be in a musical context via a roundabout process. The primary and original meaning, synonymous with 'motion', refers to the rhythmic character of the music in its totality as it results from a combination of metre, tempo prescription, and chosen note values. In the 1728 edition of Ephraim Chambers's *Cyclopaedia* 'Motion, in Music' is defined somewhat vaguely as 'the manner of beating the Measure, to hasten or slacken the Time of the Pronunciation of the Words or Notes'.[1] This sense, which goes back at least as far as the sixteenth-century theorist Zarlino, who employs the term 'movimento', is shared by French and Italian writers of the period. Brossard identifies one meaning of the word, in its various alternative forms (*motto/moto/movimento/mouvement*), as 'la *Lenteur*, ou la *Vitesse* des Nottes & de la mesure'.[2] The *Vocabolario dell'Accademia della Crusca* published in Florence in 1733 has no musical meanings listed in its entries for 'moto' and 'movimento', but the definition of 'tempo' as applied to music—'...si dice la Misura del moto delle voci, e de' suoni per lunghi, o brevi intervalli, per moderare il ritmo, secondar la battuta, e regolar la velocità, le tardanze, e le pause'—uses 'moto' in exactly the same sense.[3] We may add that in French and Italian this primary sense has never disappeared, as such instructions as 'reprenez le mouvement' and 'il doppio movimento' remind us. The change

---

[1] Ephraim Chambers, *Cyclopaedia: Or, an Universal Dictionary of Arts and Sciences* (London, 1728), ii. 96. The 1738, 1751–3, and 1779–83 editions retain this entry word for word.

[2] Sébastien de Brossard, *Dictionnaire de musique* (Paris, 1703), art. 'Motto'.

[3] *Vocabolario degli Accademici della Crusca* (Florence, 1729–38), v. 34. The phrase 'la misura del moto delle voci e de' suoni' could be translated freely as 'the measure governing the movement of the sung and played parts'.

in meaning of the word 'movement', which appears to have begun to occur no earlier than the very end of the eighteenth century, was made possible by one simple fact. In early music changes of metre and/or tempo (or within mode, time, and prolation in medieval nomenclature) nearly always correlate with significant structural divisions. Even though the sections demarcated by changes of 'movement' may not yet be sufficiently free-standing to rank as movements in the modern sense, since one such section may lead seamlessly into the next, they carry within them the seeds of autonomy. After this relative autonomy was eventually realized, in the second half of the seventeenth century, the emphasis of the term gradually shifted in parallel with music's growing preference for larger, more discrete units (in contrast to the fluid, multisectional designs of most previous instrumental music). By the middle of the nineteenth century the modern meaning is dominant. Notwithstanding the gradualness and inconspicuousness of this process, we have today come so far from the original meaning as to be prepared to conceive, in theory at least, of a change of movement (signalled by a thin-thick double barline, a move to a new system, and a large numeral at its head) without any corresponding change of metre, tempo, or rhythmic activity.

A similar development affected the understanding of the German word 'Satz', which is cognate with our 'set' and 'setting'. Its primary meanings embrace both the abstract and the concrete. As an abstract term, still current today, it denotes the act of composition itself (hence 'zweistimmiger Satz' for two-part writing and 'homophoner Satz' for homophonic writing). More concretely, it can refer to any connected passage or piece of music. The compounds 'Hauptsatz' (main subject) and 'Nebensatz' (subsidiary subject) preserve the older use of 'Satz' to refer to subunits of a longer piece. Indeed, Heinrich Christoph Koch's *Musikalisches Lexikon* of 1802 gives priority to this meaning. Koch's definition begins: 'Any individual component of a piece that makes complete sense in its own right'.[4] However, Koch also recognizes a newer meaning. Further on, he writes: 'The word "Satz" *very often* [my emphasis] denotes a complete whole in pieces of music that consist of several different wholes. For example, one says that the last "Satz" of a concerto is a rondo or that the second "Satz" of a symphony comprises variations, etc.' 'Very often' is of course different from 'nearly always' and implies that the second usage was not yet firmly entrenched when Koch wrote his dictionary.

What, then, did people call movements before that word took on its modern meaning? The answer is that they made do with very untechnical words such as 'piece' and 'part'. Even a composer as late as Berlioz could refer to a work—the *Symphonie fantastique*, Op. 14 (1830)—as being written 'en 5 parties'.

[4] Heinrich Christoph Koch, *Musikalisches Lexikon* (Frankfurt am Main, 1802), 1289–93 at col. 1289.

So far, so good. But we have not yet addressed the even thornier problem of what we mean by a 'movement' today. One way to do this would be to take an ultra-pragmatic approach and admit to movement status any group of continuously running bars bounded on both sides by a thin-thick double barline, or bounded on one side by a thin-thick double barline and on the other by the silence at the edge of the work. This would not be an entirely frivolous operation since it would at least deliver clear and usually acceptable results. Its grave weakness, however, is that it is theoretically barren since it puts the cart before the horse. The modern (post-1800) typographical conventions concerning the use of thin-thin and thin-thick double barlines do not themselves bring into being the classification of groups of bars as sections or movements: they are merely a means—admittedly, a remarkably clear and economical one—of confirming graphically the type of division (into sections or into movements) that the composer, or sometimes the publisher or editor, already has in mind. The fact that the notational distinction between thin-thin and thin-thick is of relatively recent (nineteenth-century?) origin says something about the lack of a clear and necessary distinction between section and movement in earlier ages. In sources of sonatas and canzonas from the seventeenth and eighteenth centuries a change of tempo and/or metre does not invariably cause a barline to be doubled or a double barline to be specially inserted (in the case of a mid-bar change); double barlines, nearly always thin-thin, tend to occur at points that we would identify with the end of movements or at least major sections. But whatever follows rarely moves to a new system or line and therefore gives the impression, at least to the eye, of being a continuation rather than a fresh start.[5] Early sources commonly use as a terminal indication for the whole work an elaborated version of the thin-thin double barline—followed by additional, often tapered, barlines or decorated with flourishes.

Another pragmatic approach, even less serious than the first, would be to term a movement the music that occurs between two points at which etiquette permits a player to retune his instrument or a member of the audience to cough. Once again, of course, we would be confusing causes and effects. But the effects themselves are interesting since they show that the idea of what is, and is not, a movement impinges in a very real way on how we listen to music and train our attention span. We are saying that to break the musical continuity and introduce extraneous sounds between movements, though never desirable, is less harmful than at any other points during the performance of the work because the break is in some way natural. And there is a good reason why this is so.

This reason bears directly on what a movement is in analytical terms, as viewed from the page. In a nutshell, it is the 'different whole' within the 'complete whole', to adopt Koch's rather clumsy formulation. John Daverio

---

[5] Undeniably, the high cost of paper in former times contributed equally to this reluctance to move to a new line before the end of the work.

has found a neater definition. He calls it a unit 'capable of functioning as a complete musical discourse when removed from its original surroundings'.[6] This description is especially apt since the removal of a movement from its original surroundings is not a hypothetical condition but a real one that has occurred countless times from the very beginnings of its existence in instrumental music up to the present day. Indeed, the success with which this operation has repeatedly been carried out and its evident acceptability to the broad mass of music-lovers almost make one wonder whether it is the movement or the multimovement work that is the construct most needful of explanation.

We still have to establish the criteria for this relative autonomy, and this is the hardest task of all. There is no single, idiot-proof criterion (leaving aside notational statements of intention such as thin-thick double barlines) by which one can say with certainty that a given group of bars is not a section but a movement, or vice versa. In the end, we have to fall back on an 'open' definition in the Wittgensteinian sense: that is, a multifactorial, composite definition in which the balance of the several elements rather than any one element informs our judgement. We can illustrate this by a simple comparison that places side by side features typical (in a statistical sense) of sections and movements respectively:

| Sections | Movements |
|---|---|
| Tonally open or closed | Tonally closed |
| Connected to surrounding material | Disconnected from surrounding material |
| Monothematic | Polythematic |
| Progressive or rounded form | Rounded form |

It is only too easy to find examples of undisputed movements that contradict each of the first three criteria in the right-hand column, taken singly. The opening movement of Mahler's Seventh Symphony, which 'progresses' from B minor to E minor, violates the first criterion. A movement such as the 'largo e sostenuto' of Haydn's Sonata for keyboard in D major, Hob. XVI/37, which ends with a half-close in preparation for the finale, violates the second. And 'polythematic' is hardly the term to apply to the first prelude of Bach's '48'. However, the fourth criterion, rounded form, does seem to apply. The quality of being rounded applies in particular to tonality and to thematic organization, although other elements (style, texture, instrumentation) can also participate. In most cases, tonal and thematic rounding are synchronized: they then act as mutually reinforcing signals. Only in 'bifocal' recapitulations (the term was coined by Mark Evan Bonds by analogy with 'bifocal' closes) are the tonal and thematic reprises placed 'out of synch' with each other.[7]

---

[6] John Daverio, 'Formal Design and Terminology in the Pre-Corellian "Sonata" and Related Instrumental Forms in the Printed Sources' (Ph.D. diss., Boston University, 1983), 76.

[7] See Mark Evan Bonds, Wordless Rhetoric: Musical Form and the Metaphor of the Oration (Cambridge, Mass., 1991), 189. Bifocal closes (the term is Robert Winter's) in sonata-form

The validity of the rounding criterion can be tested by considering the groups of bars in slow tempo that introduce fast movements (generally the first or last). Are these bars to be regarded as a slow introduction to the fast movement—thus part of it, formally speaking—or do they make up a discrete movement? In the case of the slow movement of Beethoven's 'Waldstein' Sonata, Op. 53, the twenty-eight bars comprising the 'Introduzione', marked 'adagio molto', that leads into the final rondo at first seem to have the status of a dependent introduction, as the heading would suggest. The absence of tonal closure—the movement begins in F major (with a strong inflection of A minor) and cadences into the C major finale—tends to reinforce this interpretation. But the reprise (following a contrasting, cantabile theme) of the opening theme in the original key at bar 17, which gives formal shape to the whole, does enough to establish the independent status, the movementhood, of the 'adagio molto' in defiance of its title.[8] In contrast, the eighteen-bar 'adagio cantabile' that introduces the 'allegro vivace' finale of Beethoven's Cello Sonata in A major, Op. 69, starting in E major and closing with an *ad libitum* flourish on the dominant seventh of A major, is too through-composed to aspire to the same status. The same is true of the long-drawn-out G minor 'adagio' introducing the G major 'allegro' ending Mozart's String Quintet in G minor, K. 516, which unfolds in a single, huge arc. Undeniably, there are occasional grey areas where the decision (by composer and/or commentator) in favour of slow-movement or slow-introduction status are a matter of judgement or customary bias. Ethan Haimo expresses a similar point when he writes: 'Slow introductions occupy an intermediate position between independent movement and dependent section.'[9] (His choice of words is perhaps a little clumsy, however, since by classifying something as an introduction, one concedes its dependence in advance!)

But even if rounding (of some kind) is a necessary condition for movement status, it is not a sufficient one, since sections, too, may be rounded. In fact, most rondo refrains and variation themes, sections par excellence, exhibit perfect thematic and tonal roundedness. So to become beyond doubt a movement, a group of bars really has simultaneously to exhibit more than one of the criteria listed above.

The Golden Age of the movement (and perforce of the multimovement work) as regards instrumental music can be situated between Bach and Mahler. Before the eighteenth century we find a period where, by and

---

movements are half-closes in the tonic at the end of the first subject group (or the following bridge passage) introducing a second subject that in the exposition begins straight away in the dominant but in the recapitulation is transposed to begin in the tonic.

[8] It is amusing to note that in Tovey's edition of this sonata (1931, for the Associated Board) the movement ends with a thin-thin barline as if it were no more than a slow introduction. But Tovey gives the game away by counting the number of bars from '1' again when the rondo begins.

[9] Ethan Haimo, *Haydn's Symphonic Forms* (Oxford, 1995), 128.

large, the movement is coextensive with the piece and therefore needs no separate description as such. However, already in the late medieval period we discover groups of dances, originally no more than two or three, arranged in a conventional sequence (at first based on contemporary dance practice rather than purely musical considerations), and during the course of the seventeenth century the choice of dances and the sequence in which they are grouped (according to the preference of individual composers) solidifies to produce the more or less fixed, multimovement structures we know variously as suites, partitas, balletti, and chamber sonatas.[10] Concurrently, the sonata proper, the so-called 'church' sonata, expanded in length and by a process of fission evolved from a multisectional to a multimovement condition.

Everyone is agreed that such a change took place and that it occurred in the middle of the seventeenth century. What is harder to fix is the point of change and the relevant criteria for evaluating it. It has already been suggested that the presence of rounding is crucial. We can expand the argument presented above by proposing a simple rule of thumb: rounding is a device that sets a frame around the unit to which it applies and in so doing defines its extent. In other words, if we have a 100-bar piece and the theme announced in bar 1 returns in bar 80, the unit is the whole 100 bars, giving us a single-movement composition. If, on the other hand, the theme announced in bar 1 returns in bar 30, to be followed in bar 60 by a new theme that returns in bar 80 we have a composition in *at least* two movements. (There may in fact be three rather than two, since there could also be a central movement whose boundaries were fixed by those of the outer movements.)[11] This rule of thumb works very well for music up to the midnineteenth century, even though we have to set it aside when we come to works featuring the cyclic recurrence of themes (with or without metamorphosis) in different movements.

To appreciate this point, we can examine Sonata 16 from the second book (1629) of Dario Castello's *Sonate concertate in stil moderno*. Castello, a wind player active in Venice, was among the most progressive sonata composers of his day, and as their title suggests, these sonatas are conceived as models of the most up-to-date style. This sonata for four-part strings (violin, soprano and alto violas, and bass violin), which in structure is typical of

---

[10] The fusion process by which dances became more regular companions has been much studied in recent years. On developments in 17th-c. Italy, see especially Daverio, 'Formal Design and Terminology', and the present author's 'The *Taiheg*, the *Pira* and Other Curiosities of Benedetto Vinaccesi's *Suonate da camera a tre*, Op. 1', *Music and Letters*, 75 (1994), 344–64. I qualify 'fixed' by 'more or less' because in practice, as one sees in the contemporary sources, dances were not infrequently omitted, inserted, or reordered. Some suite-like multimovement compositions were not based on dances; one might cite Byrd's *The Battle* and Munday's *Faire Wether* fantasia, which are early specimens of programme music for keyboard.

[11] This point becomes relevant when we consider slow movements in Baroque sonatas and concertos that although through-composed and tonally open qualify as movements by virtue of being enclosed within other movements.

TABLE 2.1. *Plan of Dario Castello, Sonata 16 (1629)*

| Section | Metre | Tempo | Textural type | Bars |
|---|---|---|---|---|
| 1a | C3(/2) | Allegro | fugue on two subjects | 1–50 |
| 1b | | Allegro | dialoguing chorus | 51–82 |
| 2 | C | Mixed | *battaglia*-like dialoguing chorus | 83–119 |
| 3 | 3(/2) | Allegro | fugue on two subjects, cadencing into: | 120–43 |
| 4 | 3/(2) | Adagio | dialoguing chorus, cadencing into: | 144–65 |
| 5a | 3(/2) | Allegro | fugue based on material of 1a | 166–205 |
| 5b | C | Adagio | chorus | 206–14 |

C = time signature

the collection (and of its predecessor of 1621), falls into five main sections, the first, third, and fifth of which can be further subdivided. In Table 2.1 I use the term 'fugue' in the older, wider sense to mean an imitative passage, and 'chorus' to mean a homophonic section. Each section remains firmly in the Ionian (white-note C) mode, closing with a perfect cadence on the final, except for the second, which concludes with a Mixolydian (dominant) cadence on G. The irregularity of barlines in the original printed source makes the numbering of the bars open to varied interpretation; I have followed the barring of the edition by Eleanor Selfridge-Field.[12]

The 214 bars are organized in what one might describe as a chain form. The sections, all through-composed, follow one another with no break in continuity more emphatic than a perfect cadence ending in a sustained note and possibly ushering in a change of metre and/or tempo. These units are paratactic rather than hypotactic; or, as Charles Rosen has expressed it in a different context, not syntactical but cumulative.[13] None of the five main sections is subordinated to, or dependent on, another. Castello's sonata clearly betrays its formal indebtedness to the sixteenth-century motet and chanson, which are constructed on similar principles, save that their general avoidance of changes of metre and tempo allows overlaps between sections to be the norm rather than the exception. From the sixteenth-century chanson (and cognate genres) comes the idea of bringing back the opening material as a framing device aiding closure. In a chanson (one may take Janequin's ribald *Au joly jeu du pousse avant* as an example) the reprise reintroduces the opening text, following the general principle of vocal music (at least, in earlier ages) that musical and textual elements must have a one-to-one relationship: that is, one cannot arbitrarily reintroduce musical material without providing it with the same, or a clearly related, textual underlay. In some but not all cases, the author of the chanson text will have anticipated the musician's desire to reintroduce the opening music as a closing device and contrived the meaning and syntax of his lines

[12] Dario Castello, *Selected Ensemble Sonatas* (A-R Editions; Madison, Wis., 1977), ii. 63–80.
[13] Rosen, *The Classical Style*, 453, with reference to 19th-c. approaches to form.

accordingly (with echoes of the old *formes fixes*).[14] In an instrumental composition this constraint is of course absent, and rounding becomes a purely
musical device (although one could argue, as Castello's contemporaries
liked to do, that it wordlessly reproduces the rhetorical organization of a
textual statement).

The reprises in Castello's sonatas have two interesting properties. The
first is that they return not to the actual beginning of the work but to an
entry of the subject some way into the piece. In Sonata 16 the reprise 'picks
up' the music at bar 14. The composer's main motivation seems to have been
brevity; the fact that the reprise is followed, and sometimes introduced, by
other material justifies condensing it for the sake of overall balance. The
other feature is that although a clean break before the reprise (unlike at
many other points in the movement) is avoided, the dovetailing is minimal,
with the result that the dramatic effect of the return of the opening subject is
maximized. Example 2.1(*a*) shows, for contrast, the reprise in Janequin's *Au
joly jeu* (in the interests of clarity, only the top part has been texted). Here the

Ex. 2.1.    (*a*) Janequin, chanson *Au joly jeu du pousse-avant*, bars 25–30; (*b*) Castello, Sonata 16
(1629), bars 163–71

[14] This prior understanding, by the poet, of the composer's needs is most strikingly evi-
denced in the texts for da capo arias penned in the 17th and 18th cc.

Ex. 2.1.   (*contd.*)

reprise follows on from the previous material so seamlessly that a second or two will elapse before it is recognized as such. In Castello's sonata, as illustrated in Ex. 2.1(*b*), the reprise establishes its identity from the very first note. In other words, despite paying lip-service to the old ideal of continuity, the structure of a sonata is becoming de facto more segmented.

In a recent book by Andrea Dell'Antonio that examines in great detail sonatas and canzonas from Castello's period the author takes Selfridge-Field to task for attempting artificially, and therefore arbitrarily, to impose movement divisions on the sonatas in her anthology.[15] In Sonata 16, for instance, Selfridge-Field takes the opportunity, whenever a clean break in continuity presents itself, to insert a thin-thick double barline and return to '1' in the bar-numbering. This results in three movements, which correspond to sections 1, 2, and 3–5 in Table 2.1.

Dell'Antonio's criticism is valid. However, Selfridge-Field's anachronistic act shows the shape of things to come. To reach the evolutionary stage

---

[15] Andrea Dell'Antonio, *Syntax, Form and Genre in Sonatas and Canzonas, 1621–1635* (Lucca, 1997), 27.

represented by a Corelli church sonata of the 1680s, a sonata has to do three things. First, the sections that are to become movements have to be made physically disjunct. Castello has already started down this path. Second, the would-be movements have to be tonally rounded. Such rounding is mean-ingful only if the music at some point strikes out from the home key, because it is otherwise tonally featureless. In this respect, Castello has hardly started to move. Third, the thematic rounding has to take place not at the level of the whole work but at that of its component movements.

Although Corelli's sonatas fulfil these conditions more than adequately, they preserve some vestiges of their single-movement ancestry. Internal slow movements are often both tonally open and through-composed, and mixed-tempo movements such as the one that opens the last sonata in Op. 1 (1681) recall the play with contrast motifs common in both vocal and instrumental music of the early seventeenth century (and exploited in the second movement of Castello's Sonata 16).[16] Most significantly for our present purposes, the themes of final quick movements often have the appearance of *tripla*-like paraphrases of the first quick movement (which is most often the second movement of the cycle). The second sonata of Corelli's Op. 3 demonstrates this connection clearly: Exs. 2.2(*a*) and 2.2(*b*) give the openings of the first violin part in the second and fourth move-ments respectively.

Although such overt thematic links between the outer fast movements become greatly attenuated in the course of the eighteenth century, they maintain a shadowy presence, reasserting themselves once more in the

Ex. 2.2.   Corelli, Trio sonata in D major, Op. 3 No. 2: (*a*) first movement, opening; (*b*) last movement, opening

[16] The single bar of *Adagio* separating the two allegros of Bach's Third 'Brandenburg' Con-certo is the ultimate reduction of a vestigial section. It is neither a slow conclusion to the first movement nor a slow introduction to the second but a mere separator, like a bookmark.

nineteenth and twentieth centuries. They are, indeed, one of the most commonly used means of making a finale, whatever its individual character, give the appearance of returning to the point of origin of the cyclic work, which in music as in literature is a potent signal of the coming closure of the cycle. A back-reference to the opening movement at its very start is the first opportunity that many a finale has to claim a role that extends beyond itself.

At what point in the history of the sonata and its cognate genres do we stop thinking in terms of a multisectional single movement and start thinking of a cycle of movements? The question is impossible to answer with precision because, for all its inexorability, the process is gradual and uneven. (One is reminded of the difficulty of tracing the evolution of the ritornello form model for the first movement of a Classical concerto into that of a sonata form with double exposition.) Willi Apel thought he knew the answer. In his compendious survey of Italian violin music of the seventeenth century he identified the *Canzoni a tre*, Op. 2 (1642), of the Bolognese composer Maurizio Cazzati as the first collection to show clearly a division into discrete movements.[17] Apel's criteria are not spelt out in sufficient detail for his claim to be examined critically, and without knowing the totality of the seventeenth-century sonata and canzona repertory—of which a large proportion, even among the prints, no longer survives—it is impossible to be confident about claims for priority. However, one can easily agree that from about 1650 onwards the 'cycle' model becomes more appropriate in virtually all cases than the 'single movement' model. The process intensifies in the following decades, so that by the 1680s, when Corelli's highly influential sonatas begin to come on stream in published form, all the major instrumental genres in the Italian tradition (and to some extent, also those in the French tradition, with its *livres d'orgue*, *pièces de clavecin*, and *suites de symphonies*) adopt a cyclic layout.

The completion of this formal evolution shortly before 1700 correlates with a change in what David Burrows has identified as the 'cultural style' of the period, manifested across the arts.[18] The kernel of Burrows's thesis is that in the last part of the seventeenth century public taste came to prefer artworks composed of only a few—but large—elements to ones featuring many—but small—ones. The artefact (libretto, painting, or musical composition) is not necessarily larger in its total dimensions but its structure is more streamlined. In opera librettos, for example, the reformers around Apostolo Zeno retain the traditional number of acts but reduce the number of scenes and the number of closed pieces (arias, ensembles, and choruses) contained in them. In paintings the 'clutter' is reduced so that the main elements stand out more sharply. The typical number of movements in the instrumental

---

[17] Willi Apel, *Die italienische Violinmusik im 17. Jahrhundert* (Wiesbaden, 1983), 96 and elsewhere.

[18] David Burrows, 'Style in Culture: Vivaldi, Zeno and Ricci', *Journal of Interdisciplinary History*, 4 (1973–4), 1–23.

cycle goes down first from five to four, then (at the beginning of the next century, initially in sinfonias and concertos) from four to three. Despite our customary insistence on a distinction between the 'late Baroque' and 'Classical' phases of the eighteenth century (with the optional interposition of 'galant', 'rococo', 'empfindsam', and 'pre-Classical' mini-periods according to taste), the eighteenth century shows unwavering adherence to the cultural style just described. A Vivaldi sonata is more similar in this respect to an early Beethoven sonata than it is to a chronologically and regionally closer sonata by Legrenzi. It is possible to argue that the option for longer (though fewer) units of itself made it necessary to give the component parts an individually rounded structure and so favoured the emergence of discrete movements.

If we now skip over the 'Golden Age of the movement' and take our bearings in the twentieth century, we see here and there signs of a rejection of organization by movements. This discomfort with movements is, naturally, only one current among countless others in that century, whose salient artistic hallmarks are its eclecticism, modishness, and capacity to revert to old approaches under the guise of radical innovation. The midwife of this rejection is the drive for ever greater unity. As Janet Levy reminds us in a gently trenchant essay, the praise of unity (alongside that of organicism, thematic economy, chamber-music textures, concentration, and counterpoint) is one of the great 'motherhood statements' of twentieth-century (and some nineteenth-century) music criticism and analysis.[19] It is difficult to conceive of a context in which unity might be negatively regarded. Gérard Genette has bravely tilted at this shibboleth (with special reference to literature), deploring the elevation of unity in all its manifestations (of subject, method, or form) into 'a sort of dominant value, a value as imperious as it is unconsidered, almost never subjected to scrutiny, accepted ... as a matter of course'.[20] It is easy to agree that unity of some kind is desirable: the problem is to locate it and establish on what plane it should operate.

Separate movements are an easy target for the more radical apostles of unity. By definition, they have autonomy at some level. This means that they make a statement about themselves that is not shared by the rest of the work. Between movements, not only have coughing and retuning taken place but, in the past, even completely foreign musical items have notoriously been inserted, as in Mozart's 'academy' at the Burgtheater, Vienna, on 23 March 1783, when, after the first three movements of the 'Haffner' Symphony (K. 385) had been heard, the finale was held back until the end of the concert, ten items later. How much better, according to the seekers after unity, to make the parts of a work so interdependent that movement divisions become meaningless.

[19] Janet M. Levy, 'Covert and Casual Values in Recent Writings about Music', *Journal of Musicology*, 5 (1987), 3–27.

[20] Gérard Genette, *Paratexts*, trans. Jane E. Lewin (Cambridge, 1997), 204.

The identity of movements is further subverted by the new premium set on continuity. In the nineteenth century and earlier a run-on relationship between one movement and its successor is usually a form of elision, a means of creating tension (the long dominant pedal preceding the C major outburst at the start of the finale of Beethoven's Fifth Symphony is a case in point), or a deliberate attempt to keep the audience attentive, as in Mendelssohn's concertos. It is only in the twentieth century that the 'link' as transmutation comes into its own. (It hardly needs saying that the enemy of movements is also the enemy of bridge passages that serve merely as functional connectors.)

A more subtle influence working in the same direction is the re-establishment of the primacy of the score as main carrier of the identity of a work. (In fact, to speak of a 'work' is in itself to acknowledge the subordination of the performance event to a notated blueprint.)[21] Music is in reality both an experience in time (when heard in performance) and an experience in space (when perused).[22] *Qua* temporal experience, it is evanescent, like a cinema film, and moves in only one direction. The whole of the structure is created by the listener's memory in relation to past events, and by his anticipation in relation to future ones. *Qua* spatial experience, it is more like an architect's plan. It has a left and right, and a top and bottom. Unless abnormally long, it can be comprehended synoptically. A *canon cancrizans* and the permutations of a note row can be seen clearly on the page, regardless of any difficulty with hearing them. (And so it was, of course, in music of the Middle Ages.) It is only the spatial aspect that makes sense of the palindromic prelude and postlude framing Hindemith's *Ludus tonalis* (1942). Without electronic trickery, there is no true reversal of a note as sound: it comes in with an attack and goes out with a decay. But as symbols on the page a crotchet followed by a quaver are perfectly and satisfyingly reversible.

Thus in the twentieth century the one-movement symphony, concerto, or sonata are privileged. If we consider nineteenth-century and early twentieth-century experiments with composite, continuously running forms—such works as Weber's *Konzertstück* in F minor for Piano and Orchestra (1821), Alkan's two *Concerti da camera* (1832–3), the two Liszt piano concertos (the first completed in its original version in 1839), the same composer's Piano Sonata in B minor (1853), and the last six Skryabin piano sonatas

---

[21] This argument is developed in my essay 'The Work-Concept and Composer-Centredness', in Michael Talbot (ed.), *The Musical Work: Reality or Invention?* (Liverpool, 2000), 168–86. Several other essays in this volume make a similar point. Works (and, by the same token, movements) hardly exist outside the Western art-music tradition, which, in the context of world musics, is a remarkable oddity for its refusal to accept the performance event as the full essence of music.

[22] In making these remarks, I am influenced by ideas advanced in Philip Downs, 'Beethoven's "New Way" and the *Eroica*', *Musical Quarterly*, 56 (1970), 585–604 at 599. Downs associates the temporal aspect with music's dramatic, discursive, and narrative properties, the spatial aspect with its formal and recapitulatory properties.

(1907–13)—we notice a strange thing. Although in some later examples the whole work is subject to a single over-arching form (usually sonata form), the topoi of the traditional three or four movements have been reassigned to sections within that form (take, for example, the scherzoid fugato that dominates the development section of Liszt's sonata). The single-movement work thus continues to pay homage, doubtless consciously, to the expressive identities of the separate movements even as it repudiates their separate existence.

In the twentieth century, one-movement structures begin to escape from these stereotypes. Richard Strauss's *Alpine Symphony* (1915), with its twenty-two named sections, uses a simple narrative programme (which gives concrete expression to the old musical metaphor of a visit and subsequent return) to acquire its shape. Sibelius's Seventh Symphony (1924) artfully dovetails different speeds into one another to give the impression of total seamlessness. Shostakovich's second (1927) and third (1929) symphonies offer a bizarre, unpredictable procession of vivid, contrasted episodes—a feast of the paratactic principle and the so-called progressive form.

In their broad mass, however, twentieth-century composers have been surprisingly content to inherit the legacy of the Classical and Romantic forms, even where no neo-Classical or neo-Romantic urge is evident. It is indeed surprising how some composers who are absolutely non-traditional in the nuts and bolts of their musical language—the composers of the Second Viennese School (Schoenberg, Berg, and Webern) spring to mind—succumb meekly to the three-movement or four-movement layout that was good enough for Mozart or Brahms.[23]

An interesting twentieth-century tendency, which is the swing of the pendulum to the opposite side from the urge towards one-movement form, has been to expand the number of movements, sometimes to a colossal degree. In the eighteenth, and to some extent also the nineteenth, century, to raise the number of movements above four (five at the outside) is to give notice that the work is 'light': a divertimento, serenade, or suite rather than a sonata, symphony, or concerto. Beethoven's 'Pastoral' Symphony (1808) legitimized the five-movement symphony, as we see from its imitations by Berlioz (*Symphonie fantastique*), Schumann (Symphony No. 3, 'Rhenish'), Goldmark (*Rustic Wedding Symphony*), Tchaikovsky (Symphony No. 3, 'Polish'), and Mahler (his First Symphony, as originally conceived; subsequently, his second, fifth, and seventh symphonies). But the line is firmly drawn (for symphonies) at six movements until Mahler's Third Symphony (1896) arrives to break the mould (using picturesque movement titles as a cloak of respectability). For sonatas, there is a similar semi-liberation. Schumann's

---

[23] Schoenberg was also notably traditional in his approach to rhythm and phrase structure. The charge of 'wrong-notery' with which Prokofiev and Poulenc are so often taxed would in justice apply equally well to him (ironically, in view of the rigorous method with which he selected pitches).

Piano Sonata in F minor, Op. 14 (1836, revised 1853) had five movements in its original version before the composer decided to retrench one of the two scherzos. Brahms, who had employed conventional four-movement form for his first two sonatas, Op. 1 in C major (1863) and Op. 2 in F sharp minor (1852), chose a five-movement plan for his third (Op. 3, in F minor, 1853). Chamber music in the 'serious' genres (duo sonata, trio, quartet, quintet, and sextet) remains more conservative in this respect, even though Beethoven's late quartets (Opp. 130, 131, and 132 in particular) might have been expected to release a riot of invention. For concertos, to have more than three movements is an innovation, so the question hardly arises.

In the twentieth century, the floodgates open for those who wish to pass through. It is hard, however, to escape the impression that some of the extravagance results from a misprision, or at least a reinterpretation, of some of the collections and anthologies of the past. The London musicians who greeted the arrival of Corelli's *Concerti grossi*, Op. 6, by playing through their partbooks from cover to cover at a single session were not under any illusion that they were performing a 'super-work' arching over twelve nominally separate concertos (even if not all modern record-collectors are fully aware of the boundaries between consecutive works!). Nor did Bach intend, in the two books comprising his '48', twice to produce a colossal, $(24 \times 2)$-movement edifice. The sequence of keys—chromatically up the scale, with alternation of the major and minor modes—is certainly calculated to ensure that keys are not duplicated; additionally, it acts as an effective aid to the performer who wishes to find his piece quickly without bothering to consult a list of contents. It is definitely not meant as a mechanism for making a smooth tonal transition from one major-minor pair to the next. However, the conventions of modern concert (and naturally recording) practice allows such collections to be presented to the public as if they were indeed 'super-works'. Even *The Art of Fugue* and *The Musical Offering* should be understood as collections that have a unity 'on paper' that does not, however, license their performance as single compositions. It may therefore be a productive 'misreading' of Bach that has inspired mammoth works in the mould of Messiaen's *Visions de l'Amen* and *Vingt Regards sur l'enfant Jésus*. Even such an apparently imitative collection as Shostakovich's *24 Preludes and Fugues* seems to stray from the model in this respect. The progression of the pairs through the keys follows the method pioneered by Chopin for his *Preludes*: sharpwards through the circle of fifths, with relative major and minor keys alternating. This makes for a smooth tonal transition if one chooses to perform, say, a group of four consecutive preludes and fugues. But is to present all twenty-four in one sitting the ideal? The unmistakably climactic character of the final movement, a massive double (i.e. three-stage) fugue saturated with hermeneutic significance (an initial 'Russian' subject combined harmoniously with a later 'Jewish' subject), demands that it come after something very substantial. Should that something be the twenty-three preceding pairs?

The 'gigantistic' current in twentieth-century instrumental music (which, inevitably, is balanced by its opposite, the 'miniaturistic' current) can be read as an attempt to make work and performance event coextensive. A full-length opera or oratorio forms an entire programme, a complete listening experience, in itself. An instrumental work lasting an hour or more, either multimovement (in the style of Hans Otte's *Buch der Klänge*) or multisectional (in that of Ronald Stevenson's *Passacaglia on DSCH*), begins to demand the same level of undistracted absorption on the part of the audience and to claim for itself the same artistic status. The advent of the CD, with over an hour of playing time, can be expected to keep such works in favour—indeed, to stimulate their composition.[24]

This discussion of real and factitious entities, or structures on paper that may or may not be translatable into structures in sound, takes us straight into the territory of the 'multi-piece' as identified by Jonathan Dunsby.[25] Dunsby's contention is that in certain nineteenth-century collections of character pieces, in which there is no overt compulsion to perform the pieces in their totality and in sequence, their conformity to the general norms of cyclic works (the sonata, in particular) makes this the intended and most desirable outcome. Dunsby approaches the matter cautiously and rightly insists on examining the question on a case-by-case basis, even in relation to the six ostensibly very similar collections of character pieces for piano, each containing between two and eight movements, that Brahms produced between Op. 10 (the four *Ballades*) and Op. 119 (four *Klavierstücke*). However, I think that he is a little too categorical when he states: 'Whereas it was tolerable, even desirable, and certainly the case, for Classical movements from multi-movement pieces to be performed separately, this was no longer either Brahms's or his audience's expectation.'[26] It is very true that the rise of the 'work' (in its full, constitutive sense as described by Lydia Goehr in *The Imaginary Museum of Musical Works*) led it successfully to challenge the 'number' as the principal sorting category in a public performance event.[27] The dismemberment (as opposed to the extracting of an individual movement) of a Mozart symphony, as described earlier for K. 385, would certainly have been unacceptable to professionals and connoisseurs by the mid-nineteenth century. But not all performances of Brahms's time were public, and not all of them were free from non-musical constraints (such as the availability of time or the ability of the performer to master every piece technically). So it is better to think in relative terms: on

---

[24] Already, the extended playing time of CDs has encouraged artists and producers to conceive factitious 'works' (not so called but marketed and consumed as such) assembled from originally independent short pieces after the model of the popular music album.

[25] Jonathan Dunsby, 'The Multi-Piece in Brahms: *Fantasien* Op. 116', in Robert Pascall (ed.), *Brahms: Biographical, Documentary and Analytical Studies* (Cambridge, 1983), 167–89.

[26] Ibid. 168.

[27] Lydia Goehr, *The Imaginary Museum of Musical Works: An Essay in the Philosophy of Music* (Oxford, 1992).

one hand, an ideal performance of the complete set in the style of a multi-movement work; on the other hand, a not quite ideal but still acceptable performance of less than the full set in a pragmatically determined order.

At the extremes, the distinction between a mere collection and a multi-piece is very sharp. Dunsby writes: 'We would lose a critical tool in our understanding of Romantic form if we . . . equated the overall structure of [Schumann's] *Carnaval* with that of, say, Chopin's Op. 17 Mazurkas.'[28] Quite so, for Chopin's grouping is one of mere convenience that creates a package of just the right size and homogeneity for the marketplace (in saying which, one means no disparagement). To demonstrate that this set is not a multi-piece, one merely has to experiment with rearranging the order of the four pieces and consider whether any harm has been done. In Schumann's case—thinking also of comparable extended collections such as the *Papillons, Davidsbündlertänze, Kreisleriana*, and the *Novelletten*—dismemberment is not only unacceptable but also impractical, given the dense intertextual reference between movements, the complex rondo-like arrangements (sometimes featuring 'rondos within rondos'), and the frequent run-on relationships.[29]

As his case study, with especial relevance for Brahms's practice, Dunsby chooses the seven *Fantasien*, individually entitled either *Capriccio* or *Intermezzo*, of Op. 116 (1892). The movements are briefly characterized in Table 2.2.

The second column of this table, which gives the keys (following the normal convention of upper case for major, lower case for minor), already suggests a cyclic work. D minor begins and ends the sequence, and the

TABLE 2.2.   *Brahms*, Fantasien, *Op. 116*

| No. | Key | Tempo, Metre | Title: Form | Length[a] |
|-----|-----|--------------|-------------|-----------|
| 1 | d | Presto energico, 3/8 | *Capriccio*: Sonata form with mirror recapitulation | 2.12 |
| 2 | a | Andante, 3/4 | *Intermezzo*: Variations | 3.26 |
| 3 | g | Allegro passionato, barred C | *Capriccio*: Simple ternary | 3.14 |
| 4 | E | Adagio, 3/4 | *Intermezzo*: 'Free' rondo | 4.18 |
| 5 | e | Andante con grazia, 6/8 | *Intermezzo*: Rounded binary | 3.36 |
| 6 | E | Andantino teneramente, 3/4 | *Intermezzo*: Simple ternary | 3.00 |
| 7 | d | Allegro agitato, 2/4, with coda in 3/8 | *Capriccio*: Ternary with coda | 2.23 |

[a] Durations in minutes and seconds taken from the Nimbus recording (NI 1788) by Martin Jones.

[28] Dunsby, 'The Multi-Piece in Brahms', 169.

[29] To be sure, Schumann also provides more clear-cut (and more conventionally scaled) examples of multi-pieces, such as the five-movement *Faschingsschwank aus Wien*, as well as collections that have no multi-piece aspirations (*Waldscenen, Album für die Jugend*).

internal movements are all placed in keys closely related by the circle of fifths (e/E, a, g). Moreover, movements 4–6 form, in tonal respects (and arguably also in terms of character and tempo), a coherent subunit: an expansion into three movements (almost equivalent, as a structure, to a minuet with a *maggiore* trio) of what could otherwise have been a single intermezzo in slow tempo. It is interesting to learn that, according to a letter to his publisher, Simrock, Brahms originally conceived the opus as a five-movement group.[30] Since Brahms liked to cover his compositional tracks well, there is no documentary evidence pointing to which two pieces were the late additions. One suspects, however, that two out of the three consecutive intermezzos (which two would be difficult to say) were the afterthoughts. With only one intermezzo between the second and third capriccio, one would have not only a strict pattern of alternation between the two quasi-genres but also a good approximation of the structure (first movement–slow movement–scherzo and trio–slow intermezzo–finale) of Brahms's Third Piano Sonata. In fact, there is little to distinguish the *Fantasien* from a five-movement sonata of the period, except—and the point is not trivial—for the restricted scale of every movement, which removes the possibility of extended development. As Dunsby has noted, the nature of the coda of the final capriccio, which reverts to the 3/8 metre of the first capriccio and gives special emphasis to the augmented triad (a pungent harmonic effect that occurs in all seven pieces, lending them a strong common identity), has all the hallmarks of a coda in the finale of a genuine cyclic work.[31]

All the same, this is perhaps not the ideal specimen of a multi-piece, because of the problematic triad of intermezzos in the second half. Arguably, the set would function even more successfully as an integrated cycle if only one movement out of Nos. 4–6 were performed. Omitting Nos. 5 and 6 would preserve modal unity and reduce the incidence of simple ternary form, whose occurrence in two movements (Nos. 3 and 6, discounting the more elaborate version of the form in No. 7) mars Brahms's otherwise obvious intention to put on show an 'anthology' of miniature forms. But there are plenty of collections by Brahms and Schumann that validate flawlessly Dunsby's concept of the multi-piece, and one must be grateful to him for coining the term.

To complete our investigation into movements as components of larger works and to prepare for the next chapter, we must briefly consider the vast repertory of vocal music composed in the two centuries or more leading up to the seventeenth century, the 'cradle' of the idea of a movement as far as instrumental music was concerned.

Unlike instrumental music, vocal music is constrained by something much more concrete than just a general notion of length, coherence, balance,

---

[30] Dunsby, 'The Multi-Piece in Brahms', 173.
[31] Ibid. 187.

repetition, development, and so on: it has a text. Throughout history, a text has been more than a simple peg on which to hang an autonomous musical structure (though a few twentieth-century compositions, such as Arvo Pärt's *Summa*, attempt to prove the opposite as a tour de force). Its structure—phonetic, metrical, formal, and semantic—informs the musical setting. Tension and contradiction between the literary and musical dimensions is often present, but it is regarded more as a necessary but perhaps unfortunate price to pay for bringing music and words together than as a desideratum to be actively promoted. Where words themselves suggest a structure that is compatible with, or runs parallel with, a musical structure envisaged by the composer, the opportunity is usually seized with both hands.

In the case of church music based on liturgically prescribed texts, the coincidence of textual and musical form (in both analytical and hermeneutic respects) is not guaranteed. It arises more by chance than by design. A prime instance, as we shall see more closely later, is the text of the Ordinary of the Mass, set as a cycle of (up to) six movements from the fourteenth century (Machaut) onwards. One may use the term 'movement' unapologetically, since the separation of all six items by other musical (and non-musical) events during the service rules out a run-on relationship between any two of them, and hence the possibility that they might count as sections rather than movements according to our chosen definition.[32] However, their separation concerns only the 'performance event' (their singing during the liturgy), not their status as movements written or printed consecutively on the page. This is another example of how Western art music, uniquely as it would seem, enshrines the identity of works (or, if this term is contentious: of compositions, pieces, etc.) in permanent, written form rather than evanescent, oral form. Indeed: without notation, there would be no works at all.

This is not the place to rehearse the varied means by which composers before 1700 imparted coherence to their Mass settings, using such devices as head-motifs, plainsong (and other) cantus firmi, and parody techniques. Suffice it to say that the degree of sophistication shown, the evidence of forward planning, and (to borrow Cone's term) the 'synoptic comprehension' of the whole are on a level that Bach and Beethoven do not surpass.

The other great liturgical 'genre' regularly to exhibit multimovement construction is the Magnificat, the Canticle at Vespers. Like a psalm used liturgically in the Catholic rite, the Magnificat consists of a series of verses (here, numbering ten) followed by the Lesser Doxology ('Gloria Patri... Amen'), which supplies two further verses. The Magnificat was often set in *alternatim* fashion, odd-numbered (or less commonly, even-numbered)

---

[32] The six movements (Kyrie, Gloria, Credo, Sanctus, Benedictus (sometimes absorbed within the Sanctus), Agnus Dei) may of course themselves divide in turn either into sections or into formally distinct movements.

verses being left in plainsong.[33] This meant that the verses set polyphonically were *ipso facto* separated from one another, forming independent
movements. Even when all twelve verses were set polyphonically to different music (a 'direct' setting, to use the modern terminology) or when some
or all of them shared the same music (a 'strophic' setting), the division into
separate movements usually remained.[34]

As cantus-firmus material, or as a thematic basis for its melodic substance, the Magnificat has the eight ancient psalm tones at its disposal.
Particularly in view of the enforced brevity of their movements and the
relatively consistent length of the texts for each verse, pre-Baroque Magnificats tended to be shaped after the fashion of chorale variations: they
present a series of movements of roughly equal length based on common
primary material. Because of this background identity, the differences
between one 'variation' and another (we are especially interested, of course,
in the final variation) acquire added significance. Polyphonic settings of the
Magnificat offer an unrivalled opportunity to find out how far modern
conceptions of 'finale character' go back.

Both sacred music (motets) and secular music (chansons, Lieder, madri-
gals, etc.) before 1700 offer limitless examples of freely written (or compiled)
verse and prose texts devised (or appropriated) for musical setting. Here,
the textual influence on the music is likely to be stronger, since the words
are already organized artistically into regular patterns, using such devices
as division into stanzas and line repetitions. Where two or more stanzas or
prose paragraphs exist in the text, these normally become discrete 'parts' in
the musical setting. Once again, we can often speak de facto of a series of
linked movements collectively forming a work.

The scene is now set for a preliminary discussion of final movements.

---

[33] One may observe in passing here that the preference for a polyphonic conclusion to the
Magnificat corresponds to the modern (but evidently not only modern) expectation of a
climactic end to a work.
[34] We will ignore here single-movement settings (Palestrina wrote one for eight voices),
which in any case are rare before 1600.

# 3

# *The Idea of a Finale*

VIEWED naively, and of course quite improperly, as a belletristic text, the Ordinary of the Mass reveals many oddities, not to say short-comings. The start is propitious: three statements of 'Kyrie eleison', three of 'Christe eleison', and three more of 'Kyrie eleison'. Here, there is economy of utterance and perfect ternary proportion on two levels. Were it not for a Trinitarian scruple that makes the subject of the second 'Kyrie eleison' the Holy Spirit, in contradistinction to God the Father in the first, even more composers would have chosen a purely ternary musical structure for the movement. The Gloria is more problematic. Its eighty-four words and lack of simple repetition (although some phrases show parallelism) mean that unless special measures are taken, its length will greatly exceed that of the Kyrie, possibly with adverse consequences for the overall bal-ance. From the Baroque period onwards, the Gordian knot is often cut, in that the Gloria is segmented to become sometimes as many as ten or eleven movements (as against the three of the Kyrie). Most pre-Baroque settings retain the Gloria as a single movement (albeit one often subdivided into sections) and adopt various expedients to cut down its length: severe rationing of melisma and word repetition, homophonic texture or imitation at exceptionally close time intervals, and *in extremis* simultaneous presenta-tion of different portions of text.

In cases where the Mass setting terminates at the Gloria (this is the case with the Lutheran *Missa brevis* and its Catholic counterpart from the Bar-oque onwards), the ending of the text is very well suited to accompany a coda (in a single-movement setting) or a finale (in a multimovement set-ting). The last two sentences run: 'Cum Sancto Spiritu in gloria Dei Patris. Amen'. Here, 'gloria' is a keyword that lends itself excellently to animated and florid exultation, while the 'A-' of 'Amen' is the perfect vehicle for an ecstatic melisma in the style of a vocalise. This is music's first great labora-tory for the joyful conclusion.

The Credo, which runs to 163 words (many of them polysyllabic), has the advantages and problems of the Gloria, only more so. The word 'saeculi' (literally, 'of the age') in the penultimate sentence (the last sentence is once again a simple 'Amen') is a heaven-sent opportunity to practise word-painting by employing musical devices connoting length: extra-long notes, extended sequences, and so forth. This is music's first great laboratory for the monumental conclusion.

The Sanctus and Benedictus revert to the smaller scale of the Kyrie, allusive reference to the Trinity returning with the threefold enunciation of the word 'Sanctus'. The twofold statement of 'Hosanna in excelsis' framing the Benedictus is a welcome rhetorical intensification to which composers commonly respond with an *ut supra* repeat of the first music, often animated in scherzo-like fashion and because of its brevity and distinctiveness, easily tolerating an unaltered second hearing.

Closing the cycle, the Agnus Dei matches the Kyrie by conforming to an overall ternary structure and running (with all the repetitions observed) to a very similar number of words. More precisely, we have 'bar' form as cultivated by the Mastersingers of medieval times and comprising two identical *Stollen* ('Agnus Dei...miserere nobis') and an *Abgesang* ('Agnus Dei...dona nobis pacem').[1] Before the seventeenth century the three statements were normally set as separate movements, in which (just as in the three movements of the Kyrie) the outer portions were more closely related to each other in musical substance than either was to the central portion.

The 'dona nobis pacem' concluding words are highly unusual for a liturgical text in terms of affect. They are the prototype for a restful conclusion, whether this is interpreted as 'peace', 'sleep', or 'passing away'—these three concepts having in common the quality of calm inertia. In late Baroque and Classical Masses the coincidence that the cycle's opening 'Kyrie eleison' (with a hiatus between the adjacent Es) and its concluding 'Dona nobis pacem' had the same number of syllables and an identical stress pattern tempted many composers into making the latter simply a retexted version of the former—what James Webster has called the *Dona ut Kyrie* practice.[2] This rather facile solution, which allows the rounding function of a conclusion to take precedence over all expressive factors, is less characteristic of earlier settings.

To sum up, the endings of the Gloria, Credo, and Agnus Dei texts already harbour in embryo the three characteristic moods (joy, monumentality, rest) that we shall encounter later in the codas and finales of instrumental music.

Leaving aside its distinctive mood, derived from its text, the Agnus Dei conclusion to the Mass (and especially its third portion, a kind of 'finale within the finale') has commonly displayed since the late fifteenth century, if not earlier, two structural properties that are both very important for the formation of our modern concept of the finale. The first I shall call 'cumulation'. This entails the expansion of the music in any appropriate way that registers aurally. The expansion may be 'horizontal', so that the movement

---

[1] We ignore here abbreviated versions of the Agnus Dei in which one or two of the three statements are entrusted to plainsong.

[2] James Webster, *Haydn's Farewell Symphony and the Idea of Classical Style: Through-Composition and Cyclic Integration in his Instrumental Music* (Cambridge, 1991), 186. The use instead of a retexted 'Gratias agimus tibi' for the 'Dona nobis pacem' of J. S. Bach's Mass in B minor deviates from custom. Perhaps the clinching factor for Bach was the desire to retain D major tonality at the close.

spreads over more bars (to use the modern, anachronistic unit). It is note-worthy in this connection that the third 'Agnus Dei' quite often dwarfs its two predecessors in size. Alternatively, the expansion may be 'vertical', supernumerary parts being drafted in to swell the sonority or augment the polyphonic complexity. One well-known example is the 'Hercules' Mass (*Missa Hercules Dux Ferrariae*) of Josquin des Prez (*c*.1450–1521). Until the final 'Agnus Dei' the Mass is scored for four parts (SATB), with the cus-tomary more lightly scored interludes (two voices in the 'Pleni sunt caeli' from the Sanctus and the whole of the Benedictus, and three in the second 'Agnus Dei'). In the final movement a second superius and second bass join in. The widely spaced entries in cantus firmus style of the subject (derived from the solmization syllables of the Duke's name) in the first soprano (superius) and tenor voices, coupled with the dense imitative play of the other four voices, produce a thrillingly climactic effect genuinely in the spirit of the old motto *Finis coronat opus* (The end crowns the work). Josquin's *Missa L'homme armé sexti toni* and *Missa Malheur me bat* expand similarly from four to six voices for the final 'Agnus Dei'. (In both Masses this movement is especially impressive, since the two extra voices are extracted canonically, obviating the need for separate notation.)

The second structural property defies easy naming. It is close to 'liquid-ation' in Schoenberg's sense, but that term seems unhappy when used in English. I propose to call it 'regression', using this word in a wholly value-free sense. The 'going back' can be literal, as in a *Dona ut Kyrie* repetition, where it has the force of a simple return to the source. But it often reaches back beyond previously heard material to strive for something more basic. It is, so to speak, development by stripping down rather than by the more usual process of elaboration. Josquin shows how poignant the effect can be in the final 'Agnus Dei' of his late *Missa Pange lingua*, based on a plainsong hymn for Corpus Christi in the Phrygian (white-note E) mode. The opening of this movement is shown as Ex. 3.1 (original note values are halved and only the top voice is texted). Josquin begins by subjecting a paraphrase of the chant's first notes to imitation after every bar at the interval of the unison or octave. In previous movements imitation has nearly always been at the fourth or fifth, so the choice of a more 'primitive' interval (the description is justified in a historical as well as an expressive sense, since the unison and octave were the earliest intervals of imitation to be regularly employed) achieves a strong effect. The chime-like oscillation between two triads (E minor and D minor) creates an air of spaciousness and expectancy—for, paradoxically, there is no better way of drawing attention to impending change than ostinato repetition.

Change duly arrives in bar 5, when the soprano, having rested for four bars, sails in with a statement of the chant's opening in doubled note values, clearly audible over the busy but now subordinate lower voices. The sudden move to a hypermeasure of two bars (this is an instance of the device known

Ex. 3.1.   Josquin des Prez, *Missa Pange lingua*, Agnus Dei III, opening

as 'hemiola') makes a majestic effect. This is the first and only time in the
Mass when the texture approximates to that of accompanied solo song.

Regression of a remarkably similar kind occurs in a Mass by Claudio
Monteverdi (1567–1643).[3] This Mass for four voices and continuo is constructed with extraordinary thematic economy. Its basic motif is a descending tetrachord (G–F–E–D), which in the course of the work is elaborated in
two main ways: by 'scrambling' the four notes in the order 1, 3, 2, 4 (G–E–F–
D), and by decorating notes 1 and 3 of the 'scrambled' version with auxiliary
notes (G–F–G–E–F–E–F–D).

Until the Agnus Dei, of which only the opening statement is set, Monteverdi employs predominantly imitative texture, offset by a few lively
block-chordal passages. The final movement signals its special character
right at the outset, where, just as in Josquin's *Missa Pange lingua* (though
doubtless coincidentally), Monteverdi briefly imitates a tolling bell with
imitation at the unison. The music then reverts to a more conventional
imitative treatment until bar 16, where for the first time the phrase 'miserere
nobis' is heard. As a response to the expressive content of these words, a

---

[3] It was published posthumously in 1651, and was therefore the last of Monteverdi's three
complete Mass settings to appear in print. Its date of composition is harder to determine.

Ex. 3.2.   Monteverdi, *Messa III*, Agnus Dei, bars 15–19

plea for divine mercy, but also as a way of lending the movement as a whole
a grandeur appropriate to its closing function, Monteverdi at last drops his
bombshell. The 'scrambled' version of the basic motif is presented, faux-
bourdon style, in close-position parallel chords, shown in Ex. 3.2 (where
only the bass has been texted). Their rate of movement (in regular minims)
is unexpectedly slow, which creates a solemn, almost processional effect,
and the false relations between the outer voices introduce an acerbic tone
not heard before. Like Josquin, Monteverdi has husbanded his resources
well, saving up his strongest and most direct effects till last.

Cumulation and regression occur in just the same way in the final movements of polyphonic Magnificats. The text of the Lesser Doxology that
is obligatorily appended to the Canticle (as also to every psalm) is exceptionally favourable towards a climactic ending. In the eleventh verse
('Gloria Patri, et Filio, et Spiritui Sancto') there is the same scope for joyful
expression as at the end of the Gloria in the Mass, while the invocation of
eternity ('Et in saecula saeculorum. Amen') at the end of the twelfth verse
parallels the 'Et vitam venturi...' closing the Credo. Moreover, the opening
of the twelfth verse with 'Sicut erat in principio...' offers the composer a
heaven-sent opportunity to refer back to the opening of the composition in
punning fashion, thus achieving a rounding that can claim textual justification.

From the start, composers give special treatment to the twelfth verse (or
the eleventh and twelfth verses, if combined in a single movement). There is
extant from Antoine Brumel (*c*.1460–*c*.1515) a celebrated eight-part setting of
the twelfth verse, published posthumously in 1553, in which each part
paraphrases one of the eight psalm tones: a *quodlibet* and *summa* rolled

into one.[4] The set of eight Magnificats ('direct' settings including all twelve verses) by the Roman composer Costanzo Festa (c.1490–1545), which were published in 1554, displays this urge to climax in extreme form. Nominally in four parts, each setting expands to between five and ten voices for the setting of the twelfth verse. Nearly all of these final movements include strict canonic imitation, sometimes multiple or otherwise recondite. As in Josquin's 'Hercules' Mass, the monumental treatment is, paradoxically, also regressive, since it allows the primary material, taken from plainchant, to assert itself in long, often uniform, note values. Here, too, the polyphonic complexity demands an increase in movement length in order for the musical processes (imitation, antiphonal contrast, etc.) to play themselves out.[5] It is noteworthy that Festa reserves the most extravagant expansion for the last two Magnificats in the set: No. 7, ending *a 7* (perhaps with punning intent), and No. 8, ending *a 10*. The eight settings seem almost to constitute a 'multi-piece' with its own final climax.[6]

Similar to Festa's cycle is one by Nicolas Gombert (c.1495–c.1560), copied in 1552. Gombert's eight *alternatim* (i.e. six-verse) settings likewise introduce up to four extra voices for the final verse. An interesting difference is that the Netherlander likes to anticipate the build-up in the settings of the verses preceding the last. After the opening verse has established the four-part norm, the texture may thin to as few as two voices before the gradual ascent to the summit begins.

Baroque Magnificats take the same approach, although the musical means of achieving climax have now become more diverse. A *ne plus ultra* of 'colossal Baroque' monumentality is achieved in a wonderful eight-part Magnificat for two choirs with string accompaniment by Bonaventura Rubino (born c.1600), *maestro di cappella* at the cathedral of Palermo from 1643 to 1665.[7] Rubino sets the Doxology as a single movement. This movement ('Gloria Patri...') opens conventionally enough with imitative treatment of a partly declamatory, partly melismatic, motif in lively quavers and semiquavers. But in bar 4 the tenor of the first choir steals in with a statement of the unadorned plainchant melody in extra-long notes (initially, two tied semibreves) that unhurriedly fights its way forward against the

---

[4] The issues surrounding the authenticity of this movement and its relationship to the otherwise four-part Magnificat to which it apparently belongs are not yet fully resolved. Together with other Magnificat settings by Brumel, it has been edited by Barton Hudson in the Corpus mensurabilis musicae series (1972).

[5] We shall return later to the important, but often overlooked, question of the relationship between length and complexity.

[6] This point is made in the introduction by Alexander Main to his edition of the cycle in the Corpus mensurabilis musicae series (1968). It is quite legitimate to regard the cycle on paper (that is, in its abstract, ideal form) as a single opus, even though the circumstances for its practical realization as such did not exist at the time of composition.

[7] Modern edition in Bonaventura Rubino, *Vespro dello Stellario con sinfonie ed altri salmi*, ed. Giuseppe Colisani and Daniele Ficola (Florence, 1996), 445–81. This setting is the *Magnificat secundo* from Rubino's *Salmi varii*, Op. 5 (Palermo, 1655).

continuing imitative and antiphonal play of the other ten parts (seven voices, two violins, and continuo). After twenty bars the end of the chant is reached. Immediately, with a change of metre from common time to 3/2, the setting of the last verse begins. After four bars the soprano of the first choir enters with the chant melody, in *Pfundnoten* as before, and the process is repeated. The climax is therefore double; but the change of metre and the transfer of the chant to the highest voice (cf. the third 'Agnus Dei' of Josquin's *Missa Pange lingua*) do enough to ensure that the second statement 'caps' the first. So great is the contrast between the rate of movement of the cantus-firmus notes and all the others that the music gives the impression of being in two tempi at once: a cosmic tempo (of the chant) and a terrestrial tempo (of the surrounding motivic play).

Motets and secular pieces in two or more *partes* from the Renaissance regularly show the same processes of cumulation and regression. From well back in the Middle Ages it is common to present borrowed material (the cantus firmus) initially in very long note values and then, for its subsequent appearances, in progressively shorter notes. This is a form of cumulation based on metric and/or rhythmic acceleration. But as the part carrying the borrowed material speeds up, its rate of movement is brought more into line with that of the other parts, which makes it possible to move to a more homophonic texture. The increased simplicity of utterance and transparency of texture constitute regression. In this instance, cumulation and regression become partners, each enabling the other.

The dual process is beautifully illustrated by Josquin's six-part motet *Praeter rerum seriem*. It is based on a strophic devotional song for Christmas, the text for each stanza forming a sestet. The three stanzas are organized by Josquin as two *partes*; the first is coextensive with the opening sestet, while the second is itself bipartite, moving to a new mensuration (in modern terms, a new metre and tempo) precisely at the point where the third sestet succeeds the second. The setting of the third stanza could aptly be described as a coda to the second movement.

In the *prima pars*, whose opening is shown (with note values halved and resting parts omitted) as Ex. 3.3(a), the borrowed melody, in the first tenor, moves too slowly to come through clearly as a melodic line, although its effectiveness as a scaffolding for the more mobile bass parts is plain. The first section of the *secunda pars* reduces the extreme disparity of note values between the cantus firmus and the other parts but keeps their functions essentially the same (see Ex. 3.3(b), where the note values are original). The coda-like second section presents the borrowed material in antiphony between the upper and lower voices, and for the first time the music becomes genuinely song-like, revealing the melody in its pristine glory. Its opening is quoted as Ex. 3.3(c), for which the note values have been halved and only the two lines with the borrowed melody are texted.

Ex. 3.3. Josquin des Prez, motet *Praeter rerum seriem*: (*a*) Part I, opening; (*b*) Part II, opening; (*c*) Part II, bars 53–8

Ex. 3.3.  (*contd.*)

As we turn now to instrumental music, we need to put into perspective the significance for the instrumental tradition of the foregoing observations on vocal genres. It is not claimed that the movement cycles and final movements of vocal genres acted as actual models for composers of sonatas and suites. What is claimed, however, is that familiarity with such cycles and their conclusions made musicians and their audiences aware from the very start of certain universal aesthetic principles of composite structures, and of some of the associated problems, potentialities, and solutions. The composers of the first instrumental cycles did not need to invent these principles from scratch.

The cycles in question were groups, usually comprising no more than two or three items, of dances in a common mode or key that often advertised their affinity by being thematic paraphrases of each other. In extreme cases, the paraphrase was little more than a metrical conversion (as if one were to invent a complementary version of 'God save the Queen' in common time). This is the classic *Tanz–Nachtanz* ('dance and afterdance') relationship, whose roots go back to medieval times. One characteristic of such pairings and the occasional longer grouping is that the weight of the cycle falls on the first dance and reduces progressively in the successive movements.

This is the right moment to establish what one means by 'weight', which, like so many other descriptive terms used in musicology, is a metaphor whose suitability as an analytical concept demands scrutiny.

Does weight have to do with length in terms of the number of bars? Not necessarily, since barring is an artificiality that is not even guaranteed to accord with the patterns of musical pulse, accent, and phrase structure. Many are the pieces that have doubled or halved their number of bars as a result of a change of mind by the composer or publisher. And what about pieces with repeated sections? Is a 'Goldberg' Variations on two CDs with all repeats played weightier than one on a single CD with none played?

Does weight have to do with length in terms of minutes taken for performance? Not necessarily, since this is dependent on tempo, over which the composer lacks full control. In any case, an 'adagio', for the same number of bars, will take longer to perform than an 'allegro', and no one has suggested that in a Haydn or Mozart symphony, where the slow movement often occupies more time than any of the others, this movement bears the greatest weight.[8] Particularly in music written before the nineteenth century, the problem of how to bring repeats into the equation is also present.

Does fuller instrumentation confer extra weight? Here, the answer is probably yes, although in most earlier music instrumentation is a constant that cannot be used as a factor in the comparison of different movements.

Does the 'tone' of a movement affect its weight? Yes, obviously—except that this factor is something incapable of objective measurement and categorization. Two people may perceive a different 'tone' in the same piece. Nevertheless, a serious demeanour as conveyed by conventional indicators (predominance of the minor mode, to give just one instance) makes a contribution towards weight.

The only factor that is both measurable and always relevant is complexity of structure. The number of significant events in a movement—its rhythmic, harmonic, and tonal changes, as well as the thematic and textural patterns woven by the composer—has relevance for its weight. The controversial 'presto' finale of Chopin's B flat minor Piano Sonata compensates for its brevity (it covers only a third as much paper as the first movement), its bare texture (plain octaves throughout), and its uniform rhythm (a *moto perpetuo* of triplet quavers) by having an extremely active harmonic and tonal evolution, which is hardly less complex than that of the first movement. Arguably, it gains sufficient weight thereby to balance the three preceding movements. Conversely, one knows of many extended movements (dare one suggest the finale of Mendelssohn's String Quartet in E flat, Op. 44 No. 3?) in which the number of significant events is not commensurate with the length.

---

[8] This has been suggested for Bruckner (by Paul Bekker, among others), but for no other composer, to my knowledge.

To sum up: musical weight is a product of many factors, including bulk, duration, fullness of scoring, and 'tone', but is validated primarily by structural properties.

Most early suites (I use the term generically and include cyclic groupings that have no collective title) are 'front-weighted', and their final movement is the lightest of all.[9] Doubtless, ballroom custom set them on this path. The processional dances for the full company (pavane, intrada, balletto, allemande, etc.), which are commonly in quadruple metre (itself traditionally associated with seriousness of tone), were danced first. These were complemented and succeeded by couple dances in 'shorter', usually triple, metre (galliard, sarabande, courante). Solo dances, such as the jig, came last.[10] The four-movement basic framework that we know from J. S. Bach and elsewhere—allemande–courante–sarabande–gigue—derives the sequence of its movements ultimately from the ballroom, although by Bach's time the traditional arrangement had long since acquired an autonomous aesthetic value. The preference for a light ending is part of the general cultural style of the Renaissance, Baroque, and Classical periods alike, and can be observed in culinary practice (where it persists to the present day) and literature (think of the epigrammic *envoi*).

The rise of organicist theories and ideals in the nineteenth century has given front-weighting a bad name. If one adopts the metaphor of an oak tree rising from an acorn, it appears tantamount to dying back rather than to growing. However, even for a confirmed organicist the objection is valid only if one equates musical development exclusively with elaboration ('progression', as one might term it) and not with simplification (or 'regression', as we called it earlier). Take the first variation suite in Johann Hermann Schein's *Banchetto musicale* (1617), of which the incipits of the five movements are given in Ex. 3.4. The difference between the relative weight of the movements emerges all the more clearly because their material is common. The opening 'Padovana', with its three repeated strains, is clearly the most elaborate of the movements in every respect: formal, contrapuntal, and textural. Then the 'Gagliarda', in two long strains, begins the process of progressive simplification that the 'Courente' continues. The concluding 'Allemande' and 'Tripla', both short and notably homophonic, are related in the classic manner of *Tanz* and *Nachtanz*, presenting well-nigh identical material in alternative metrical stylizations.

The 'Tripla' is indisputably the lightest movement of all. However, precisely because it presents the basic idea informing all the movements in its

---

[9] 'Front-weighted' and 'end-weighted', or close equivalents to them, are terms used quite often in recent musicological literature. Alexander Ringer has coined the alternative expressions 'push' forms (front-weighted) and 'pull' forms (end-weighted), which appear in 'Clementi and the *Eroica*', 466.

[10] A good introduction to 17th-c. ballroom practice and dance stylization remains William C. Klenz, *Giovanni Battista Bononcini of Modena* (Durham, NC, 1962), 99–123.

Ex. 3.4. Schein, *Banchetto musicale*, Suite 1: (*a*), 'Padovana', opening; (*b*) 'Gagliarda', opening; (*c*) 'Courente', opening; (*d*) 'Allemande', opening; (*e*) 'Tripla', opening

simplest, most essential guise, it makes a very satisfying point of final arrival. After all, synoptic comprehension of a work becomes no more difficult and no less rewarding when one closes in on a point than when one expands out of it.

That said, front-weighting works best when the general dimensions are small and the disparities not too extreme. Once a listener becomes consciously aware that a first movement is long, expectations for the length of the rest are raised. Arguably, the contrast between the dimensions of the opening movement of many late Baroque orchestral suites (*ouvertures*) and that of the last of the dances (consider, for example, the 'Badinerie' of J. S. Bach's *Ouverture* in B minor) is too extreme to be entirely successful; similarly, the extended preludes that open Bach's 'English' Suites, while magnificent in their own right, do nevertheless tend to overshadow and thereby devalue the rest of the cycle.

In this perspective, the drift towards end-weighting—or, at least, to the abandonment of extreme forms of front-weighting—in virtually all instrumental genres (the suite has shown resistance up to the present day) was probably as much a factor of steadily increasing movement length during the eighteenth century as it was of changing aesthetics and cultural style. To read certain twentieth-century authors on end-weighting in the symphony (I am thinking in particular of Paul Bekker, Bernd Sponheuer, and Karl

Wörner), one might imagine oneself to be confronting a revelation comparable with the invention of monotheism. A saner attitude is to regard both front-weighting and end-weighting (not forgetting the *via media* of perfect balance) as absolutely right—in their proper place.

When the sonata, as explained in the previous chapter, split into separate movements, the de facto chamber suite (still rarely given an overall title) provided a formal model. Almost from the start, 'church' and 'chamber' sonatas contaminated each other freely, and it is ironic that Corelli's sonatas, long treated as textbook models of the generic distinction, evidence this cross-fertilization in an advanced stage, with final movements *alla giga* in the first type (see Ex. 2.2(*b*) for an instance) and 'abstract' slow movements in the second.

In a very few cases, but ones that have importance for the future, seventeenth-century sonatas end in slow tempo. Sometimes, the 'grave' or 'largo' conclusion is best regarded as an addendum to a preceding quick movement, especially when it exhibits no patterned structure. One is reminded here of the 'molto ritenuto' endings in nineteenth-century compositions; the seventeenth-century English term for a slow coda—'drag'—expresses the situation nicely. There do, however, occur instances of genuine slow final movements in the trio sonatas of Purcell, one example being the first sonata of the 1683 set, which ends with a 28-bar 'largo'. One suspects that this represents a survival of the Renaissance–Jacobean aesthetic earlier expressed via the ensemble fantasia.

Another prophetic development is the injection of humour (albeit only very rarely) into the finale. Seventeenth-century musical humour tends to be very different from the elegant wit of the Classical period, gravitating as it does towards the bizarre and grotesque. For a striking manifestation one may take the last movement of a four-movement trio sonata (entitled 'Sÿmphonia à 2 violini e basso') by Alessandro Stradella (1639–82), of which the first bars are shown as Ex. 3.5. The movement refuses to settle down into a stable rhythmic or melodic pattern; it is all rests, leaps, and syncopations. This is 'lightness' with a twist!

Before leaving the Baroque, we must consider one exceptional and conspicuous case of end-weighting in sonatas and suites: that of final movements in variation forms, principally the passacaglia and the chaconne. Throughout musical history, theme-and-variations structure has never been popular for introductory movements, but it was a recognized option for finales long before Haydn had the idea of using it in a slow movement (in Symphony No. 47, from 1772).[11] Part of the reason may be intrinsic to the nature of the form: the theme with which a variation movement opens is usually regressive in character in comparison with the material of the other

---

[11] Information from Elaine R. Sisman, *Haydn and the Classical Variation* (Cambridge, Mass., 1993), 8.

[Allegro]

Ex. 3.5.   Stradella, Trio sonata in F major, last movement, opening

movements—it has to be, in order to serve its purpose well. One must also consider the function of the passacaglia and chaconne as 'applied' forms. The passacaglia was used for public processions and for 'continuity music'; the chaconne, in French ballet and opera, was the dance with which a happy ending was customarily celebrated by all the characters. One might say that the export of the passacaglia to the sonata and suite was a present of the operatic finale to the instrumental finale.

Many seventeenth-century passacaglias and chaconnes (and the sectional variations that closely resemble them) are, at least ostensibly, free-standing works. In Corelli's Op. 2 (1685) the 'Ciacona' makes up the entire twelfth sonata, as 'La folía' does in Op. 5 (1700). But already before 1700 we find some examples of chaconnes and passacaglias used as final movements. One relatively well-known example is the 'Passacaglia' in G major ending the fifth and last sonata in Georg Muffat's *Armonico tributo* (1682). Lasting over ten minutes, it almost matches in duration the preceding four movements taken together. This vast movement, in which the theme itself recurs at intervals in the manner of a rondo refrain, is particularly well integrated into its cycle, its thematic material having been prefigured earlier.

It would be inappropriate here to speak of a 'finale suite' or insist on a historical link to the 'finale symphony' of the nineteenth century, except to point out that the first composer to cast a symphonic finale in passacaglia form, Brahms (in his Fourth Symphony), was a connoisseur and a practising editor of Baroque music. Nevertheless, these unquestionably end-weighted suites and sonatas at least establish that on the comparatively few occasions before 1700 when players and audiences were treated to them, they were found aesthetically acceptable.

As we approach the threshold of the 'Golden Age of the movement', the outlines of a basic typology of finale types are already visible. In instrumental music the dominant type is the one we have characterized as 'light': short, simple, and sometimes humorous. (We must recognize, however, that this lightness is only relative, for in the sonata, and even more in the emergent concerto, finales can almost attain the weight of the first movement.) In a number of instances, we encounter a second type that aspires to monumentality (i.e. the variation movements just mentioned). Here and there, but very rarely, we find a slow concluding movement that ends the cycle on a note of calm.

What names shall we give to the three types? There are no 'off the peg' labels for them in musicology, whether in English or in German, although many authors have devised labels for one or other of them. It is important, however, to propose names in the hope that these will be useful for the future discourse on finales.

The 'light' type I will call the relaxant finale. 'Relaxant' has here the dictionary meaning of 'inducing relaxation'. The term implies that in relation to the interplay of tension and release throughout the cycle the finale is mostly about the second. It also implies, albeit less insistently, that the finale has been written in such a way as to tolerate a lower level of concentration on the listener's part. These criteria apply as much to passionate minor-key finales such as those of Haydn's symphonies Nos. 39, 44, 49, and 52 as to their more cheerful (and more common) major-key counterparts. In a broader sense, the relaxant finale is related, in its function as a narrative (or quasi-narrative: one should not use the term too glibly), to the 'happy ending' in opera and oratorio.

The 'weighty' type may be called the summative finale. 'Summative' conveys the idea that such a finale aims to sum up the cycle as a whole. This implies a more overt thematic (and hermeneutic) relationship to the earlier movements than the first type has. Because a summative finale has dual loyalties of commensurate importance—to itself and to the cycle as a whole—it is most often unconventional in form, its structure exhibiting hybrid features.

To the 'restful' type I give the name of valedictory finale. The hermeneutic connotations of 'valedictory' are not prescribed: the farewell may precede a departure into rest, sleep, death, or the unknown. In Haydn's not inaptly nicknamed 'Farewell' Symphony (No. 45), the departure represents, in mime, the orchestral musicians' wish for a vacation in order to visit home and family. For a departure of this kind, a slow tempo is mandatory.

There are two main ways in which one may seek to map the three finale types on to the vast repertory of instrumental music of the past three hundred years. The first is to consider them in relation to individual composers and their works, and the second is to do the same in relation to genre. In the next four chapters, each devoted to a single 'species' (with hybrids discussed in Chapter 7), the emphasis will fall on individual works, their composers, and various points of special interest not so far considered. In Chapter 8 lines of development in the principal genres (symphony, sonata, concerto, etc.) will be surveyed. Detailed discussion of a complete corpus of music by a single composer (Shostakovich's string quartets) is left for Chapter 10.

# 4

# *The Relaxant Finale*

T HE relationship of any finale to its companion movements is partly one of similarity, partly one of difference. If it is totally similar, it loses its *raison d'être* as a separate movement; if it is totally different, it violates the broad principle of unity or (if one prefers) coherence. In a conventional three-movement or four-movement plan its relationship to the first movement is crucial for two reasons: the two movements are both fast (a factor that makes their direct comparison appropriate), and they occupy strategically equivalent (though, as we saw, very different) positions framing the rest of the work. To a lesser extent, a finale has to position itself vis-à-vis the interior movements, and in particular the minuet, scherzo, or similar movement in a four-movement cycle. Its relationship to the minuet (etc.) is naturally most conspicuous when the two movements are adjacent: that is, when the minuet comes third rather than second, as it does most often from Haydn onwards until the late nineteenth century.

If there is a universal principle concerning the relationship of the finale to the other fast (or moderate) movements in the cycle, it is that there has to be a complex trade-off of similarities and differences so that the right overall balance is achieved. Suppose that both the first and last movements employ conventional sonata form. This similarity compels there to be a compensatory difference effected by means of a contrast in one or more of the other elements: tempo, metre, rhythmic-melodic character, texture, 'tone'. Conversely, if the form of the outer movements is different, their contrast in other respects need not be so pronounced. Udo Zilkens has correctly observed that when Beethoven, in the finales of his piano sonatas, opts for a very fast tempo such as 'presto', he employs sonata form for preference; but when he chooses a different form, the tempo is unlikely to exceed 'allegro' (a possible final *stretta* excepted).[1] To put this another way: Beethoven increases the tempo contrast to compensate for a deficiency of formal contrast.

The 'classical' minuet or scherzo, which is cast in a form *sui generis* (a ternary grouping of binary movements), struggles less hard to establish its distance from both outer movements, but as soon as sonata-form designs become applied to it (an early example is the scherzo of Beethoven's First 'Rasumovsky' Quartet, Op. 59 No. 1), it too enters fully into the equation.

---

[1] Zilkens, *Beethovens Finalsätze in den Klaviersonaten*, 22–3.

The above remarks apply with greatest force to the relaxant finale, since this is the type that insists most strongly on its autonomy. A summative finale, precisely because it refers back to the material of the earlier movements, is likely to be so distinct in form that overall tempo contrast is rendered less important. A valedictory finale is slow virtually by definition, so the contrast is inbuilt.

We can put the principle stated above to the test by tabulating the tempo, metre, and metronomic marking (adjusted so that it applies in every case to the note representing the notated beat) of the first, third, and final movements of Beethoven's symphonies Nos. 1–8 (Table 4.1).[2]

TABLE 4.1. *Tempo, metre, and metronomic markings in Beethoven's symphonies*

| No. | Movement | Tempo | Metre | M.M.[a] |
|-----|----------|-------|-------|------|
| 1 | I | Allegro con brio | 2/2 | 224 |
|   | III | Allegro molto e vivace (Menuetto) | 3/4 | 324 |
|   | IV | Allegro molto e vivace | 2/4 | 176 |
| 2 | I | Allegro con brio | 4/4 | 220 |
|   | III | Allegro (Scherzo) | 3/4 | 300 |
|   | IV | Allegro molto | 2/2 | 152 |
| 3 | I | Allegro con brio | 3/4 | 180 |
|   | III | Allegro vivace (Scherzo) | 3/4 | 348 |
|   | IV | Allegro molto | 2/4 | 152 |
| 4 | I | Allegro vivace | 2/2 | 160 |
|   | III | Allegro vivace (Scherzo) | 3/4 | 300 |
|   | IV | Allegro ma non troppo | 2/4 | 160 |
| 5 | I | Allegro con brio | 2/4 | 216 |
|   | III | Allegro (Scherzo) | 3/4 | 288 |
|   | IV | Allegro | 4/4 | 168 |
| 6 | I | Allegro ma non troppo | 2/4 | 132 |
|   | III | Allegro (*Réunion joyeuse de paysans*) | 3/4 | 324 |
|   | V | Allegro | 6/8 | 60 |
| 7 | I | Vivace | 6/8 | 104 |
|   | III | Presto (Scherzo) | 3/4 | 396 |
|   | IV | Allegro con brio | 2/4 | 144 |
| 8 | I | Allegro vivace e con brio | 3/4 | 207 |
|   | III | Tempo di Menuetto | 3/4 | 126 |
|   | IV | Allegro vivace | 2/2 | 168 |

[a] The metronomic markings are those published with Beethoven's authority in the *Allgemeine musikalische Zeitung* on 17 Dec. 1817. Whether Beethoven's metronome was defective or not makes no difference to the argument, since what counts is only the ratio between the speeds.

[2] The Ninth Symphony is omitted not because it has a choral finale but because its complex form does not permit us to pinpoint any individual section as the one bearing the basic tempo and metre. The table disregards the slow introductions to the first movements of Nos. 2, 4, and 7 and all other occasional deviations from the main tempo (including those in 'trio' sections).

It is true that metronomic markings do not determine by themselves the effective speed of a composition. One has to take into account the note values used, the harmonic rhythm, and most of all the presence of hypermetre (which turns whole bars into beats or even smaller units) or hypometre (which turns units nominally smaller than a beat into beats).[3] For this reason the 'one-in-a-bar' scherzos and scherzo-like movements (in Symphonies Nos. 1 and 6) in Table 4.1 all have an effective metronomic speed that makes the bar equivalent to a beat (Beethoven himself uses the bar as the metronomic unit). The longer movements move in and out of hypermetre freely. Consequently, one can rarely say that a finale is *consistently* faster or slower than the first movement. What does emerge from the table, however, is that the first and last movements nearly all have metronomic rates that are distinct but not overly so. This means that even if its effective speed is doubled or halved the audible distinctness of each movement remains. In our sample there is only one case where two fast movements have an identical pulse: that of the outer movements of Symphony No. 4. One can verify this by thinking of a passage in one of these movements and then 'cutting' to a passage in the other. Nevertheless, the finale appears quicker throughout because its basic harmonic rhythm moves at twice the rate of that of the first movement: there are very few bars in either that would fit well into the other. Example 4.1, which gives the opening bars of the main theme of each movement, brings out the difference clearly.

What can happen, on the other hand, when the basic pulse of two movements is too close for comfort is seen in Mendelssohn's Octet in E flat major, Op. 20. The scherzo, in 2/4 and marked 'allegro leggierissimo', moves at exactly the same rate as the finale, in 2/2 and marked 'presto'. It is therefore

Ex. 4.1. Beethoven, Symphony No. 4 in B flat major, Op. 60: (*a*) first movement, bars 43–8; (*b*) last movement, opening

---

[3] Hypometre (as I call it by analogy with hypermetre) is uncommon in the Classical and later periods but very common in the Baroque period, where movements notated in simple or compound quadruple metre often operate as if in duple metre, so that their phrases and periods begin indifferently on the first or the third beat of the bar.

little surprise when, during the development section of the finale, the scherzo theme irrupts in note values twice as long as before but aurally indistinguishable. Conventionally, this appearance of the earlier theme is regarded by commentators as, at worst, a pleasant *jeu d'esprit* and, at best, an inspired stroke demonstrating cyclic unity. I prefer to view it as an apology masquerading as a justification.[4]

The Beethoven symphony in which the finale moves most conspicuously faster than the first movement is the Seventh. Although not quite a *moto perpetuo*, it belongs to the tradition of the finale as a 'poem of speed'. This tradition, which has its roots in the late Baroque period (consider the last movement of Bach's Third 'Brandenburg' Concerto), continues in such works as Haydn's 'Lark' Quartet (Op. 64 No. 5), Beethoven's Piano Sonata, Op. 54, and Third 'Rasumovsky' Quartet (Op. 59 No. 3), Chopin's Piano Sonata (No. 2) in B flat minor, Bizet's Symphony in C major, Prokofiev's Seventh Piano Sonata, and John Adams's Violin Concerto (1993). Although strong and unbroken, this tradition has never been truly dominant: it is only one 'variant' of the finale concept among many.

Zilkens's remark that a difference in form from the first movement tends to slow down a finale applies just as well to Beethoven's symphonies as to his piano sonatas. The two finales among the eight symphonies that are not in sonata form—the variation movement in No. 3 and the rondo in No. 6— are among the slowest (the latter emphatically so). There is naturally no rule that rondo finales have to be more moderately paced than the allegro movement or movements that precede them (the fourth movement of Haydn's 'Lark' Quartet is one of the *moto perpetuo* movements just mentioned), but evenly paced 'allegrettos' (often marked 'grazioso') are strikingly well represented among them in the Classical period. Mozart's eighteen keyboard sonatas contain eleven rondo finales, of which five are marked 'allegro' or faster, and six 'allegretto'. Significantly, the slower tempo predominates among the most mature sonatas (including four out of the last six, which all have rondo finales). As for variation movements, the theme has to be in a slow to moderate tempo in order to permit the kind of melodic ornamentation that was de rigueur at the time.

With the music of the Classical period especially in mind, Wilhelm Seidel, among many others, has noted that whereas 'long' metres such as 4/4 and 3/4 are characteristic of opening movements, 'short' metres such as 2/2, 2/4, 3/8, and 6/8 belong more to finales.[5] This tendency is certainly borne out by Mozart's keyboard sonatas, which yield the following statistics:

---

[4]  Carl Dahlhaus has commented on the problematic nature of a finale following immediately on a scherzo, writing: 'The relationship between a scherzo and a finale is sometimes precarious, and the superimposed mediation, or connecting passage, in Beethoven's Fifth Symphony betrays rather than conceals the difficulty' ('Studien zu romantischen Symphonien', *Jahrbuch des Staatlichen Instituts für Musikforschung Preussischer Kulturbesitz* (Berlin, 1972), 104–19 at 115).

[5]  Wilhelm Seidel, 'Schnell–Langsam–Schnell: Zur klassischen Theorie des instrumentalen Zyklus', *Musiktheorie*, 1 (1986), 205–16 at 209.

| Metre | First movements | Third movements |
|-------|-----------------|-----------------|
| 4/4 | 9 | 0 |
| 3/4 | 4 | 1 |
| 2/2 | 1 | 5 |
| 2/4 | 2 | 8 |
| 6/8 | 2 | 2 |
| 3/8 | 0 | 2 |

(In passing, we should note that, in accordance with the principle of mutually compensating similarities and differences, the tempo of the outer movements is contrasted on the rare occasions—only in K. 330/300h and K. 533—when their metre coincides.)

There is an entrenched tradition among musicologists of considering the shorter metres associated with pre-1800 finales as dance-related. Everything works towards this interpretation: the teleologically inspired view of the gradual evolution of 'applied' music into 'pure' music (or of music as entertainment into music as edification); the wish on the part of semiotic analysts to identify concrete 'topics' (for which the names of dances provide convenient labels); the growing interest in the gestural and mimetic properties of music.

So we read, for example, that the gigue with which the Baroque suite often ended provided a precedent for the 'distinctly melodious character' and the metrical characteristics (the preference for 3/8 or 6/8) of symphony and sonata finales of the mid-eighteenth century.[6] The statement is accurate inasmuch as the convergence of the church and chamber sonatas after *c*.1700 led to the concentration of elements derived from the first at the head of the sonata, and from the second at its end. The Trio Sonata in C major, BWV 1037, once attributed to J. S. Bach and now thought to be by his pupil Johann Gottlieb Goldberg, is a case in point. But the gigue was by no means the only dance that influenced the nature of the sonata finale (had it so been, we would have expected to see 12/8 metre appear more often): other types employed in the late Baroque period to conclude sequences of dances—including the gavotte, the minuet, and the courante (each with its Italian as well as French stylization)—made an equal mark on finales in sonatas, and to a lesser extent in symphonies (sinfonias) and concertos as well.

Many writers have supplemented the repertory of dance types introduced to the sonata and other 'abstract' genres from the suite with further examples taken from the ballroom of the later eighteenth century: notably, the *contredanse* (country dance) and the *Kehraus* (a lively dance, usually in 6/8, that traditionally ended balls in Germany). To the dance models proper has been added the *chasse* (hunt), revealed by fast 6/8 metre and 'horn fifths'. A neat synthesis of the modern view is pronounced by

[6] Michael Tilmouth, 'Finale', in *The New Grove Dictionary of Music and Musicians*, ed. Stanley Sadie (London, 1980), vi. 558.

Leonard Ratner in his influential book on Classical music: 'Final movements are frankly entertainment music, with gigue or contredanse styles preferred.'[7]

The problem with the reduction of finales to specific dance types is that a label assigned, possibly a little hastily, to a 'topic' does not convey all the properties and nuances of a dance in its real, historical existence. If we describe the theme of the finale of Beethoven's 'Eroica' Symphony as 'contredanse-like', we are, for once, spot on, since this theme originated as an actual *contredanse* (No. 7 in a set of twelve, WoO 14). But that fact should not give us licence to affix the 'contredanse' label to each and every movement in 2/4 metre moving at a moderately brisk pace. Between them, the dance models, if interpreted with enough latitude, can be made to account for the majority of theoretically possible metres and rhythmic styles found in an early Classical symphony or sonata. But if this point is reached, the dance description pays diminishing returns: we end up using 'contredanse' as a simple code word for 'moderately fast 2/4'.

A better way to approach the relationship of dance types and finales is to start by acknowledging that the many Classical finales displaying consistent, repetitive rhythmic patterns and a periodic phrase structure do indeed share this property with dance music in general. In other words, one does not need to classify a finale as a gavotte or a *contredanse* before agreeing on its non-specific 'dance-like' qualities. The recognition of a generalized relationship to the dance needs, however, to be coupled with a much more rigorous definition of individual dances. One should never be tempted to call a movement a 'gigue' simply because a modern semiotician has assigned this word as a handy label to a given 'topic'.

Nor should one forget the many Classical finales that are on any analysis totally devoid of dance connotations. What steps would one choose for the fierce, rhythmically unstable finale of Haydn's Symphony No. 39 in G minor, or that of his 'Passion' Symphony, No. 49?

We reach firmer ground when we discuss the formal types favoured by the relaxant finale. Besides sonata form and its linear ancestor binary form, we find two forms to be especially favoured in instrumental finales: rondo and variation. Both are what Gretchen Wheelock has described as 'reiterative' forms: they tolerate (indeed, derive their identity from) the repetition

---

[7] Leonard G. Ratner, *Classic Music: Expression, Form, and Style* (New York, 1980), 322. Similarly Zaslaw: 'The finales [of Mozart's symphonies of the 1760s and 1770s] are generally based on rustic or popular dances: gavottes, *contredanses*, jigs or quick steps' (*Mozart's Symphonies*, 417). It is surprising that the minuet is not given pride of place in this context, since *tempo di minuetto* finales, styled either as rondos or as variation movements, figure prominently from the 1720s up to the end of the 18th c. László Somfai states that as many as fifteen finales in the thirty-four Haydn keyboard sonatas written after the end of the 1760s are minuet derivatives ('Vom Barock zur Klassik: Umgestaltung der Proportionen und des Gleichgewichts in zyklischen Werken Joseph Haydns', in Gerda Mraz *et al.* (eds.), *Joseph Haydn und seine Zeit* (Jahrbuch für Österreichische Kulturgeschichte, 2; Eisenstadt, 1972), 64–72 at 67).

rather than the development of their primary material.[8] Where development does occur, it is often merely decorative and does not amount to a 'taking apart' of the material. Ethan Haimo has bluntly stated: 'A higher degree of repetition was acceptable [for Haydn and his time] in a finale than in a first movement.'[9] This is absolutely correct. Neither of the two reiterative forms occurs with any significant frequency as the first movement of a multi-movement cycle in any period or genre—I cannot even cite an instance of a first-movement rondo (as distinct from a free-standing rondo or a 'double variation' opening movement).[10]

Wilhelm Fischer did not exaggerate when he termed the rondo 'the second most important form of Viennese Classical allegro movement'.[11] According to the researches of Malcolm Cole, a scholar who has made the Classical (and later) rondo his speciality, 'rondomania' (my term) peaked during the years 1773–86.[12] Burney noted disapprovingly the fashion for rondo finales and criticized Ernst Eichner for acquiring the habit from J. C. Bach in London, which this minor German composer visited in 1773.[13] Statistics tell their own story. Whereas Haydn's first fifty-two symphonies (numbered by chronology) contain a modest five rondo finales, the next thirty-five (dating from 1773 to 1786) contain sixteen, while the last seventeen have as many as twelve.[14] We have already seen how the rondo established its supremacy in the finales of Mozart's later keyboard sonatas. It is significant, too, that he composed rondos as substitutes for the original ritornello-form finales of the Keyboard Concerto in D major, K. 175, and the Violin Concerto in B flat major, K. 207.[15] In particular, the rondo gained ground at the expense of the simpler variants of sonata form—that without

[8] Gretchen A. Wheelock, *Haydn's Ingenious Jesting with Art: Contexts of Musical Wit and Humor* (New York, 1992), 106.

[9] Haimo, *Haydn's Symphonic Forms*, 6.

[10] Among the rare instances of an opening variation movement one may cite Mozart's Piano Sonata in A major, K. 331/300i, and the Haydn piano sonatas Hob. XVI/ D1, 39, 40, and 42. Since, as explained, variation movements cannot be in quick tempo, placing one at the head of the work tends to cause a transposition in the normal tempo sequence (fast–slow–moderate/fast–fast). In that sense, an opening variation movement (such as the one in Haydn's 'Razor' Quartet, Op. 55 No. 2) can often be regarded as a second movement that has merely exchanged position with the first movement.

[11] Wilhelm Fischer, 'Zur Entwicklungsgeschichte des Wiener klassischen Stils', *Studien zur Musikwissenschaft*, 3 (1915), 24–84 at 74.

[12] Malcolm S. Cole, 'The Vogue of the Instrumental Rondo in the Late Eighteenth Century', *Journal of the American Musicological Society*, 22 (1969), 425–55 at 425–6.

[13] Discussed in William S. Newman, *The Sonata in the Classic Era* (New York and London, 1983³), 164.

[14] Cole, 'The Vogue of the Instrumental Rondo', 425. Some of the rondos in the last two groups might alternatively be viewed as sonata-form movements with strong rondo character-istics, but the conclusions of Cole's survey are too emphatic to be affected by debates over a few individual movements.

[15] The replacements were K. 382 (1782) and K. 269/261a (1776) respectively (K. 382 is arguably a variation movement in strict formal terms). It is interesting, however, that the mature Mozart never used a rondo to end a symphony.

a development section (so-called 'sonatina' form) and that without a re-capitulated first subject (the unhappily named 'binary variant')—both of which persisted well into the Classical period.[16]

Rondos established their presence in slow movements and (especially) finales across the genre spectrum. We find them in symphonies, diverti-menti, sonatas, *opera buffa* overtures, and concertos (in the last-named genre the rondo has remained the normative form for a finale up to the modern period). In his piano sonatas Mozart uses rondo form for both the second and the third movement of a work on five occasions (K. 311/284c, 457, 545, 570, 576). Then there are some free-standing concert rondos that include works as significant as Mozart's K. 511 in A minor for solo piano and Schubert's *Rondo brillant* in B minor for violin and piano, D. 895. Rondos are also found in the vocal numbers of some comic operas.

Strangely enough, the rondo had blossomed once before and then all but withered away. In secular French instrumental music of the *Grand Siècle* the rondo equals, and in some repertories and collections surpasses, binary form in the frequency with which it is chosen for dance movements and character pieces of equivalent length. It is still strongly represented in François Couperin's four great *Livres de clavecin* published between 1713 and 1730, even though its incidence tends to diminish with each collection. The Baroque rondo (for which, in modern musicology, the original French spelling *rondeau* is often preferred, rather as *sinfonia* is used today to denote the Baroque symphony) is in many respects very different from its Classical successor. Its refrain and the alternating couplets all form self-contained periods that need no extra introductions, links, or codas. The couplets reach their tonal destinations quickly (sometimes in the first few notes) and fre-quently make their final cadence in a foreign key, thus creating a hiatus (but usually a pleasant one) with the returning refrain.

Multimovement works on the Italian pattern make little use of the rondo as a finale during the Baroque period, but there are a number of examples from the German concerto, including Bach's E major Violin Concerto, BWV 1042, as well as various concertos by Telemann.[17] In its mathematically precise balance between sections (the refrain and the couplets are all based on a sixteen-bar unit, the fourth and final couplet being double-length), its consistent figuration for the solo instrument within each couplet, and its well-organized plan of modulation, Bach's rondo finale for BWV 1042 is a model of its kind:[18]

---

[16] 'Binary variant' is a very unsatisfactory description since, historically speaking, it was sonata form that arose as a variant of binary form—not the other way round.

[17] These include a concerto for recorder and transverse flute in E minor and another for flute, oboe d'amore, and viola d'amore in E major.

[18] For a similarly cogent example by Bach, see the 'Rondeaux' movement in his Second Partita for harpsichord, BWV 826. There, however, we encounter a *rondeau varié*, in which variation technique is applied to every recurrence of the refrain.

| Section | Bars | Tonality | Section | Bars | Tonality |
|---------|------|----------|---------|------|----------|
| Refrain | 1–16 | E → E | Couplet 1 | 17–32 | E → B |
| Refrain | 33–48 | E → E | Couplet 2 | 49–64 | c♯ → c♯ |
| Refrain | 65–80 | E → E | Couplet 3 | 81–96 | E → A |
| Refrain | 97–112 | E → E | Couplet 4 | 113–44 | E → g♯; g♯ → g♯ |
| Refrain | 145–60 | E → E | | | |

In the late Baroque the popularity of rondo form begins to dwindle even in its French heartland. It is notable how, in Rameau's last two books of *Pièces de clavecin* (1724, c.1729), the 'big' pieces employ large-scale binary form in preference to rondo form. The decline is probably related to the creeping Italianization of French music during the period.

However, towards the middle of the century the fortunes of the rondo begin to pick up again. The revival is certainly related to the rise of Paris as the major centre of music publishing for all Europe, including Italy and Germany, and to the new *galant* sensibility that set a premium on melodiousness and transparency of structure. However, the new-style Classical rondo that emerges differs in important respects from the old Baroque one, notably by admitting transitions and codas, and by allowing sections to expand to the point where they can become polythematic.[19] The refrain is no longer necessarily repeated in full when it returns, and can even be omitted (the ABACBA/coda form used by Mozart for the rondo finale of the Piano Sonata in C major, K. 309/284b, is exemplary). In fact, the schematic description of Classical rondos as ABACABA, etc., perfectly adequate for Baroque rondos, loses its ability to capture the full essence of a movement. A 'B' section, for instance, may have as many as four different components (and in so doing come to resemble the entire bridge passage, second group, and codetta of a sonata-form movement): a modulating transition, a first theme, a second theme, and a link back to the refrain.

One great attraction of the rondo during the whole of its existence has been its flexibility, hence adaptability. Even in the Baroque period, the possibilities range from a 'first' rondo (to use Edward Cone's neat terminology)—a simple ABA structure with a single couplet, such as represented by the *Menuet en rondeau* prefaced as a fingering exercise to Rameau's 1724 collection—to the massive 'eighth' rondo exemplified by the *Passecaille* in B minor contained in the eighth *ordre* of Couperin's second book. Late Baroque French rondos even include examples (by Jean-Marie Leclair, for instance) of rondos embedded within rondos, in which one episode (normally in the parallel key) becomes the refrain for a rondo of its own.[20]

This flexibility continues into the Classical period, except that the general expansion of section lengths, together with a concern not to allow the

---

[19] For this reason, Joel Galand (see below, n. 25) speaks of a 'refrain-complex' rather than a refrain *tout court*.

[20] 'Parallel' is used here in the English (rather than German) sense to denote the key, major or minor, that shares a tonic with the main key.

movement to become too diffuse, limits the maximum number of couplets to three or at most four. Not all Classical rondos have extended codas, but many do, and the opportunity can be taken there to demonstrate virtuosity or develop earlier material further (usually regressively).

The variant that we know today as sonata-rondo form is a special adaptation of the 'third' rondo. The third couplet is made into a version of the first ('B'), transposed from the original dominant (or equivalent key) back to the tonic, and all or part of the second couplet ('C') is turned into a development section for the refrain material. Rudolf von Tobel, the doyen of musical taxonomists, identified Mozart's String Quartet in C major, K. 157 (1772 or 1773), and Symphony in D major, K. 181/162b (1773), as the pioneering works.[21] Malcolm Cole has counted eighty-six subsequent appearances of sonata-rondo form in Mozart's instrumental music; Haydn used it first in Symphony No. 77 (1782).[22] Heinrich Koch noted the variant in his *Musikalisches Lexikon* (1802), and it was left to Adolf Bernhard Marx in 1845 to devise a name for it ('das sonatenartige Rondo').[23]

From Beethoven onwards, most rondos employed in prestigious genres (symphony, sonata, string quartet, etc.) have been sonata-rondos. Their sonata-like features (to translate Marx's 'sonatenartig' literally) have been their passport to respectability in the company of ever more elaborate sonata-form structures. They transform the rondo, originally a paratactic form par excellence, into a hypotactic form in which function, length, and proportion are as carefully controlled as in sonata form proper.

But the influence has not travelled only in one direction. From the late eighteenth century onwards we can also speak of 'rondo-like' sonata-form movements. Their characteristic formal features are the self-contained nature of the first subject (which may resolve into a perfect binary form, as in the finale of Haydn's Symphony No. 95), the reappearance of the opening theme in the tonic at the start of the development and/or coda, and, naturally, the absence of repeats at the end of the exposition and recapitulation. Their typical stylistic features can be described as bubbling effervescence and good humour.

Not surprisingly, the convergence of sonata and rondo form has led to situations where either model can plausibly be used in analysis. This convergence lies at the root of the imprecision of nomenclature noted in Chapter 1. With his usual perceptiveness, Tovey remarked:

The only important criterion is that of style [in distinguishing rondo and sonata forms]. Mozart is not particular. If a movement begins with a square-cut tune, he

---

[21] Rudolf von Tobel, *Die Formenwelt der klassischen Instrumentalmusik* (Bern and Leipzig, 1935), 181–3.

[22] Malcolm S. Cole, 'Haydn's Symphonic Rondo-Finales: Their Structural and Stylistic Evolution', *Haydn Yearbook*, 13 (1982), 113–42 at 122.

[23] The English equivalent, 'sonata-rondo form', seems to have originated with Ebenezer Prout, in his *Applied Forms* (London, 1895).

may call it a rondo, even when it has exactly the repeat marks and shape of a first movement; and for some obscure reason it is seldom that a movement will be labelled as a rondo unless it happens to be a finale.[24]

Joel Galand makes the same observation in the musicological language of the 1990s when he observes: 'for eighteenth-century composers, the rondo was not a strict form but rather a more loosely defined genre which could be adapted to various formal procedures: sectionalized ternary form, variation, and expanded binary structures'.[25]

Hence all the rondos that are not really rondos. Schumann took the composer Camill Grillparzer to task in 1837 for publishing a new work as a Rondo when analysis revealed it to be in sonata form.[26] But even Berlioz slipped up, when, in his celebrated essay on Beethoven's symphonies, he referred to the 'final rondo' of the First Symphony.[27] And Hugo Leichtentritt, amazingly, describes the finale of Beethoven's two-movement Sonata in F major, Op. 54, as a 'rondo with only one theme', perhaps out of an unwillingness to recognize the twenty bars leading up to the repeat sign as a highly compressed sonata-form exposition.[28] Similar instances are legion.

Rondo form also influenced variation form. The 'double' variation form (ABA'B'A"B", etc.) based on alternating *minore* and *maggiore* (or the other way round) versions of the same idea, popularized and possibly invented by Haydn, can be viewed as an expanded 'first' rondo (ABA). Further, the introductions, transitions, developments, and codas of the Classical rondo find their way into the more ambitious variation structures. Modern analysts tend to regard sonata form (or even the multimovement cycle) as the modifying agent that turns the finales of Beethoven's 'Eroica' Symphony and Ninth Symphony into outsize and out-of-the-ordinary variation movements, but a better case can be made for rondo form, which is less prescriptive in tonal terms.[29]

[24] Donald F. Tovey, *Essays in Musical Analysis* (London, 1935–9), i. 15. Mozart's free-standing Rondo in D major for Piano, K. 485, has a repeat sign at the end of the first couplet. This movement employs a version of rondo form pioneered by C. P. E. Bach in which intermediate statements of the refrain occur in foreign keys.

[25] Joel Galand, 'Rondo-Form Problems in Eighteenth- and Nineteenth-Century Instrumental Music, with Reference to the Application of Schenker's Form Theory to Historical Criticism' (Ph.D. diss., Yale University, 1990), 141; quoted in David A. Grayson, *Mozart: Piano Concertos No. 20 in D minor, K. 466, and No. 21 in C major, K. 467* (Cambridge, 1998), 74.

[26] Quoted in Nicholas Marston, *Schumann: Fantasie, Op. 17* (Cambridge, 1992), 25. The finale of Schubert's Piano Trio in B flat major, D. 898, is another 'false rondo'.

[27] Hector Berlioz, *The Art of Music and Other Essays (À travers chants)*, trans. and ed. Elizabeth Csicsery-Rónay (Bloomington and Indianapolis, Ind., 1994), 9–37 at 12. Berlioz was probably misled by the fact that the coda leads off with a restatement of the first subject's opening—a common 'rondo-like' feature.

[28] Leichtentritt, *Musikalische Formenlehre*, 118.

[29] It is the same fixation with sonata form as the 'normative structural model' of the Classical and Romantic periods that prevents analysts from identifying the opening movement of Schumann's *Fantasie*, Op. 17, as a rondo—more precisely, a 'third' rondo that is also an 'arch' rondo (ABACABA/coda). In other words, the proper connection to make is with the first movement (in rondo form) of a cycle such as the *Faschingsschwank aus Wien*, rather than with

Something needs to be said about the use of variation form in general for finales. Never a normative choice, variations have been an option from the days of the Baroque chaconne and passacaglia (and the air or dance with *doubles*, well represented in Handel's harpsichord suites) onwards. The period of their maximum popularity probably occurred in the second third of the eighteenth century, when minuet-variation finales were fashionable; the last movement of Vivaldi's Flute Concerto in G major, Op. 10 No. 6 (RV 437), published in 1729, is an early example.

Because of their essentially primitive, paratactic structure, variations are highly adaptable. With the right customization, they can be turned happily into relaxant, summative, or valedictory finales. As relaxant finales, such movements tend to favour decorative, rather than more thoroughgoing, methods of variation, to maintain a playful spirit (akin to that of the 'character variation'), and to submit readily to clear sectional divisions, whether or not the variations are individually numbered. It is normal for the last variation to be extended or replaced by a long coda in which, for the first time, developmental processes or *stretta*-like intensification can occur. Good examples of such codas are found in the finales of the two Mozart piano concertos (K. 453 and 491) that end with variations.[30]

In her magisterial survey of variation form in the Classical period, with especial reference to Haydn, Elaine Sisman comments that in multimovement genres variations require more melodic resemblance between theme and variations (hence between one variation and another) than in independent sets.[31] This is certainly true as an empirical observation, and one can see why it should be so. Whereas a free-standing set of variations is preoccupied above all to achieve 'unity in variety' (since the only variety it can achieve lies within itself), a variation movement within a larger cycle, irrespective of its position, has to aim at 'variety in unity' (since the cycle itself is the main guarantor of variety). This limitation on the ability of variation movements within larger cycles to maximize their potential (in a technical sense) may account for the popularity of the double variation in Haydn and, to a lesser extent, in Beethoven. Doubling the number of themes means that one exhausts the stock of simple possibilities less quickly.

Another form that makes an occasional appearance in a finale is fugue. It is necessary to distinguish here between a 'complete' fugue (a movement constructed from start to finish on fugal principles) and a fugato (a section

Schumann's sonata-form movements. It is pertinent to add that the first movement of the *Fantasie* originated, in 1836, as a stand-alone composition, which implies that Schumann at that stage did not even need to consider it from the perspective of an opening movement.

[30] In K. 453 the coda, ushered in by a short extension to the preceding variation, is individually titled 'Finale'—a literal example of what Zilkens felicitously calls 'Finale im Finale' (*Beethovens Finalsätze in den Klaviersonaten*, 120). In K. 491 the last variation and coda, which follow a cadenza, emphasize their separateness by moving from 4/4 to 6/8 ('hunting') metre and beginning (for the whole of the variation proper) with unaccompanied piano.

[31] Sisman, *Haydn and the Classical Variation*, 257 n.

of a longer movement constructed as a fugal exposition), although in the context of the present discussion, what applies to one usually applies to the other. In late Baroque instrumental music, the drive towards homophony (or the flight from counterpoint, as some prefer to call it) greatly reduced the incidence of fugues and fugal ritornellos, but there is an interesting difference in this respect between sonatas and concertos. Sonatas, which around 1700 frequently had both their first and their last fast movements styled as fugues, tended to abandon their contrapuntal pretensions more readily in the last movement (which commonly adopted binary form) than in their first, although in time both usually succumbed. In concertos, however, fugue was not an original feature (the very *raison d'être* of the primitive concerto, as cultivated in northern Italy in the 1690s, was to exploit homophonic sonorities) but one introduced for special effect. In the short term, this made it more durable. The classic early examples are the fugal finales in each of the twelve *Concerti a cinque*, Op. 5 (1707), by the Venetian Tomaso Albinoni. Here, we see the birth of the *concertante* fugue, in which display writing for a soloist (if present) is happily accommodated within the episodes separating entries of the subject. The fugal finales in Bach's Second 'Brandenburg' Concerto, BWV 1047, and his Concerto for Two Harpsichords in C major, BWV 1061, operate within the same tradition. At the same time, Vivaldian ritornello form gave composers the opportunity, if they so wished, to cast all or part of the ritornello as a fugato. Ultimately, however, fugal finales became as rare in concertos as anywhere else.

When fugues found favour again in multimovement instrumental works, it was as finales in the symphony and in chamber genres. Since fugue is ordinarily regarded as a 'learned' form that makes particular demands on the listener, we must examine why it was available as an option at all—and especially why it was placed in the very part of the work where, at the time, lightness was considered a prime aim.

The paradox is that the very learnedness of fugue and its historical association with the sacred and the vocal make it the ideal vehicle for parodistic treatment. An exaggeration here or an incongruity there can turn a fugue into a feast of wit. Carl Dahlhaus writes, apropos of fugues in Classical chamber music, that 'musical erudition and ostentatious pedantry were prohibited' and links this fact to the long-established humanistic and egalitarian ethos of social music-making.[32] Quite so; but there was no ban on poking fun at erudition and pedantry. If we look at the three fugal finales in Haydn's Op. 20 string quartets (1772), which are landmarks in their genre even though not quite the actual prototypes, we can see the truth of this. In No. 5 the 'antique', quasi-vocal character of the principal subject, which begins with four *Pfundnoten* outlining what Warren Kirkendale has termed the 'Pathotype' (configurations of notes based around degrees 7, 1, 5, and 6

[32] Carl Dahlhaus, *Nineteenth-Century Music*, trans. J. Bradford Robinson (Berkeley and Los Angeles, 1989), 260.

of the harmonic minor scale) is subverted by the chattering complementary subject (or countersubject), which begins with three chirpy repeated notes followed by a written-out appoggiatura.[33] Even before the episodes are reached, the parody has begun. In No. 2 a slurred chromatic slither and in No. 6 a *gruppetto* deliberately trivialize the principal subject in the opening few notes. In the couplet of the rondo finale of Haydn's 'Lark' Quartet and the finale of Beethoven's Third 'Rasumovsky' Quartet, Op. 59 No. 3, the helter-skelter of the subject is already incompatible with a straight face.[34]

If the subjects themselves lack comedy, this can be supplied from without. In the finale of Haydn's Symphony No. 70 (*c*.1779) the fugue is framed by a mysterious-cum-comic introduction and conclusion that emphasize the 'tapping' motif with which the subject begins. In that of Mozart's famous G major Quartet, K. 387, the solemnity of the fugal first subject is offset by an impudently homophonic transition that conveys the cheap thrills of *opera buffa*. Similarly in the even more celebrated finale of the 'Jupiter' Symphony, K. 551, where the undulating quavers in the second violins that accompany the principal fugue subject (like that of K. 387 and Haydn's Symphony No. 3, an 'off the peg' theme of four semibreves) introduce *opera buffa* levity from bar 1.

Contemporary writers were perfectly aware of these comic intentions. The redoubtable contrapuntist Simon Sechter, teacher of both Schubert and Bruckner, recognized the light-hearted quality of the 'Jupiter' Symphony's finale, and Koch related how, when 'combined with comic ornaments to provoke laughter' an instrumental fugue could win the hearts of amateurs.[35]

This is not to argue that there is anything inherently comic about instrumental fugue. In fact, we shall later see that in summative finales fugal writing can represent a grand culmination of serious intentions. The ruminative kind of fugue (Shostakovich's Eighth String Quartet provides a good example) can even contribute to a valedictory finale. Ultimately, fugue is only a technique—and one that can serve many masters.

In the finales of instrumental compositions from the first half of the eighteenth century binary form is frequently adopted in preference to the form used in the first movement, whether 'motto' form (in sinfonias), ritornello form (in concertos), or through-composed form (in sonatas).[36]

---

[33] Warren Kirkendale, *Fugue and Fugato in Rococo and Classical Chamber Music*, trans. Margaret Bent and the Author (Durham, NC, 1979), 91–2. Kirkendale's study remains not only the most comprehensive survey of the use of fugue in chamber music but also the best available introduction to fugal technique and its terminology.

[34] Kirkendale, *Fugue and Fugato*, 238, discusses the humorous aspects of the Beethoven movement.

[35] Sechter's view is reported in Elaine R. Sisman, *Mozart: The Jupiter Symphony* (Cambridge, 1993), 32; Koch's observation (in his *Versuch einer Anleitung zur Composition*) is cited in Agawu, *Playing with Signs*, 29.

[36] 'Motto' form is my term for the primitive version of ritornello form in which the material restated in successive keys is not a complete musical period but only a head-motif. This remained normal for the first movements of sinfonias until the 1740s, when they came increasingly to adopt binary form.

Binary-form finales in concertos often mimic the alternation of *tutti* and *solo* scoring practised in ritornello-form movements, so that the first repeated section is organized as T–S or T–S–T, and the second repeated section as T–S–T or S–T–S–T. The more extended of these two schemes reproduces the same pattern of four tuttis and three solos that remains standard in concerto first movements up to the time of Mozart.

With or without repeats, the symmetrical version of binary form (i.e. the one lacking a reprise of the opening), which some musicologists have christened the 'binary variant', persists for a while in Classical sonata and symphony movements, primarily in slow movements. Haimo has found it in twelve Haydn symphonies written before 1766, though only once (Symphony No. 21) in a finale.[37] It soon dies out, not because it is an unsophisticated or inherently unsatisfying structure (otherwise, we would not listen to Scarlatti sonatas and Bach suites), but because it is unsuited to movements beyond a simple length. When that length is reached, it becomes appropriate to insert a reprise, and once that is done, stylistic pressures virtually compel a *rapprochement* with sonata form.

There is, however, one extraordinary nineteenth-century sonata finale that should be regarded as a throwback to Baroque binary form. This is the 'presto' in 12/8 ending Chopin's Piano Sonata in B flat minor. Chopin, fairly unusually for his time, was brought up on the keyboard music of Bach, whom he revered, and this movement is his most eloquent tribute.[38] It conflates, as it were, two species of movement cultivated by Bach. The first

Ex. 4.2.   Chopin, Piano Sonata in B flat minor, Op. 35, last movement, opening

[37] Haimo, *Haydn's Symphonic Forms*, 64 n.

[38] Chopin's debt to Bach and the Bachian features that manifest themselves in his music are examined in Jean-Jacques Eigeldinger, 'Placing Chopin: Reflections on a Compositional Aesthetic', in John Rink and Jim Samson (eds.), *Chopin Studies 2* (Cambridge, 1994), 102–39. Since, as Eigeldinger notes (p. 120), we do not know very precisely which Bach works Chopin owned or knew, Bachian influence on him has to be inferred directly from the music.

is the restless, freely evolving type of prelude based on elaborations of a small group of motivic-cum-technical ideas that we find in the Third Partita for unaccompanied violin (BWV 1006) and the six Suites for unaccompanied cello (BWV 1007–12).[39] As Ex. 4.2 shows, Chopin even translates their monophonic (though harmonically complex) texture into pianistic terms by retaining bare octaves until the very end. The second source of influence is the binary form with a reprise (and usually also with repeats) encountered in the '48'. The ground plan of Chopin's finale is the following:

| Bars | Key | Description | Comment |
|---|---|---|---|
| 1–8 | b♭ | first theme | establishing tonic |
| 9–22 | modulating | transition | chromatically unstable |
| 23–30 | D♭ | second theme | diatonic |
| 31–8 | modulating | retransition | sequential progressions |
| 39–46 | b♭ | first theme | reprise of bars 1–8 |
| 47–56 | modulating | transition/second theme | based on bars 9–30 |
| 57–75 | b♭ | coda | largely diatonic |

Although we have distinguished first and second 'themes', the music is remarkably featureless, flowing onwards in a ceaseless torrent. The alternation between (relatively) diatonic and chromatic passages, not the pattern of tonal or thematic succession, is the element that orients the listener most strongly.

How successful is this movement? Had Chopin called it a study and given it a title such as 'Comme le vent' (after the fashion of the first of Alkan's Op. 39 studies), it would doubtless have joined the 'Raindrop' Prelude in the hall of fame. But as the last of four movements, following on from an impressive 'Marcia funebre', it seems a little too 'light' for its context, even allowing for the fact, noted in Chapter 3, that its harmonic density increases its effective length. Pianists tend to accentuate the problem by playing it at breakneck speed; a tempo not much faster than that of the 'presto ma non troppo', also in 12/8, that concludes Chopin's Third Piano Sonata (in B minor) and a 'fingery' style of articulating the quavers would substantially improve matters.

Having now considered movements written according to a design not prefigured in the first fast movement, we must return to those finales—in some repertories, the great mass—which establish their identity, as Hans Keller puts it, not through form but through character.[40] Keller was writing about a work from the Classical period, the last of Haydn's Op. 76 quartets, but his remark would apply equally to the concertos of the late Baroque. In Vivaldi and Bach we find well-differentiated first movements and finales, all in orthodox ritornello form, where the separate character of each is

---

[39] Although doubtless known only to connoisseurs, Bach's unaccompanied music for violin and cello was available in published form already in Chopin's day.
[40] Keller, *The Great Haydn Quartets*, 233–4.

established by the cumulative effect of small factors. These factors include not only obvious ones such as metre, tempo, rhythm, and melody, but also less tangible ones such as touches of humour and fantasy (more appropriate in finales than in opening movements). Although Vivaldi was an inveterate recycler of his material, it is extremely seldom that we find a ritornello theme (or even part of one) from a first movement re-employed for a finale, or vice versa.[41] Moreover, even when the main theme is the same, the structure is always different.

In relaxant finales, from the late Baroque onwards, there is a tradition of using popular or popular-sounding thematic material for the main theme and/or subsidiary themes. The popular song (or sometimes the folk song) is to the relaxant finale what the hymn will become to the summative finale: something that by virtue of its real or feigned origin (with all the social or spiritual connotations of that origin), encapsulates the 'tone' of the whole movement.

Example 4.3 offers a small selection of finale opening themes that display their popular credentials openly. They come from:

Ex. 4.3.  (a) Vivaldi, Cello Concerto in C major, RV 399, last movement, opening; (b) Haydn, Symphony No. 104 in D major, last movement, opening; (c) Schubert, String Quartet in A major ('Italian'), D. 804, last movement, opening; (d) Brahms, Piano Quintet in F minor, Op. 34, last movement, opening; (e) Shostakovich, Cello Sonata in D minor, Op. 40, last movement, opening

[41]  One example is the opening theme of the finale of a sinfonia in G major, RV 147, used again in the first movement of a concerto without soloist, RV 150.

(a) Vivaldi, Cello Concerto in C major, RV 399
(b) Haydn, Symphony No. 104 in D major
(c) Schubert, String Quartet in A minor, D. 804
(d) Brahms, Piano Quintet in F minor, Op. 34
(e) Shostakovich, Cello Sonata, Op. 40 (1934)

Oddly enough, two of the themes seem to have 'Slavic' features (Vivaldi, Haydn), while the other three present a 'Hungarian' face (Schubert, Brahms, Shostakovich)—the Hungary being that of a hussar's song or restaurant band rather than that of the Puszta.[42] Whether from other lands or from the composer's own, popular melody is always 'exotic' in terms of art music, but taking it from another country accentuates its alterity. It is interesting that the first four incipits are characterized by gapped-scale tendencies: the leading-note is either absent or introduced quickly in passing. Simplification of the musical raw material is, of course, a prime case of regression and therefore a feature suited to last rather than first movements—which must be why, in 'serious' genres, popular elements rarely intrude into the latter.[43]

'Regression' implies that the thematic material exists initially in a relatively complex state and is then whittled down to something simpler. But there is nothing to stop the regressive version from being the original one, the Urbild as Wörner terms it.[44] In the case of borrowed popular themes that make their first appearance in a finale, this is the only possible interpretation (barring an incredible serendipity). The thème russe that launches the finale of the first of Beethoven's 'Rasumovsky' Quartets, Op. 59, is undoubtedly the progenitor of the noble first-movement opening theme, even though in the process its characteristic motivic elements (the descent 6–5, the ascent 5–6–7–8, and various combinations of 1–2–3 and 5–4–3) have been thoroughly shuffled. The incipits are shown in Ex. 4.4.[45]

It has to be stressed that from an aesthetic or analytical point of view, it is hardly material which of the two themes existed prior to the composition and served as the basis for the other. What matters, rather, is their location in the composition and their style of treatment. Ernst Gombrich sets the

---

[42] The association of Vivaldi with central Europe is not often made, but the Riva degli Schiavoni where the Ospedale della Pietà was located was named after the Dalmatian sailors who frequented it, and Vivaldi travelled to Bohemia in 1729–30. One of the compositions he wrote during his visit was a 'characteristic' concerto (Conca, RV 163) that, as its title suggests, mimics the sound of a conch-shell, as blown for ritual purposes by Bohemian peasants.

[43] The fact that Brahms used a parody of the Haydn theme quoted as Ex. 4.3(b) for the first movement of his Serenade for Orchestra in D major, Op. 11, shows only that he regarded the genre as 'light' and wished to advertise the fact to his audience without delay.

[44] Wörner, Das Zeitalter der thematischen Prozesse, p. xx. 'Modellvariante' is this author's useful term for a theme that is a variant of a more fundamental model.

[45] Alexander Ringer calls a germinal idea of this kind a 'reference theme', noting (specifically in connection with Beethoven's 'Eroica' Symphony) that it is 'a motivic body that does not really belong to it [the work] but has been assigned to it, as it were, for continuous reference' ('Clementi and the Eroica', 464). Ringer's supposed model for the theme of the 'Eroica' finale comes from a Clementi piano sonata (Op. 7 No. 3).

Ex. 4.4. Beethoven, Quartet in F major, Op. 59 No. 1: (a) first movement, opening; (b) last movement, opening

question nicely in perspective when he comments (in connection with pictorial art) on the difficulty of distinguishing between a thought and an afterthought.[46] He might well have added: the near-pointlessness.

Even when a finale theme is not itself strongly characterized as such, its style of treatment often betrays its position and function in the work. The gallery of special effects to which a finale theme may be subjected (not necessarily at the very beginning) includes the long-drawn-out preparation (Mozart, K. 516: the 'adagio' in G minor); the false start (Beethoven, Symphony No. 1: the upbeat ascents); the dislocation (Beethoven, Symphony No. 8: the 'screwing up' into F sharp minor); the abrupt slowing down (Beethoven, Symphony No. 4: the slow-motion presentation of the theme shown in Ex. 4.1(b) just before the end); the abrupt speeding up (Beethoven, 'Waldstein' Sonata: the 'prestissimo' coda); the dissolution of the theme into fragments (Haydn, String Quartet in C major, Op. 33 No. 3 ('The Joke'): the final bars). All these devices are capable of producing a comic effect ranging from good humour to rough humour;[47] already in 1802 Koch noted that a typical finale was marked by 'cheerfulness, gaiety, or jocularity'.[48]

One fairly common expression of this light-hearted mood is the off-tonic opening. To use a chord other than V or I to open a movement is not restricted to finales but comes more naturally to them since (in tonally rounded cycles) their tonic is implanted in the listener's ear before they begin, and they can therefore take more liberties. The sonata-rondo finale of Beethoven's Fourth Piano Concerto, which begins on a C major (subdominant) chord, is brilliantly eccentric, since every time the refrain returns, it is prepared in the manner of a theme in C major—that just happens to gravitate unexpectedly quickly to the 'dominant'. Other Beethoven finales

[46] Ernst Gombrich, *The Sense of Order: A Study in the Psychology of Decorative Art* (Oxford, 1984²), 79.

[47] Or from the 'ludic' to the 'frankly ludicrous', in Wheelock's words (*Haydn's Ingenious Jesting with Art*, 107).

[48] Koch, *Musikalisches Lexikon*, 575: 'den letzten Satz der Sinfonien, Parthien, Balleten, u[nd] d[er] gl[eichen], dem gewöhnlich der Charakter der Munterkeit, der Freude, oder des Scherzos eigen ist'.

that exploit the ambiguity of an off-tonic opening chord are those of the early Cello Sonata in G minor, Op. 5 No. 2, and the Second 'Rasumovsky' Quartet (in E minor); in both cases, the opening chord is that of C major.[49]

Even if the main theme itself is treated straightforwardly, subsidiary themes can inject an element of the grotesque or diversionary. A very common device in the relaxant finale is the unforeseen interpolation. This interpolation may be of an introduction to the finale itself, as occurs with the 'Muss es sein?' motto of Beethoven's String Quartet in F major, Op. 135; it may reach back into a first movement (Haydn: Symphony No. 31 in D major 'mit dem Hornsignal'; Mendelssohn, String Quartet in E flat major, Op. 12); a slow movement (Schubert, Piano Trio in E flat major, D. 929, and Fantasy in C major for Violin and Piano, D. 934);[50] a minuet or scherzo (Haydn, Symphony No. 46; Beethoven, Symphony No. 5). It is important to clarify that such quotations, even when taken with little or no alteration from an earlier movement, serve a different purpose in a relaxant finale from that in a summative finale. In the latter, they act to bind the movements closer to one another, to demonstrate interconnectedness. In the former, they are a *jeu d'esprit*, a diversion.

This becomes clearer when we consider another kind of interpolation, which takes the form of a 'fragment' of a contrasting piece only imagined for the occasion (as it were) by the composer. Such are the 'Minuet' in the finale of Mozart's Piano Concerto in E flat major, K. 482, the 'Gavotte' in the Violin Concerto in D major, K. 218, the 'Turkish' episode in the Violin Concerto in A major, K. 219, and the 'adagio' in the Piano Concerto in C major, K. 415.[51]

These seeming digressions and unexpected twists are part and parcel of the ending process, as literary theorists know. They are an ingredient of *peripeteia* (also known as 'the peripeties'), which Frank Kermode defines as 'that falsification of simple expectations as to the structure of a future'.[52] Kermode comments on the function of *peripeteia* thus: 'It is one of the great charms of books that they have to end.... But unless we are extremely naïve...we do not ask that they progress towards that end precisely as we have been led to believe.'[53] In the same spirit (but with reference to poetry rather than the novel), Barbara Herrnstein Smith argues that 'our pleasure in a poem does not consist in having all our expectations gratified

[49] Both the original finale of Beethoven's String Quartet in B flat major, Op. 130, and the finale of Schubert's Piano Sonata in B flat major, D. 960 (clearly modelled on it), open with the dominant chord of the supertonic minor, which, in similar fashion, becomes the initial destination of all returns of the main theme.

[50] It is no accident that Schubert, the lyricist par excellence, should have favoured the reintroduction of song in the middle of a finale. In D. 934 the finale is preceded by another reminiscence—of the opening, Hungarian-flavoured slow movement (where the piano tries to sound like a cimbalom).

[51] I am indebted for these four examples to Jeffrey Kallberg, 'The Rhetoric of Genre: Chopin's Nocturne in G Minor', *19th Century Music*, 11 (1987–8), 238–61 at 245.

[52] Frank Kermode, *The Sense of an Ending* (New York, 1967), 23.

[53] Ibid. 23–4.

but, on the contrary, ... the effective power of poetry lies in what it can do with those expectations'.[54]

Because *peripeteia* is a generic device, it applies in some measure not only to finales but also to all the movements that precede it. Hence it is likely to be present in most codas. However, a last movement may need a 'double dose' of it in order to bring the complete work to a satisfactory close.

A common peripety is the modal transformation of thematic material—usually from minor to major—in the latter part of a movement or cycle. This modal shift operates much more often, at a structural level, from minor to major than the other way round, and our theory of regression can explain why. Occurring naturally in the 'chord of nature', the major triad over the fundamental note (reproduced in a higher octave) is traditionally, and perhaps not mistakenly, considered more basic than the minor triad and also more consonant. Hence the minor-major shift is a reversion to a simpler form (or a 'release' according to the tension/release model), whereas the reverse is a complication. Looking at the full spectrum of tonal music between 1750 and 1900, one comes across huge quantities of finales in major keys serving works in (or, at least, beginning in) minor keys. We have already had cause to mention Mozart's String Quartet in G minor, K. 516, Beethoven's Cello Sonata in G minor, and Schubert's 'Italian' Quartet, D. 804. Against this, we find for (nominally) major-key works only a miserable quantity of finales that both begin and end in minor. Of these by far the best known is that of Mendelssohn's 'Italian' Symphony, which does its best to compensate for the anti-regressive effect with its vivacious tarantella rhythms.[55]

The position is complicated, however, by the ability of a movement to shift mode (when in the tonic key) at several different structural points. A movement otherwise in major may have an introduction in minor. Somewhat less commonly, a movement in minor may have an introduction in major (as in the opening movement of Beethoven's 'Kreutzer' Sonata for Violin and Piano, Op. 47). A movement otherwise in minor may escape to the major in its closing bars in a glorified *tierce de Picardie*; this occurs in the finale of Haydn's Symphony No. 70 in D major and in that of Berwald's *Sinfonie singulière*.

An even more typical case, however, is that of a Classical or later movement in minor that, by placing the second subject group and (if present) coda in the tonic major, achieves 'progressive modality'. This procedure was

[54] Smith, *Poetic Closure*, 110.
[55] Another example is Brahms's Piano Trio in B major, Op. 8 (in both its versions). Brahms's liking for the minor mode to figure strongly in a finale (as in those of his First Violin Sonata, Op. 78, and his Third Symphony) is perhaps related to his habitual *Ernsthaftigkeit*. It may also have something to do with his penchant for Baroque and earlier music, in which the major/minor antithesis (as distinct from the more complex and nuanced question of modal ethos) does not carry the hermeneutic significance it has held from the Classical period onwards.

almost unknown before the middle of the eighteenth century.[56] French late
Baroque music groups together (as movements of a suite, couplets of a
rondo, or variations of a chaconne) major- and minor-key units sharing a
*ton* (the French word for key that embraces both modes on the same tonic),
but it merely juxtaposes them as adjacent blocks without any sophisticated
transition. Italian late Baroque music in major keys has occasional enclaves
in the minor for 'pathetic' contrast but is careful to preserve overall modal
unity.[57] In binary-form movements, where the option of a modulation to
the relative major in the first section is taken—unlike in the Classical period,
the dominant minor is a common alternative choice—its restatement (in the
fashion of a sonata-form second subject group) in the second section is
invariably in the tonic minor.

Even before the Classical period arrived, a change in the status of the
minor mode was observable. From the position of parity with the major
mode that it had enjoyed in the period of Corelli, the status of the minor
mode (as the key-centre of a movement and, still more, of a work) declined
dramatically. The process was already under way by the time of Vivaldi,
whose published collections of concertos show a 3:2 preponderance of major
keys. The decisive turn coincided with the advent of the 'Neapolitan' style,
which became dominant in the mid-1720s and remained so (it is the
immediate precursor of the Classical style). Newman calculates that in
Haydn's sonatas minor-key works represent under 10 per cent of the total;
in Mozart's they account for about 10 per cent; in those of Beethoven, who
prefigures the minor mode's return to favour in the Romantic period, it
reaches just over 25 per cent.[58]

Its relative rarity (even in slow movements, which in major-key Baroque
works had traditionally used the relative minor key for preference) caused
the minor mode to be treated as a special case: a vehicle for exceptional
passion or melancholy. Textbook sonata form, which although not codified
by theorists until the end of the eighteenth century was a reality in practice
long before then, made no allowance for the peculiarities of the minor mode
beyond insisting that the second subject group be placed in the relative major
key instead of the dominant. The result was that every composer approaching the recapitulation of this group had a hard choice to make. If the formerly
major-key material were recast in the tonic minor, modifications would
undoubtedly have to be made (theory and experience show that one cannot
successfully turn a section in the major mode into one in the minor mode
simply by manipulating accidentals), although the movement's modal unity

[56] In a broader context, I discuss the question of major–minor relationships (with especial
reference to Domenico Scarlatti's sonatas) in 'Modal Shifts in the Sonatas of Domenico Scarlatti',
*Chigiana*, 40, NS 20 (1985), 25–43.

[57] A notable exception is Corelli's 'Christmas' Concerto in G minor (Op. 6 No. 8), where the
concluding pastorale—an optional and overtly extraneous movement—switches to major.

[58] Newman, *The Sonata in the Classic Era*, 137.

would be respected. If, on the other hand, the major mode were retained (which would enable the composer simply to transpose the original material if he had no higher ambition), the movement would end in a mode different from one in which it had begun.[59] The new musical aesthetic obligingly allowed all composers who so wished to follow the easier course: the *lieto fine* option was simply extended to all movements, regardless of mode.

However, this gave composers a chance to obtain modal variety between the outer movements (a useful means of giving the finale individuality) without sacrificing modal unity at the level of the work. The finale of a major-key work can proceed as if in minor until the recapitulated second subject group, at which point a *deus ex machina* restores the major mode of the first movement. Well-known instances are the finales of Haydn's String Quartet in C major, Op. 76 No. 3 (the 'Emperor' Quartet), and Schubert's String Quintet in C major, D. 956. A facile technique has become, ironically enough, the vehicle for a sophisticated realization of the tension/release model. And in the Romantic period, when the summative finale sets the trend, the turn to major at the end can bring forth a blaze of glory rather than just a happy ending.

In twentieth-century music, which rarely deals in the simplicities of the Classical–Romantic tonal system, an equivalent to the shift from minor to major has been found. This is the shift from chromaticism to diatonicism, which is likewise a regressive technique, considering that the diatonic scale can be viewed—in a theoretical rather than historical perspective—as a simplified version of the chromatic scale (just as the pentatonic scale represents one further simplification). Béla Bartók (1881–1945), whose neo-Classical approach to composition, especially marked in his later years, led him to parody Baroque and Classical techniques, was especially fond of this transformation. His *Music for Strings, Percussion, and Celesta* (1937) and *Sonata for Two Pianos and Percussion* (1942) offer brilliant instances.

Many of the points covered in this chapter are brought out by the finale of Schubert's Piano Trio in B flat, D. 898 (1827). This is a good example to study in more detail since it illustrates to perfection the ambiguity of a sonata-form structure married to rondo style. It also enables us to consider more closely the case of a composer whose finales, perhaps more than those of any other person, have been found problematic (a euphemism for 'weak') by commentators.[60]

---

[59] I am of course oversimplifying, since more complex solutions (a 'variable-mode' second subject group and/or coda) are possible. Not until Beethoven did such solutions become common, however.

[60] The same movement is the subject of a close analysis in Thomas A. Denny, 'Articulation, Elision, and Ambiguity in Schubert's Mature Sonata Forms: The Op. 99 Trio Finale in its Context', *Journal of Musicology*, 6 (1988), 340–66. My conclusions are similar to Denny's: we at least agree on the classification of the movement's structure as sonata form despite its 'Rondo' heading. However, I think that his view is a little one-sidedly taxonomic, underrating the extent to which we nevertheless 'hear' the movement as a rondo.

Some perceptive remarks by Charles Rosen, who in his *Sonata Forms* devotes a separate section to what he calls 'Finale Sonata Form', will set the context. Rosen observes:

Finale Sonata Form is more loosely organized [than first-movement sonata form] and tends by its very looseness to a resolution of tension. What is essential is a squareness and clarity of rhythm and phrasing, and generally an emphasis on the subdominant as well as a broad use of the tonic equivalent to the similar emphasis in a recapitulation... The first theme is generally rounded off by a full cadence on the tonic, and does not move directly into a modulation. The square phrase structure which isolates each theme is especially suitable for rondo form.[61]

Interesting, and relevant to the case we are about to consider, is Rosen's mention of the subdominant emphasis (which one may interpret broadly as encompassing all areas to the flat side of the home key). 'Normal' sonata form, at least in major keys, has a definite sharpward bias. The dominant key for the second subject group lies, of course, on the sharp side—but so, too (as a rule), do the various substitutes for it used by composers from Beethoven onwards.[62]

Rondo form, in contrast, has always treated visits to the sharp side as non-mandatory. Baroque rondos tend to be very even-handed in their distribution of keys for the couplets, and in simple rondos from the Classical period this approach persists. In Mozart's Piano Sonata in B flat major, K. 570, the central 'adagio', a 'second' rondo, has couplets in the relative minor (neutral in respect of sharpness and flatness) and the subdominant, while the final 'allegretto' has couplets in the tonic and the subdominant. Both movements therefore place the emphasis unequivocally on the flat side.[63] In a sonata-form movement informed by the rondo style one would not expect to find the subdominant displacing the dominant, but one would anticipate its presence in the development section, the coda, or transitional sections.

Schubert's movement fulfils Rosen's criteria. Table 4.2 presents an outline of its form. The 'loose organization' of which Rosen writes is certainly in evidence in this movement. It resolves into six clearly demarcated main sections forming an ABCABC pattern where 'C' represents (i) the central episode, including the small amount of development following it, and (ii) the bipartite coda. The joins are enviably smooth (note how the cadential B flat opening Ex. 4.5(*b*) immediately becomes reinterpreted as III of the relative minor), and this easy transition from one section to the next is aided by Schubert's extreme thematic economy. As Exs. 4.5(*a*)–(*d*) already suggest, the principal themes are dominated melodically by the progression

---

[61] Charles Rosen, *Sonata Forms* (New York, 1988²), 123–4.

[62] For example, the mediant, as found in the first movements of Beethoven's 'Waldstein' Sonata and Brahms's Third Symphony.

[63] The pronounced subdominant emphasis in the first movement of Schumann's *Fantasie*, Op. 17, is one (but not the only) reason why this rightly celebrated movement is more appropriately analysed as a rondo than as a sonata-form movement.

TABLE 4.2.   *Plan of the finale of Schubert, Piano Trio in B flat major, D. 898*

| Bars | Description |
|---|---|
| 1–52 | First subject group, closing in B flat major. The first-subject theme, whose opening is shown as Ex. 4.5(*a*), is bipartite, its second half starting in bar 26. It follows the thematic pattern abcb, where 'c' tonicizes the supertonic minor. |
| 52–176 | Transition, beginning on the cadential chord and leading seamlessly into the second subject group. The transition and second subject group cohere in a single block, the greater part of which is stated twice (in bars 68–112 and 132–72, respectively): the first time, the music modulates from G minor to A flat major; the second time, from G minor to F major, the dominant. The opening is shown as Ex. 4.5(*b*). |
| 176–249 | Closing group, remaining overall in F major (with brief divagations). Bars 246–9 move, via an interrupted cadence in the parallel key, F minor, to D flat major. The opening is shown as Ex. 4.5(*c*). |
| 250–344 | Development section, comprising: |
| 250–80 | Episode based initially in D flat major, the flattened submediant. A D♭ bass pedal note is maintained until bar 265. In conformity with the hypermetre (a *ritmo di tre battute* equivalent to the one occurring in the scherzo of Beethoven's Ninth Symphony) the metre changes to 3/2 (i.e. 3 × 2/4) in bar 250. In bars 265–77 the new material is developed conventionally, reaching an imperfect cadence in C (minor) in bar 277. The G major chord is then used as a dominant substitute to introduce E flat major in bar 279. The opening is given as Ex. 4.5(*d*). |
| 281–318 | 2/4 metre is restored. Bars 1–38 are recapitulated in a transposition to E flat major. This is initially assumed to be the start of a subdominant recapitulation, but... |
| 318–44 | a developmental continuation steers the music back to B flat major, in which key... |
| 345–70 | bars 1–26 are recapitulated in B flat major. Retrospectively, bars 281–318 can now be interpreted as a *fausse reprise* mimicking a regular (in Schubert's terms) subdominant recapitulation. The 'real' recapitulation starts, therefore, only in bar 345. |
| 370–85 | A developmental interpolation, beginning and ending in the tonic. 3/2 metre returns, and the first subject theme combines contrapuntally with that of the episode. |
| 385–509 | Transition and second subject group. 2/4 metre is restored. Largely as in the exposition, with an adjustment in bars 293–6 to keep the music in the tonic. |
| 509–82 | Closing group as before (but with the conventional transposition). The section closes in G flat major, the key used to introduce... |
| 583–611 | First section of the coda. This reproduces, with transposition, the start of the central episode but is diverted via a French Sixth to a dominant pedal (with alternating tonic and dominant harmony) in the home key. |
| 611–54 | Second section of the coda. 2/4 metre is restored, and the tempo quickens from 'allegro vivace' to 'presto'. Opening with a reminiscence of the transition (bars 52– ) and later revisiting the material of the closing group of the exposition, this section has the character of a *stretta*. |

Ex. 4.5.  Schubert, Piano Trio in B flat major, D. 898, last movement: (*a*) opening; (*b*) bars 52–7; (*c*) bars 176–82; (*d*) bars 250–2

5–(6)–7–8 and rhythmically by Schubert's beloved dactyls (crotchet plus two quavers—in the 3/2 passages also present in augmentation as a background rhythm of minim plus two crotchets). 'Loose' therefore refers to the sheer number of sections and subsections (and perhaps also to some unconventional aspects of their arrangement), not to any haphazardness or crudity.

The strong presence of the subdominant, and of the flat side generally, hardly needs comment. In the exposition we have A flat; in the episode-cum-development, D flat; in the coda, G flat. Whether we identify the restatement of the opening theme in bar 281 as part of the development section, as a *fausse reprise,* or as the actual start of a subdominant recapitulation will depend on the extent to which we are prepared to count what is indisputably a Schubertian idiosyncrasy in relation to the practice of other composers (the subdominant recapitulation) as a norm from which he himself can meaningfully deviate. I would say that, given the traditional use of chord III to introduce recapitulated openings in the tonic (the practice goes back at least as far as Corelli), the naive listener will initially accept the E flat chord in bar 281 both as a tonic and as the start of the recapitulation. An educated listener who can tell E flat from B flat will of course recognize that the key is not the tonic—but may have enough experience of Schubert's works to know that a subdominant recapitulation is quite possible. The likelihood is, therefore, that the subsection beginning in bar 281 will be interpreted at first as the beginning of a subdominant recapitulation, but after bar 345—when the same material appears, following a developmental episode (bars 318–44), in the orthodox key—as a kind of *fausse reprise*. Something similar happens at bar 206 of the first movement of Haydn's String Quartet in D major, Op. 20 No. 4, when, following a chord of B major (the dominant of the relative minor), the first subject theme enters in G major. Here, once again, we encounter a 'false' *fausse reprise* (with the important difference that in Haydn there would be no expectation whatever of a subdominant recapitulation).

Had the material of section A returned before or after the second C (i.e. to introduce or close the coda), it would have been tempting to see this movement as a sonata-rondo. It does not: we leave A for good in bar 385, with over 260 bars still to run. But whether we accept the sonata or the rondo model, there are some highly unusual things about this music that are typical of its composer when he writes extended instrumental movements. They are by no means restricted to his final movements, although they are accentuated there.

Edward Cone comes close to the answer when he writes: 'Schubert . . . always had trouble in controlling the rondo. It is to his finales, and especially to his rondo finales, that his reputation for rambling redundancy is due.'[64] Cone points to an imbalance between the immense length of many of Schubert's finales—he cites the 411 bars of that of the Fantasy-Sonata in G major, D. 894 and the 650-odd bars of the *Rondo brillant* in B minor for Violin and Piano, D. 895—and the simplicity of their overall form (the former is a mere 'second' rondo: ABACA). This is very true, but it masks an even more fundamental problem.

Schubert commonly infringes two general principles common to late Baroque and Classical style. These are (i) that passages earmarked for requotation should be easily distinguishable on first hearing from those intended to be stated only once, and (ii) that there should be an equitable balance between the two kinds of passage. A movement should consist, therefore, of a judicious mixture of 'developmental' and 'non-developmental' passages. Orthodox sonata form achieves this aim by making the first and second subject groups largely 'non-developmental', while the transitions, the development section itself, and the coda are 'developmental'.

In Schubert, however, material that to the ear carries all the hallmarks of being 'developmental' (e.g. bars 68–112 of the movement analysed above) frequently becomes subject to repetition (either immediate or long-range). Schubert forms his music into large blocks that are shuffled around, with adroit tonal manipulation at their points of connection, in such a way that any modulating sequence, any imitative dialogue, any harmonic *frisson*, is potentially repeatable.[65] In the whole of the D. 898 finale only a couple of

[64] Edward T. Cone, 'Schubert's Beethoven', *Musical Quarterly*, 56 (1970), 779–93 at 787.

[65] The development section of the String Quintet in C major, D. 956, is a notorious case in point.

short subsections (bars 265–77 and 318–44) present their material as a unique, 'developmental' statement. Everything else is repeated at least once.

Hence Cone's accusation of 'rambling redundancy'. It is this all-pervading redundancy that time and again turns an amble into a ramble, for length itself is not the problem. Despite that, one may continue to love Schubert's instrumental music for other reasons, while acknowledging this unusual and puzzling source of weakness.

Schubert's heading 'Rondo' reminds us that we have not yet considered what difference, if any, it makes if a composer, in addition to providing a tempo marking and possibly a generic marking ('Tema e variazioni', etc.) for a last movement, heads it 'Finale'. Practice in this regard has always been very haphazard. There is no clear pattern in how composers use, or fail to use, the description. For early music, 'finale', the Italian translation of the Latin 'finalis', denoted, as a substantive, the modal final, equivalent to the later tonic. In Lully's comedy-ballets we find 'final' and 'chœur final' used for the first time in reference to the last number of a dramatic work, and this meaning carries forward (in the shape of the operatic act finale) to the modern age. In instrumental music the name 'finale' does not appear to be applied commonly to last movements until the Classical period.[66] As a simple description, it was doubtless universally used and understood. But as a title it was, and remains to this day, sporadic. Among Beethoven's violin sonatas (the example is chosen almost at random), only Op. 30 No. 2 and Op. 47 (the 'Kreutzer') feature it.

Carl Dahlhaus writes that the prior announcement of the form of a movement (as when one heads it 'Fugue' or 'Minuet', for example) stimulates a listening strategy and can therefore assist the composer in achieving his communicative purpose.[67] It becomes what Genette calls a paratext: something surrounding the text. A finale is not exactly a genre, but using the first word as a label for a movement sets up something very similar to the 'generic contract' as described by Jeffrey Kallberg.[68] In effect, one is saying to the player and listener: 'This is the last movement. Approach it as you would the other finales that you know.' What the other finales one knows are like depends, of course, on historical, local, and even personal factors. In an age of light finales or neo-Classical tendencies, to label a movement 'Finale' is to emphasize its light quality. Conversely, if Bruckner prefaces the word 'Final' to the fourth movement of the Eighth Symphony, the intended comparators are, not surprisingly, the finales of the previous Bruckner symphonies—so the listener here has to prepare himself for something titanic.

---

[66] The *Passacaglio* ending the Op. 22 (1655) of the Brescian composer Biagio Marini (1594–1663) concludes with a six-bar epilogue in slow tempo marked 'Finale' (balancing a five-bar 'Introdutione' of similar character at the beginning of the movement). This is the earliest instance of the use of our term for a final section or movement that I have encountered.

[67] Carl Dahlhaus, *Esthetics of Music*, trans. William W. Austin (Cambridge, 1982), 78.

[68] Kallberg, 'The Rhetoric of Genre', 243.

Occasionally, the use of 'Finale' as a heading discloses something that was not already obvious. Ivor Keys remarks: 'When Brahms writes the word "finale" [as in his Second Piano Trio, in C major] it is as though he gives notice to the world that he is stripped for action of a more rhythmical, less introspective sort.'[69] In other words, labelling a last movement 'finale' is Brahms's method of conveying in words the idea of a relaxant, as opposed to summative, movement. In similar fashion, Mahler heads the last movements of his fifth and seventh symphonies 'Rondo-Finale' as if to suggest, via this twofold act of retrospection, a return to Mozartian ways. Of course, the music soon turns out to be very un-Mozartian because of its parodistic transformations of the Classical model and its huge scale, but the label is very apt as a starting point.

---

[69] Ivor Keys, *Brahms Chamber Music* (London, 1974), 51–2.

# 5

# The Summative Finale

WHAT makes a summative finale different from a relaxant one? Is the difference one of kind or only of degree? If the latter were the case, one would expect a relaxant finale to turn into a summative one if it received an increment of length or weight, or if its cumulative and regressive character became more pronounced. The choice between the descriptions 'relaxant' and 'summative' would then give up all claim to have a technical foundation and would instead resemble that between 'small' and 'large'.

The finale of Mozart's 'Jupiter' Symphony puts this problem acutely to the test. With all repeats observed, it lasts almost as long as the first movement (reckoning two bars of its 2/2 metre as roughly equivalent to one bar of the latter's 4/4 metre). The complexity of its contrapuntal treatment (not to speak of its harmony and modulation) is unarguably greater. Its coda, in which five themes that were previously heard only in a linear relationship (albeit often given individual fugal or imitative treatment) are combined contrapuntally for the first time, is nothing if not cumulative, turning the whole movement, at the last moment, into a glittering tour de force.

The quality of regression is no less marked. The four-note *soggetto* of the opening (accompanied, it will be remembered, by *buffo*-style quavers that right from the outset call mockingly into question its *stile antico* credentials) is the ultimate point of reduction of a thematic process in train since the first movement. If the principal first-subject theme of the opening movement, shown as Ex. 5.1(*a*), emphasizes reiteratively the descending two-note figure represented by notes 3–4 of the *soggetto*, its second-subject theme, shown as Ex. 5.1(*b*), does the same (in slower motion, with an interposed chromatic passing note) for the ascending two-note figure represented by notes 1–2 and also prefigures (in the second violin) the undulating accompaniment of the finale. The bass of the opening theme of the slow movement, shown in Ex. 5.1(*c*), for the first time brings the two halves of the *soggetto* almost together (the single loud chord separating them is experienced as a clearly extraneous element). The minuet builds the *soggetto* inconspicuously, at different pitch levels, into its melody (and once again anticipates the finale's accompaniment), while the second half of the trio brings the process almost to completion by quoting the *soggetto* in its final, *Pfundnoten* form, albeit in the minor mode: see Ex. 5.1(*d*). In Wörner's terms, the *soggetto* is a genuine *Urbild* towards which the three previous movements grope.

Ex. 5.1.   Mozart, Symphony in C major ('Jupiter'), K. 551: (*a*) first movement, opening; (*b*) first movement, bars 56–9; (*c*) second movement, opening; (*d*) third movement, bars 68–72

And yet: the finale does not for one moment lose its overriding relaxant quality. The teasing character of its material seldom vanishes, and is in fact only enhanced by the contrapuntal (as well as harmonic and tonal) hoops through which it has to jump. This movement is a successor to the last movement of K. 387, in the same way as that movement builds on the fugal finales of Haydn's (and other Classical composers') symphonies and quartets. It is not a precursor of, say, the finale of Beethoven's Fifth Symphony. In this case, indisputable end-weighting does not amount to a conclusive difference in concept or function.[1]

---

[1]  Wörner, *Das Zeitalter der thematischen Prozesse*, p. xiv, claims that all of Mozart's last three symphonies exhibit 'Endcharakter'. The case is far less clear, it seems to me, for the E flat major and G minor symphonies.

We could adduce very similar arguments against considering the finale of Beethoven's 'Eroica' Symphony as summative in a strong analytical sense. It is uncommonly long—but so, too, is the first movement. (We should point out here that it is the relationship of the finale to the other movements, especially the first, that is important for the present argument, not its individual qualities considered in isolation.) It has a remarkably complex form (variation form with an introduction, episodes, and coda), but not more so than the first movement. Its various cumulative devices (fugato, *stretta*, etc.) are impressive but merely match those of the latter. Once again, it features an *Urbild* (the motif eb–bb–Bb–eb) prefigured, in elaborated forms, in earlier movements. None of this takes away its essential good humour— the quality that led the ever-perceptive Berlioz, taking his cue from the symphony's Napoleonic connection and the presence of a funeral march as second movement, to liken it (and the preceding scherzo with trio) to Grecian funeral games in which joy and sorrow mingle.[2]

The qualitative difference between an unusually elaborate relaxant finale and a truly summative one has mainly to do with the position of each within the 'narrative' of the cyclic work. To put it succinctly: a relaxant finale is an *envoi*, whereas a summative finale is a dénouement.

Narrativity is one of a small number of explanatory or associative ideas that have been used, sometimes concurrently, in the history of Western art music for various purposes ranging from the justification of music as a serious and demanding cultural practice to its popularization among a mass audience. Examples of other historically significant ideas of this kind have been mathematics ('the Harmony of the Spheres'), rhetoric, the imitation of nature, and, much more recently, socialist realism. Music resists easy assimilation to these external ideas, which are never adequate as a total explanation or even as a mere analogue. They nevertheless have great historical importance, since composers themselves have often believed in their efficacy and skewed their own practice accordingly.

The mathematical association dominated in the medieval period, as is shown by the inclusion of music alongside arithmetic, geometry, and astronomy in the Quadrivium. It privileges the spatial aspect of music over the

---

[2] Berlioz, *The Art of Music*, 15. Berlioz's statement that 'the finale is nothing but a further development of the same poetic idea', which follows on directly from his characterization of the scherzo, could be taken to refer to the first three movements as a whole, but his use of the singular form ('idea') convinces me that only the third movement is intended. I am grateful to my colleague John Williamson for reminding me of this description. Alexander Ringer claims that the 'Eroica' Symphony is the first 'Finalsymphonie' in musical history ('Clementi and the *Eroica*', 466). His argument is based largely on the fact that the thematic material of the finale generates that of the preceding movements ('What followed was really that which preceded'). But this is unconvincing. First, the sequence in which a composer happened, historically, to assemble a work in many movements or sections is quite irrelevant to its musical effect when heard or read on the page. Second, if the presence of an *Urbild* in the final movement were to be the decisive criterion for a 'Finalsymphonie', 'Finalsonate', or final-whatever, we would have to go back much further than Beethoven's symphony to find the first examples.

temporal: what is evident in the notation can actually be more germane to the essence of the music than the sound of a performance. For example, in some mensuration canons (ones in which the note values of the participating voices are proportionately related) exactness of proportion resides only in the notation, since the operation of rules governing perfection and imperfection (i.e. whether a note is three or only two times the next-smaller value) modifies the ostensible note values in practice. Music of this kind often attempts to introduce reversibility into music, the equivalent of left and right in architecture and the visual arts. Without resort to electronic wizardry, this is always a fiction, since, as we saw earlier, the basic unit, the note, is itself asymmetrical, even though the symbol used to represent it (especially when written in the old manner with a centred stem) suggests otherwise. Eero Tarasti explains at a deeper level the inherent irreversibility of music: in an ABA form the second 'A' is always experienced as different from the first because of the embedded memory of what has preceded it.[3] Even if there is a return, there is no simple recovery of the initial state. Unlike an eye wandering over an image, an ear can proceed only in one direction: forward.

Nevertheless, even as a fiction (in terms of its real effect), mathematical proportioning can act as a fruitful generative force. It has come into its own again in the twentieth century, mainly because it acts as a useful filter. When so many possibilities are theoretically open, it can be attractive to apply any fixed principle, regardless of its ultimate rationale, in order to narrow down choice and draw back from what Stravinsky once called the 'abyss of freedom'.[4]

Rhetoric, a constituent of the medieval Trivium (alongside grammar and logic), was the dominant comparator for music from the age of Humanism up to the Enlightenment—that is, from the sixteenth to the eighteenth century. The analogy of music and rhetoric or, to put it more precisely, the use of rhetorical processes and effects as metaphors for musical ones, focuses firmly on the temporal aspect of music and, unlike the mathematical model, finds difficulty in accommodating the large-scale patterns created by non-immediate repetition: instead, the sequence of the ideas, their flow, becomes the all-important factor. As Brian Vickers has convincingly argued in a study that ought to be required reading for those modern historians of music who have taken on board too uncritically the rhetorical model, a linguistic system cannot so easily be translated into a non-linguistic one.[5] Whatever one's understanding of the essential nature of music—'an unconsummated symbol' (Susanne Langer)[6] and 'a medium of pure symbolic

---

[3] Tarasti, *A Theory of Musical Semiotics* (Bloomington, Ind., 1994), 61–2.

[4] Igor Stravinsky, *Poetics of Music in the Form of Six Lessons*, trans. Arthur Knodel and Ingolf Dahl (Cambridge, Mass., and London, 1970), 64. Much of the so-called 'process music' falls into this category. One may cite here Reich's *Clapping Music* and Pärt's *Summa*.

[5] Brian Vickers, 'Figures of Rhetoric/Figures of Music?', *Rhetorica*, 2 (1984), 1–44.

[6] Susanne K. Langer, *Philosophy in a New Key* (Cambridge, Mass., 1951), 240.

gesture'[7] (Edward Cone, referring specifically to instrumental music) are two good attempts at description that spring to mind—this art-form cannot be said to conduct an argument in the way that language does. (If, today, we speak of a musical 'argument', we employ this term in the same honorific, non-literal way as did the rhetoricians of old when they referred to a musical *confirmatio* or *confutatio*.) Vickers hits the nail on the head when he observes: 'A metaphor is a translation of something different, not of something identical.'[8] There are enough similarities between a musical piece and an oration (or poem, or any other literary composition) to allow useful comparisons by analogy and even the exchange of some terminology. What one can never do successfully, however, is to find a satisfactory home within music for the complete conceptual and terminological baggage of the art of rhetoric—its five constituent parts (*inventio, dispositio, elocutio, memoria, pronuntatio*), its six structural components (*exordium, narratio, propositio, confirmatio, confutatio, peroratio*), and its huge stock of figures running from *abruptio* to *variatio*.[9] To represent a musical composition as a complete and meticulously executed oratorical statement, as Johann Mattheson famously attempted to do for an aria by Benedetto Marcello, is doomed to failure.[10]

Again, however, the models provided by the oration (which for the first time identifies the beginning and the end of a musical composition as discrete sections with distinctive functions) and also by its *figurae* (which have left an indelible mark on the conventions of word-painting and onomatopoeic reference within music) have proved, in their time, a highly potent fiction that the historian cannot ignore if he wishes to get inside the minds of those who composed, performed, and heard the music of past centuries.

Leaving aside the doctrine of the imitation of nature (which connects in any case with that of the rhetorical figures just discussed), we arrive at narrativity. The narrative model, which shares with the rhetorical model an emphasis on linearity, coexisted with it for a long time before, finally, becoming dominant in the nineteenth century. The hegemony achieved by this model is perhaps surprising, since the problems with relying on narrative to supply adequate hermeneutic explanations for music are immediately apparent. We are led straight back to the non-linguistic nature of music, which includes the fact that, in the words of Jean-Jacques Nattiez, 'it is not within the semiological possibilities of music to link a subject to a predicate'.[11] Even more seriously, normal music is unable to portray a truly

---

[7] Edward T. Cone, *The Composer's Voice* (Berkeley and Los Angeles, 1974), 164.

[8] Vickers, 'Figures of Rhetoric/Figures of Music?', 18.

[9] This is not to say that these were all entities with a fixed status and meaning within rhetoric itself—which was an added source of confusion and perplexity to those who sought to transpose them to the musical sphere.

[10] Johann Mattheson, *Der vollkommene Capellmeister* (Hamburg, 1739), 237–9.

[11] Jean-Jacques Nattiez, 'Can One Speak of Narrativity in Music?', trans. Katharine Ellis, *Journal of the Royal Musical Association*, 115 (1990), 240–57 at 244.

connected, incrementally changing sequence of events. What we hear is not like a moving film but more like a succession of separate snapshots. 'Growth', a concept dear to organicists, rarely occurs literally in music, except in dynamic shading. An explicitly or implicitly programmatic piece is therefore rather like a cartoon strip, providing us with a finite number of tableaux that we have to connect in an imagined way in order to produce a story. Nattiez comments aptly that the linearity of music constitutes an 'incitement to a narrative thread that *narrativises* [his emphasis] music'.[12] He is right to stop short of claiming that music itself supplies the thread.

Nevertheless, the appeal of the narrative model is very strong, all the more so because of the universal, 'democratic' nature of story-telling. An untutored audience will follow a story more successfully than an architectural plan or an oration. Nattiez, with prudent restraint, speaks of music as 'imitating the intonation contour of a narrative'.[13] What he means by such a contour was illustrated by a practical experiment he conducted, in which a group of children had to guess the story of Dukas's tone poem *L'Apprenti sorcier* from the experience of listening to it. The only consistent result that emerged was the recognition of the sequence calm–chase–calm. This, then, is the sum total of what the most ingeniously and meticulously crafted descriptive music could achieve, shorn of its paratextual accretions!

In fact, this 'intonation contour of a narrative' (or 'plot archetype', to use a term favoured by structuralists) is so rudimentary that it merges easily into non-narrative schemes (for instance, Tarasti's *embrayage–débrayage–embrayage* cycle). In other words, the potentially narrative effect does not depend on a prior narrative intention on the composer's part. This is, of course, a strength as well as a weakness, since if the wish for a narrative explanation arises, the material lies compliantly to hand.

Instrumental programme music, which more or less precisely fixes the narrative content by paratextual means (usually in the form of words, although pictures could do the job almost as well), has existed for many centuries. In a sophisticated early example, Johann Kuhnau's six *Biblische Historien* (1700), we see how a fairly complex narrative can weave its way both within and between the successive movements of each cycle. However, the narrative, far from governing the course of the music, repeatedly succumbs to the dictates and ingrained habits of ordinary musical processes. Real-life narratives and the literary fictions that imitate them tend not to return to their starting point. The difference between the situation of the characters at the beginning and the end is part of the story's *raison d'être*. Music, in contrast, favours circularity. Whether the composition is in one movement or several, it likes to return to its original key and to recall (via thematic material, scoring, 'tone', etc.) its initial state before it closes. This basic incompatibility has to be overcome by one means or another.

[12] Nattiez, 'Can One Speak of Narrativity in Music?', 257.    [13] Ibid. 251.

One common way to reconcile programmatic (or 'narrative') and musical demands is to select a story (or 'plot archetype') that embraces circularity. Five of the six biblical episodes chosen by Kuhnau have happy endings that allow him to style the last movement as an expression of rejoicing indistinguishable from the finale of a non-programmatic sonata:

| Subject | Title of Last Movement |
|---|---|
| 1. The Battle of David and Goliath | The Common Rejoicing and The People's Dance of Joy |
| 2. Saul's Madness Cured by David's Music | Saul's Calm and Contented Mind |
| 3. Jacob's Wedding | The Happiness of the Nuptials[14] |
| 4. The Illness and Recovery of Hezekiah | The Happiness of the Convalescent King |
| 5. Gideon, the Saviour of Israel | The Happiness at the Victory Gained |
| 6. Jacob's Death and Burial | The Consolation of the Survivors |

The exception is the sixth sonata, where Jacob's burial and the attendant lamentation would seem to form the natural close (as indeed occurs in Genesis). Kuhnau, however, feels it right to introduce a restrained *lieto fine*, justifying the invention in his introduction with a little homily. The scriptural story is not allowed to interfere with general principles of sonata design.

The most perfectly circular narrative ever devised for a programmatic composition is perhaps that of Strauss's *Alpine Symphony*, which begins at night at the foot of a mountain, reaches the summit halfway through the day, and then returns to base camp in time for the following night.

In most cases, however, a complex trade-off takes place. Some of the material is recurrent, and by returning periodically satisfies the musical desire for rounding. This leaves the non-recurrent material free to develop episodically and pursue its programmatic course free of constraint. Vivaldi's programme concertos, in particular *The Four Seasons* (*Le quattro stagioni*), pioneered this solution. Their outer movements depict in the ritornellos the constant element of the scene—the backdrop, as it were—while the solo episodes develop the story in a logical sequence.[15] Exactly the same approach is taken in Richard Strauss's tone poems *Don Juan* and *Till Eulenspiegel*, both of which are shaped as rondos.

Another practical solution to the conflicting demands is to lay less emphasis on the sequence of the events depicted and more on their contrast with one another. In other words, the story organizes itself as a series of

---

[14] Amusingly, this is a literal reprise of the music that earlier accompanied Jacob's wedding to Rachel's sister Leah.

[15] Contrary to what one might think, Vivaldi's four illustrative sonnets are 'on' the music, rather than the other way round; the concertos were originally composed according to a lost scenario (which, as Paul Everett has pointed out, bears affinities to Milton's poems *L'allegro* and *Il penseroso*), and the sonnets were added as a new feature when the works were published in 1725.

independent but linked tableaux, each of which is developed at length in conventional fashion. In a multimovement work, this allows each movement to represent one episode (as in a collection of independent short stories about a single person). Berlioz's *Symphonie fantastique* is a good example. Each of the five movements introduces, in stylized form, the *idée fixe* representing the woman on whom the sleeping artist is fixated, and this is enough to ensure an overall 'thematic' coherence in both senses. The movements are disposed so that they form a five-movement cycle not very different from that of Beethoven's 'Pastoral' Symphony (the scherzo substitute comes second instead of third, and the short movement preceding the finale is a march rather than a storm). If the 'Scène aux champs' preceded 'Un bal', no violence would be done to the programme; its position in third place follows musical rather than programmatic logic. Following any strict definition, the *Symphonie fantastique* (like the 'Pastoral' Symphony before it) is not a 'programmatic' work but a 'characteristic' one that depicts rather than recounts.

The same could be said of the 'Mirjam' Symphony (No. 3, 1887) of Brahms's younger contemporary Friedrich Gernsheim (1839–1916). The four movements of this colourful and attractive work seem to mesh nicely with the story in Exodus (I: 'Bondage'; II: 'Miriam's Song'; III: 'The Flight'; IV: 'Freedom, Songs of Victory and Joy'), but what has obviously happened is that the four events depicted have been hand-picked to fit a conventional symphonic plan. The story 'illustrates' the structure, rather than the other way round. What lends this symphony memorability is not its narrative outline but the special colouring it acquires through the prominence of the harp, symbolizing Miriam herself.

Narrativity, covert or overt, is in principle compatible with any kind of finale: relaxant, summative, or valedictory. However, the choice of type cannot but radically affect the nature of the narrative the composer intends or we choose to infer. Of the three types, the relaxant finale offers least resistance to musical circularity. The happy ending is readily identifiable with a primal state (for cultural and perhaps even basic psychological reasons, we regard sadness as a deviation from a natural state of happiness rather than the reverse), and if regressive factors such as the return of material from previous movements in simplified form are present, they accentuate the sense of reversion. Both the summative and the valedictory finale refuse, in their different ways, to return to an original state of innocence. Even if many elements of circularity remain (return to the home key, recall of first-movement themes, etc.), the status of the finale (in particular, the climax or the end of the finale) as a point of arrival, a distant goal that has been attained with effort, is upheld.

The ideal of a final summation was nourished from two main sources, both intimately connected with narrativity. The first was organicism, the second biography.

The contrast between organic and mechanical form, first drawn by August Wilhelm Schlegel in 1808 (and much later plagiarized by Samuel Taylor Coleridge) is in essence one between a content-dominated form and a form-dominated content. According to a strictly organic view of form, a unique content (the prerequisite for a work of any stature) inevitably gives rise to a 'unique form, unlike in a 'conformational' view—this apt term originates with Mark Evan Bonds[16]—where content is adjusted to fit a predetermined, familiar scheme. Michael Broyles has argued that the decline in surface decoration (embellishment) in symphonies of the late eighteenth century is symptomatic of growing sympathy towards organic ideals;[17] an even more significant pointer, which he goes so far as to call a 'benchmark', is the gradual abandonment of initially the second, and later also the first, repeat in sonata-form movements.[18] Although there may be other, simpler reasons for the abandonment of repeats (I suspect that the growth of the dimensions of traditionally repeated sections outpaced that of the attention span of listeners, forcing composers to take drastic action), the growing reluctance to repeat section-length passages without alteration is certainly a symptom of the rise of organicism. One should not be surprised that such a change in thinking was well under way before it became an object of discourse. As Dahlhaus reminds us about Romanticism (of which organicism is one facet), it was a category of reception (c.1790) before it became a category of production.[19] In other words, sensibility preceded rationalization.

The hegemony of the organic view of form has if anything grown stronger since the nineteenth century (hence Genette's need to tilt against the worship of unity), and we are perhaps too easily inclined today to view it as normal, natural, and more 'evolved' than its alternatives. When, for example, we encounter something as obviously mechanistic in a twentieth-century composition as the note-for-note repeat of the scherzo after the trio in Martinů's Fourth Symphony, we are likely to be disconcerted: is the composer naive, or lazy, or what? Schoenberg's ideal of 'rhetoric without repetition' (which to a classical rhetorician would appear almost a contradiction in terms) represents in extreme form a line of musical thought that goes back to the early nineteenth century.[20]

---

[16] Bonds, *Wordless Rhetoric*, 13.

[17] Michael Broyles, 'Organic Form and the Binary Repeat', *Musical Quarterly*, 66 (1980), 339–60 at 358.

[18] Ibid. 357.

[19] Dahlhaus, *Nineteenth-Century Music*, 20.

[20] The modernist's hatred of literal repetition comes out in an introductory note by Pierre Boulez to the reprint by Universal Edition of Berg's *Chamber Concerto* (1925), in which this writer observes: 'The third movement...is assigned a repeat [of bars 536–710, counting from the beginning of the work] the numerical necessity of which is perceptible, but the structural necessity of which I, for my part, have not seen; it goes against the principle of constant variation systematically set in relief throughout the work' (translation by Felix Aprahamian).

To the early nineteenth century, too, belongs the reception of musical composition as encoded biography. I have argued elsewhere that what I term 'composer-centredness'—the idea that musical works derive their primary meaning from their association with an individual composer (rather than with a genre or a performer)—arose around then in association with the new 'mass' consumption of music in the concert hall and the drawing room.[21] To oversimplify a little: before 1800 composers existed to produce compositions; after 1800 works existed to reveal composers. For the first time, compositions as diverse as a bagatelle for piano and an opera could be brought under one roof by virtue of belonging as 'works' within the canon of a named composer.

By the middle of the century it had become orthodoxy among composers and their public that musical compositions conveyed something of the human condition. Asked what one of their compositions was 'about', composers often retreated into vagueness or improvised some more or less plausible scenario (as Bruckner did for his Fourth Symphony); what is interesting is that they did not dismiss the exercise as irrelevant. Sometimes, the work is presented or received—the distinction is not always easy to draw—as autobiography, as in Smetana's First String Quartet ('From my Life'). Sometimes, it is a fictional hero (albeit one with whom the composer may identify), as in Berlioz's *Symphonie fantastique* and his 'Harold in Italy' Symphony or Tchaikovsky's 'Manfred' Symphony. Sometimes, the human content may be generalized (as in Alkan's piano sonata *Les Quatre Âges* and Nielsen's Second Symphony, *The Four Temperaments*). In nearly every case, the biographical element is narrativized: what comes first in life comes first in the musical depiction. The distinction between the programmatic and the non-programmatic becomes attenuated: the difference lies not in content but in paratextual explicitness.

Organicism and programmaticism make happy bed-fellows. If a theme can be equated with a person (as is indeed often the composer's stated intention), its restatement or transmutation can be equated with the stable or unstable course of that person's life. The alliance persists in some twentieth-century analytical writing; only here, biography is used as an analogue for thematic development rather than the other way round, as it was originally. Take, for example, Joseph Kerman's description of a sonata-form movement in Beethoven as 'the story of a theme—the first theme', wherein 'the exciting last chapter . . . is told in the coda'.[22] Similarly Anthony Newcomb, when he describes musical themes as 'interesting characters' operating within a plot archetype.[23]

[21] Talbot, 'The Work-Concept and Composer-Centredness', *passim*.
[22] Joseph Kerman, 'Notes on Beethoven's Codas', *Beethoven Studies*, 3 (1982), 141–61 at 150.
[23] Anthony Newcomb, 'Once More "Between Absolute and Program Music": Schumann's Second Symphony', *19th Century Music*, 7 (1983–4), 233–50 at 234.

These narrative expectations, allied to a growing inclination towards end-weighting that perhaps had a more purely musical rationale, brought about the introduction of the summative type of finale, alongside the relaxant type (which it never succeeded in supplanting absolutely), in the early nineteenth century. As we saw, one characteristic symptom of a summative finale is that its form is in some way unconventional. Because it functions not as a relatively self-contained movement but as a summation of the whole cycle, it has to sacrifice some of its own coherence and tidiness in order to carry out its larger task. It gravitates towards what James Webster terms 'progressive form', which is marked by 'instability, continual development, [and] freely composed recapitulation'.[24] Not infrequently, its coda is of exaggerated length, since it aims to serve the whole work.

Although the finale of Beethoven's Fifth Symphony does not depart from the pattern of relaxant finales in many respects (for instance, it follows a clear sonata form, the only deviant feature being the famous reintroduction of scherzo material before the recapitulation), it has enough of the key elements to count as the first summative finale (in the strong sense of the word) in musical history. The build-up achieved in the extended linking passage at the end of the scherzo (bars 224–373), which acts as a massive dominant preparation, already signals something exceptional and climactic. The change of modality to major in bar 355 is nicely judged: it gives forewarning, heightening expectancy, without taking away the impact of the glorious, full C major chord opening the finale.

The first subject theme adopts a heroic 'tone' similar to that already used by Beethoven in his three 'Leonore' overtures (the link between the worlds of opera and symphony, which we will not develop here, has a bearing on the narrative dimension discussed earlier) but not encountered previously in symphonies by Beethoven or, to my knowledge, anyone else. The essence of this new 'tone' is the marriage of hymn-like to march-like elements. The first supplies broad lyricism, the second a sense of urgency and forward movement. In this way, the theme combines the dynamism of a first movement (and of a scherzo as well) with the songful nature of a slow movement. Bernd Sponheuer sees one vital function of the finale in late Haydn symphonies as being to balance (his word is 'ausbalancieren'), or mediate between, the respective spheres of the first and second movements.[25] True as this may be for Haydn, it is even truer for Beethoven.[26] It is interesting and significant that the shape of the finale's opening theme is most closely

---

[24] Webster, *Haydn's Farewell Symphony*, 7–8.

[25] Sponheuer, 'Haydns Arbeit am Finalproblem', 200. More questionable is his argument (p. 220) that this balance is a counterpart of conflict-resolution in early liberal bourgeois society.

[26] A good example for comparison would be the C major finale to Haydn's Symphony No. 95, also in C minor. Haydn's finale opens, certainly, with a songful theme (said to be based on a street song), but this has a fragile quality that lacks the element of breadth so abundantly possessed by Beethoven's opening and subsequent themes.

prefigured not anywhere in the first movement but in the tailpiece to the opening theme of the second movement (bars 10–15).

This contrast of 'tone' is in itself enough to establish the summative character of the finale to Beethoven's Fifth Symphony, but it is supported by other factors. We may first note its exceptionally long, and exceptionally recapitulatory, coda. It occupies 150 out of 444 bars—over a third of the movement (in the first movement, the corresponding fraction is a quarter). Like a typical Beethoven development section, the coda contains several distinct sections, but in contrast to the former, it remains firmly anchored in the tonic, including only such feints at other tonalities as are needed to relieve the otherwise relentless succession of tonic and dominant harmonies. In section 1 (bars 295–317), the opening of which is shown as Ex. 5.2 (a), Beethoven starts by playing with a phrase extracted from the first theme of the second subject group, which is treated in double counterpoint with a counter-theme in the violas (as in the development section at bars 92–9, but without passing through different keys), and then leads via an animated extension to a half-close. Section 2 (bars 318–61) begins with dialoguing references to a motif first heard in the transition of the exposition at bar 26 and ends (from bar 350 onwards) with a *stretta*-style reiteration, *accelerando*, of a new motif based on a diatonic descent from G to C in the treble and a chromatic descent from Bb to G in the bass, shown as Ex. 5.2(b). Section 3 (bars 362–89), now in 'presto' tempo, begins with the motif that introduced the second theme of the second subject group and ends (from bar 378 onwards) with new reiterations of the *stretta* motif; its opening is shown as Ex. 5.2(c). Finally, in bar 390, the movement's main theme returns in a modified form that permits its brief treatment in canon between treble and bass—see Ex. 5.2(d)—before the ultimate 'liquidation', the hammered alternation of tonic and dominant chords, supervenes.

A coda of this kind would make no sense if the finale were detached from its context to make an independent concert piece. Without the memory of the first three movements behind it, it will seem disproportionate, even monstrous. What gives it sense is its place within a narrative that, at a general level, can be identified with a victorious struggle against adversity and, at an autobiographical level, with Beethoven's ability to continue composing despite ever-worsening deafness.

The second factor supporting the finale's summative quality is the addition of five previously unheard instruments, which enter in the very first bar: a piccolo, a double bassoon, and a trio of trombones (once again, an 'operatic' link is evident). Although these extra forces produce an effect of cumulation similar to that described in Chapter 3 for Renaissance vocal music (with which, naturally, they have no direct connection), there is one important difference. The extra voices used in the final movements of Masses and Magnificats are obtained by the subdivision of existing parts, not by importing new musicians (similarly, Mozart, at the start of the 'Great

Ex. 5.2.   Beethoven, Symphony No. 5 in C minor, Op. 67, last movement: (*b*) bars 294–8; (*b*) bars 350–5; (*c*) bars 362–7; (*d*) bars 390–4

G minor' Symphony, K. 550, obtains two viola parts by having the regular section play *divisi*). In Beethoven's symphony the newcomers are genuine extras, who have sat (or otherwise) in patient idleness up to that point. Their entry is not only an aural but also a visual event, and the spectacle of new players joining the ensemble lends a fresh dimension to the sense of cumulation. To hold players back in reserve for a last movement was a bold step in terms of orchestral etiquette. In the eighteenth century and earlier it was normal to introduce the full ensemble in the first movement and to allow the same performers to take their leave of the audience in the last movement;

reductions in scoring, if they occurred, affected only the inner movements.[27] In this way, the personal status of the individual musicians was respected. Beethoven's innovation is remarkable for social as well as musical reasons: it identifies the individual performer as a means to the realization of the composer's ends instead of as an autonomous actor in the process of creating music.

Although none of the finales in Beethoven's later symphonies is less than long, only that of the Ninth Symphony is genuinely summative. There, a double bassoon is added—and, more unexpectedly, a choir and a quartet of solo singers. At one level, it is incidental that the singers have to perform a setting of Schiller's *Ode to Joy*. The ethical significance of the Ode and its coded socio-political implications are of course important, but Beethoven never allows it to take command of the movement, as a poem, in the way that we find in the concluding vocal movements of Mendelssohn's *Lobgesang* (Symphony No. 2) or in the last two movements of Mahler's 'Resurrection' Symphony. In other words, the Ode (whose text Beethoven does not refrain from amending in places) is raw material for a movement that, in order to fulfil his final 'narrative' intentions for the work, had to transcend the bounds of instrumental music by including voices but did not need to alight on that specific poem. The rejection of the material of the three earlier movements before the 'great tune' is allowed to enter, and the solo baritone's belated exclamation of 'O Freunde, nicht diese Töne' before the voices take up the same tune, merely dot the 'I's and cross the 'T's of what should be evident without those devices: that the 'great tune', hub of the last movement, is the final realization, the ultimate point of regression, of the thematic content of the earlier movements.[28] Chapter 8 will continue this discussion.

It is strange that in his string quartets Beethoven left no comparable examples of summative finales. One's thoughts turn immediately to the *Grosse Fuge* (Op. 133), the original finale of Op. 130, which in terms of length certainly fits the bill. But there is little overt 'inner connection' between this finale and the five preceding movements (commentators have frequently pointed out the suite-like nature of this quartet), and this seems a case of pronounced, even exaggerated, end-weighting without summation. The fact that when requested to substitute a more conventional finale Beethoven complied—and complied with notable success—shows that there was nothing in the first five movements that looked forward inevitably to a summative finale. Some may regret that he was so easily persuaded, but one cannot

---

[27] This is why, contrary to what the principles of balance and euphony would advise, the chorales ending J. S. Bach's cantatas are always fully scored.

[28] Since the form in which this finale is cast has been the subject of much discussion and disagreement among scholars in recent years, I would like to place on record my view that it is a single, elaborated variation movement (with an introduction, interludes, and coda) which reproduces in an expanded and more diverse manner the same general principles already applied in the 'Eroica' Symphony.

help thinking that such a strong-minded artist would not have abandoned his original finale (which he deemed worthy of publication as an independent piece) without, at best, lack of certainty and, at worst, grave doubts about its suitability to serve as the finale of Op. 130. Had the *Grosse Fuge* been lost without trace, I am convinced that there would have been no murmurs about the movement that replaced it.[29]

Beethoven's change of mind recalls Edward Cone's scepticism over the notion of inevitability as applied to music. At the end of five movements, Beethoven's options were still sufficiently open for him to conceive two entirely different types of movement.

One looks equally in vain among the other late quartets. Op. 131, cast in seven movements that run continuously in the manner of a fantasia, has a notably powerful and (relative to the other movements) extended finale that recalls the thematic and tonal features of its predecessors. Ironically, however, it is the most 'detachable' and structurally orthodox of any of them. We could call it 'summative' only in the sense that it makes coherent, and unites, elements that in earlier movements appeared partially and separately: in all other respects it could be compared with the fierce, unreconciled finales of some of Haydn's middle-period symphonies (for example, Nos. 39, 44, and 49), which, although they do not relax the emotions, have the vivacity, transparency, and dynamism of their major-key counterparts.

On the other hand, the five last piano sonatas and, arguably, the two cello sonatas of Op. 102 all have finales that in varying degrees deserve to rank as summative. In Op. 101 the reintroduction of the opening of the first movement in motto style before the finale (in succession to an independent slow introduction) and the lengthy fugal divagation in the development section amount to something more than mere weight; the completely fugal finale of Op. 106 achieves a similar effect. The 'classic' summative finale in the piano sonatas is undoubtedly that of Op. 110—another fugue, which breaks off mid-way through to introduce a second strophe of the 'Klagender Gesang' ('Song of Lamentation') and ends by transforming the fugue subject, which is closely related to the opening theme of the first movement via its sequence of alternate rising fourths and descending thirds, into an exalted, hymnic paraphrase of it, complete with the original swirling accompanimental figuration.

The two variation finales, in Opp. 109 and 111 respectively, are at first sight harder to classify. Were they no more than slightly scaled-down counterparts of the independent sets Op. 34 and Op. 35 ('Eroica' Variations), one would readily identify them as relaxant in the same way as the finale of the 'Eroica' Symphony. Their intellectual rigour and technical

---

[29] Many of the arguments adduced in favour of the *Grosse Fuge* seem to boil down to general propositions such as that great composers should not take advice from others, that first thoughts are always best, or that long, gritty fugues are better than moderately sized, easygoing sonata-rondo movements.

adventurousness is unchallengeable, but even those qualities did not suffice to make the *Grosse Fuge* summative. In the end, what counts most is their sustained lofty 'tone' and their ability to absorb the essentials of the preceding movement (in Op. 111) or movements (in Op. 109) and present them again in purified and enriched form. The major–minor antithesis in Op. 111 parallels that of the Fifth Symphony, except that in the former the shift to major signifies a retreat into *Innigkeit*, not a triumph over adversity. Both movements go out quietly, that of Op. 109 even reverting to the theme in its austere original guise.[30]

The works of Beethoven's middle and late period provided the matrices for finale-writing in the rest of the nineteenth century. The 'Haydn' formula for a finale (on which Beethoven had relied in his first two symphonies) proved durable as a model to be inculcated in conservatories—which is why the symphonies of Gounod and Bizet exhibit its symptoms so strongly—but was generally spurned by composers with high ambitions. Composers with 'classicizing' tendencies most often compromised by opting for finales that preserved the structural independence of the relaxant model but absorbed something of the weight and 'tone' of summative finales (exactly as in Beethoven's 'Pastoral' Symphony, in fact). However, many composers produced genuine summative finales from time to time, and there was one tradition (identified by Paul Bekker as specifically Austrian) that made the type almost normative.

The finale of Schumann's Piano Quintet in E flat major, Op. 44, composed in 1842, takes the kind of structuring seen in Beethoven's Fifth Symphony a stage further. It is essentially a generously proportioned sonata-rondo movement, but the last 207 of its 427 bars are occupied by a sequence of six sections following the final statement of the refrain; these additions bolster the central tonality, add a dash of excitement, and, by reintroducing the primary material of the first movement, produce a rounding effect for the complete four-movement cycle. The finale's structure is outlined in Table 5.1.

A remarkable fact about the main refrain theme (A) is that it is doubly off-tonic: doubly, because it is set firmly in the mediant key, G minor, but starts on its submediant chord (C minor). In its subdominant emphasis it resembles the main theme of the slow movement, with which it has strong affinities. However, E flat major is firmly in the listener's mind at the start of the movement, since it has been hammered home in the preceding scherzo, and the first statement of the subsidiary theme B (bars 22–9), which is also in E flat major, arrives early enough to make the backward

---

[30] Beethoven may have got the idea of closing with a return of the unadorned theme from Bach's 'Goldberg' Variations. In fact, the option of ending a set of variations with a return to the theme, unadorned or with only simple additions, goes right back to the virginalists of the sixteenth century. One could write a book about the different ways in which variation works end.

TABLE 5.1. *Plan of the finale of Schumann, String Quintet in E flat major, Op. 44*

| Bars | Description | Key | Notes |
|---|---|---|---|
| 1–43 | refrain group | g → B♭ | structured ABAB |
| 44–77 | episode 1 | G | |
| 78–93 | refrain | b → B | A only, with extension |
| 94–136 | episode 2 | E → g♯ | uses main theme of episode 1, with superimposed counter-melody |
| 137–78 | refrain group | g♯ → G♭ | bars 1–43 transposed, with tonal deviation at bar 149 |
| 179–212 | episode 1 | E♭ | bars 44–77 transposed |
| 213–20 | refrain | g | A only |
| 221–48 | closing theme | E♭ | |
| 249–74 | fugato on theme A | g | |
| 275–320 | episode 2 | E♭ | bars 94–136 transposed (in paraphrased form), with extension containing material from first movement in preparation for… |
| 321–70 | fugato on opening theme of movt 1 | E♭ | theme A as counter-subject |
| 371–402 | closing theme | E♭ | |
| 403–27 | coda | E♭ | extension of closing theme |

connection succinctly but effectively. Thereafter, the tonic is studiously avoided until the recapitulation of the first episode in bars 179–212. The movement divides neatly into a tonally non-repetitive first part (bars 1–178) and a tonally repetitive second part (bars 179–427).

Schumann is heavily indebted to Schubert's example for the 'laissez faire' approach to modulation that characterizes the movement's first part. It may well be that his only fixed tonal goal in the first 178 bars was to arrive eventually at E flat major, although he must have taken care also to avoid, first, any premature appearance of that key (after bars 22–9) and, second, any accidental return visits to tonal centres already visited once. He relies heavily, as Schubert did before him and Dvořák was to do after him, on nodal points in the harmonic-tonal structure: points from which continuation with identical thematic material can be effected in more than one key.[31] The unorthodox recapitulation of the full refrain group in G sharp minor at bar 137 would have led to the unwanted G sharp (A flat) major for the restated first episode in bar 179, had Schumann not slipped theme A up to D sharp (instead of G sharp) minor in bar 149, thereby breaking the pattern of strict transposition.

This manner of composing produces mixed blessings. We remarked in the last chapter on the disorientation than can arise when expository (or

---

[31] The 'bifocal' close at the end of a sonata-form first subject group (leading to a second subject opening theme in either tonic or dominant) is a well-known instance of a nodal point.

recapitulatory) and developmental sections are not clearly distinguished by their tonal treatment. On the other hand, the freedom to peregrinate through the tonal system secure in the knowledge that, where absolutely necessary, pre-set tonal destinations can easily be reached releases, for such composers as Schumann, a spontaneity that one would not wish to sacrifice.

The total success of the second half of the movement is not in doubt, however. The closing theme, with its gentle syncopations on the piano; the first fugato, with its echoes of Fuxian species counterpoint; the return of the second episode, reminiscent of the similar event in Schubert's Piano Trio in B flat major;[32] the subtle reintroduction of first-movement textures and thematic material; the second fugato on two subjects; the returning closing theme and its codal extension: all of these prolong the movement in an unexpected but wholly welcome manner. They emphasize the finale's thematic connections with earlier movements and put on display Schumann's truly impressive gifts as a contrapuntist. If this movement begins in the iconoclastic mood of the *Davidsbündler* setting off for battle, it ends on a note of tranquil traditionalism. In a way, the shifting, unpredictable tonality of the first part and the secure tonal anchorage of the second are complementary, for without the contrast between them it would have been difficult to find the resources for such a long movement.

For a different vision of a summative finale we may turn to the fourth movement of Brahms's First Symphony in C minor. This is a specimen of what could be termed, without disparagement, a pot-pourri finale. The general idea, prophetic of Mahler's inclusive ideal (the symphony as 'world'), is that a variety of different themes, contrasted in style and 'tone', process across the movement, drawing in elements from the preceding movements and forming themselves into a splendid pageant. In Brahms's day this style of organization was already familiar from the operatic and concert overture (Beethoven's overture *The Consecration of the House* is an early example). Since we are dealing with Brahms, it follows naturally that the superficially disparate elements are saturated with thematic interrelationships and that no significant theme is allowed to escape with only one appearance.

The movement begins with a succession of five short sections. These we may characterize as:

1. A mysterious, brooding 'adagio' in C minor recapturing the mood of the slow introduction to the first movement (bars 1–29) and also foreshadowing the 'great tune'.

2. A melody for solo horn in C major, 'più andante', which imitates the alphorn in *Ranz des vaches* style (bars 30–9).

---

[32] There are also thematic parallels between the two movements, in particular the three-note figure consisting of an ascending major third followed by a minor second and configured crotchet, crotchet, minim.

3. A chorale-like phrase ending in C major, whose voicing and 'antique' harmony (note especially the root-position triad on the flattened seventh degree in bar 49) recall Brahms's liking for Giovanni Gabrieli and Heinrich Schütz (bars 40–51).

4. The *Ranz des vaches* theme treated in imitation, once again in C major (bars 52–61).

5. The 'great tune', 'allegro non troppo'. Brahms's melody, which otherwise resembles that of the finale of Beethoven's Ninth Symphony, is different in one important respect: it cadences (like a typical chaconne variation) into its repeat or into whatever succeeds it. Brahms lets us hear it only twice at this stage (bars 62–93).

In bar 94 Brahms embarks on a sonata-form structure in C major, to which all of the foregoing has been preparatory. What is original and remarkably effective is how he chooses to 'drop' into the main part of the movement, at appropriate points, more or less literal restatements of all the introductory material. The development section, beginning at bar 185, reintroduces material from the 'great tune' in alternation with an idea taken from the opening 'adagio' section. The *Ranz des vaches*, in its second, contrapuntal form, separates the two subject groups in the recapitulation (bars 289–300). The pseudo-chorale irrupts with brilliant effect in the 'più allegro' coda, momentarily holding up its headlong rush.

Brahms never again attempted anything similar in his symphonies. The justly admired chaconne that ends his Fourth Symphony is noteworthy for being the earliest finale in a post-Mozart symphony to adopt 'pure' variation form (the finales of Beethoven's third and ninth symphonies fail to qualify, being too heterogeneous); it is probably also the first set of continuous variations ever to act as a symphony finale. One hesitates to classify it as summative in the strong sense (it is, rather, a 'heavyweight' relaxant movement), but its power, passion, and fastidiousness of design place it in a class above most of its many later imitations.

What Brahms did exceptionally, his contemporary and somewhat involuntary rival Bruckner did as a matter of course in his last six completed symphonies, which run from No. 3 (the first version of which dates from 1873) to No. 8 (first version completed in 1887).[33] Just as a Bruckner opening movement has to begin with 'sensuous vagueness' (Edward Lippman's term for the typically Romantic way of opening a movement with a harmonic 'shimmer', as in the first movements of Mozart's 'Great G minor' Symphony and Beethoven's Ninth Symphony and in the scherzo of Mendelssohn's 'Scottish' Symphony), its finale has to bring back the work's opening theme, and preferably others as well, at its monumental climax. Tovey described both obligations wittily and aptly, referring to a major

[33] The finale of No. 9 had not been written when Bruckner died in 1896. It can be argued that the finale of No. 7 is less emphatically summative than those of the others.

source of the composer's inspiration, when he commented that Bruckner's symphonies always begin with 'Rheingold harmonic breaths' and end with 'Götterdämmerung climaxes'.[34]

By common consent, it is the finale of the Fifth Symphony in B flat major, completed in 1878, which most completely, ambitiously, and successfully realizes Bruckner's ideal of a finale that synthesizes and crowns the preceding movements. More than any other of his symphonic finales, it reaches back into the musical past, drawing heavily on the tradition of the double fugue: the fugue that first treats two subjects independently, one after the other, and then brings them together in a grand climax as subject and counter-subject. This tradition, on which J. S. Bach sometimes drew, had been equally current in South Germany and Austria: one has only to think of the 'school' active in the late seventeenth century which included such masters as Heinrich Biber and Georg Muffat. But Bruckner no more introduces fugue in a 'neat' form than did Mozart in the 'Jupiter' Symphony. He finds room for it within what is, for him, a typical sonata-form structure, complete with a discursive *Gesangsperiode* (lyrical section) as second subject group. And—naturally—the opening theme of the first movement, germ cell of the whole work, has to force its way into the finale, capping everything at the end.

Lasting as long as 25 minutes in performance in the uncut version edited by Robert Haas, the finale is a little longer than the first movement and considerably longer than either the slow movement or the scherzo. The inner movements are very unusual in that they are both in the same key, D minor, and employ virtually the same principal theme, albeit performed at different speeds. The outer movements, which share much thematic material, are complementary in similar fashion (although their close kinship is what one would have expected from Bruckner in any case).

Three themes dominate the finale: the main theme of the first movement (theme A), shown as Ex. 5.3(*a*) from bars 55–8 of that movement; the opening theme of the main part of the finale itself (theme B), shown as Ex. 5.3(*b*); and a chorale theme first introduced in the codetta of the exposition (theme C), whose first phrase is shown as Ex. 5.3(*c*). All three themes are designed for harmonization with an initial chord of G flat and a visit to the Neapolitan region (C flat) before the first cadence in B flat. This is of course a prerequisite for their successful contrapuntal combination later on, but even before they start to combine, the unusualness of their common harmonic orientation is registered, even if only unconsciously, in the mind. So too, perhaps, is their common use of a three-note scale motif.

Before the main part of the finale begins, Bruckner juxtaposes the emergent main theme with a variety of themes drawn from the earlier movements. This technique is based on the idea of 'rejected return' first employed by Beethoven (with a specific purpose relating to the introduction of voices) in his

---

[34] Tovey, *Essays in Musical Analysis*, ii. 69 (apropos of Symphony No. 4).

Ex. 5.3.  Bruckner, Symphony No. 5 in B flat major: (a) first movement, main theme; (b) last movement, main theme; (c) last movement, 'chorale' theme

Ninth Symphony and copied less successfully by Berlioz in his 'Harold in Italy' Symphony and by Bruckner himself in the original (1873) version of his Third Symphony.[35] In the present case, the recalled themes are not so much rejected as incorporated. As they progress, Bruckner accompanies them with, or links them by, increasingly complete statements of theme B, until the point is reached when the latter is self-sufficient and ready for independent development. The thirty-bar-long introduction proceeds as follows:

1–10    An almost literal repeat of the 'adagio' introduction to the first movement, ending on the dominant of G minor. Note, however, the added interjections on the first clarinet, which present the first two notes (the descending octave) of theme B.

11–12   The first clarinet plays, unaccompanied, the first two bars of theme B in the key of G.[36]

13–22   After two bars of 'sensuous vagueness' (violin tremolos) violas and cellos play theme A, in B flat major, exactly as in bars 55–62 of the first movement. The first trumpet interjects the octave-motif.

23–4    The first clarinet, again unaccompanied, repeats the first two bars of theme B, now in C sharp.

25–8    The strings intone the opening of the slow movement in D minor, the first flute softly interjecting the octave-motif.

29–30   The two clarinets in unison present the first two bars of theme B loudly in A flat. The same theme, when it appears in bar 31 as a fugue subject, now complete with its continuation in dotted notes and *marcato* cadence in crotchets, merely continues the chromatically ascending sequence initiated in bar 29.

---

[35] In Berlioz's symphony the quotations represent Harold's memories of quieter times as he witnesses the 'Orgy of the Brigands'. Bruckner's reminiscences in Symphony No. 3 appear before the coda and seem even less firmly motivated. César Franck's String Quartet in D major (1890) is another attempt at imitation that has won few admirers.

[36] The modality of theme B appears to be minor when it opens; the turn to major occurs only at the cadence.

The exposition occupies bars 31–174. Its first subject (31–66) is a strenuous fugato on theme B. The second subject (bars 67–174) comprises a *Gesangsperiode* beginning in D flat major and moving to F major and a transition based on the octave-descent opening theme B. A codetta (bars 175–210), which reverts, unexpectedly, to the home key, introduces a chorale theme (C) delivered by the wind in four phrases separated (in a manner reminiscent of chorale fantasias in Bach's cantatas and organ works) by commentating string interludes.

The development section (bars 211–372) begins with orthodox development of the first phrase of theme C, but this is discontinued in bar 223 in favour of a fugato. At bar 270 theme C acquires a counter-subject in the shape of the first half of theme B. At bar 362 dominant preparation for the recapitulation begins.

The start of the recapitulation (bars 373–582) forms a seamless whole with the end of the development section by virtue of the fact that the first subject, theme B accompanied by its counter-subject, passes across the join without any thematic rupture. This is not unprecedented: the recapitulation of the first movement of Haydn's Symphony No. 39 occurs in similar fashion. From bar 398 to bar 459 the *Gesangsperiode* material, beginning in F major but returning to B flat major, proceeds normally. However, the end of the second subject group (bars 460–582) follows a radically new course. This is because Bruckner's purpose in the second half of the recapitulation is to reintroduce theme A from the first movement, gradually raising its level of prominence. Between bars 460 and 497 we hear fragments of the theme. In bars 506–63, following an interlude (bars 496–505) in which the opening of theme B serves as an ostinato bass-motif, theme A undergoes rigorous development. At bar 564 theme B is heard in augmentation simultaneously with its inversion.

In the coda (bars 583–635) Bruckner brings back the chorale, theme C, with interpolations from various other themes. These include theme A, whose opening phrase—transposed for the first time to become 5–3–2–1 in the home key—resounds in triumphant unison to bring down the curtain.

One can think of no last movement by any composer that deploys side by side, and with such thrilling effect, so many of the elements (expansion, cumulation, synthesis, back-reference, regression, etc.) that go to make up a summative finale. If there is any weakness in this movement, it is that its lyrical moments, usually a high point in Bruckner's finales (as, indeed, in his first movements), struggle to find an appropriate function. They remain strangely external to the contrapuntal interplay of themes A, B, and C, assuming the character of quiet enclaves removed from the main business of the movement. In that respect only, this titanic movement falls short of being exemplary.

To show that a summative finale need not occupy very many bars or minutes and is compatible with a classicizing (if not downright classical) aesthetic, one need only take the example of Sibelius's Third Symphony in C major, Op. 52 (1907). This is a three-movement symphony: the finale begins as a scherzo and ends as a hymn-like apotheosis in concise variation form, thus conflating, as it were, the third and fourth movements of the Classical symphony. Sibelius was interested in run-on relationships between movements (his later Fifth Symphony, in its definitive version, opens with a fusion of opening movement and scherzo, while his Seventh Symphony is a genuine one-movement work), but the manner of linkage is far from simple. Elements of the hymn appear intermittently with ever-increasing strength from an early stage in the scherzo (bar 77), but immediately after the hymn finally establishes its supremacy (in bars 246–65) the scherzo begins to regain its presence by stealth, though now only as a background feature. The movement can also be viewed as a conflict between ordinary metre (6/8, with as many as four changes of harmony per bar) and hyper-metre (notated variously in 6/8 and in 4/4, one bar of which equals two of 6/8). Where scherzo and hymn elements appear simultaneously (e.g. in bars 231–45), a 'counterpoint' of metres (6/8 versus 4/4) is created. Beginning only 'moderato', the movement accelerates in several successive 'waves'. Paradoxically, the increase in tempo facilitates the imposition of hypermetre and thereby brings about an effective slowing-down.

A small number of thematic characteristics inform the whole work. One central motivic idea is stepwise 'rotation' back and forth around a central note (first heard in bars 1–2 of the first movement, in the progression B–A–G–A).

Another is the 'Lydian' fourth (F♯ in C major) which coexists with the ordinary diatonic fourth. The F♯ gains prominence in both outer movements by being used as a pivotal note linking C major to E minor.

A third feature is the prominence of what Mark DeVoto has aptly called the 'Russian Sixth'—a submediant (the note A in the home key) that by virtue of its frequent recurrence and tonicization creates a 'no man's land' between a major key and its relative minor.[37] Born in what was part of the Russian empire and exposed to Russian music during the golden years of Tchaikovsky and the 'Mighty Handful', Sibelius could not but come under their influence.

In all movements the falling fifth is frequent, especially at phrase ends. The fifth is often 'filled out', either with all three notes (as at the start of the finale) or with just the third (as at the close of the same movement).

Finally, one should mention a distinct pentatonic flavour, the 'gaps' in the heptatonic major scale being its fourth and seventh degrees. In the first movement the scraps of theme beginning at bar 18 conform to this description.

[37] Mark DeVoto, 'The Russian Submediant in the Nineteenth Century', *Current Musicology*, 59 (1995), 48–76. From Glinka onwards, this feature has functioned as a national 'trademark' in Russian music. It can doubtless can trace its origin back to folk music.

The first movement is an outwardly conventional sonata-allegro, whose only unusual feature is the highly fragmentary, sometimes enigmatic, quality of its thematic development. The second movement, in G sharp minor, is in variation form with interludes. It belongs to the species of 'fast' slow movement represented by the second movement of Beethoven's String Quartet in C minor, Op. 18 No. 4, or by the 'Canzonetta' in Mendelssohn's Op. 12. In a curious way, this movement has neo-Baroque characteristics. The accompaniment of a treble line in parallel thirds (initially on flutes) by a bass moving in fairly strict contrary motion with them recalls the style of 'trio' scoring in Lully's music, which became a topos of late Baroque music everywhere.[38] The transition to the C major of the finale is smoother than might be imagined since the tonic, G sharp, can be reinterpreted as its enharmonic equivalent, A flat (the same trick is performed after the second movement of Beethoven's Third Piano Concerto).

The finale begins in a low-key, almost non-committal, manner. It opens with a cheerful cadential phrase (similar in function and effect to that introducing the first movement of Haydn's String Quartet in B flat major, Op. 33 No. 4). Then follows, up to bar 41, a chain of similar answering snippets, many of which make clear reference back to material in earlier movements. The section is held together by an ostinato on the violas that employs a version of the rotating motif described earlier; this describes the motion c–d–e–d (with extra, rapid oscillations between c and d).

Bars 43–69 form a new section based on A minor, albeit with C pedals lurking in the background. Its most prominent feature is an ostinato string figure in unison canon whose billowing motion recalls the surges of Wagner's Rhine. At bar 70, marked 'più allegro', C major is re-established and the chain of snippets resumes. In bars 77–84 the upper woodwind dialogue among themselves in a series of two-note phrases which, though still at this stage enigmatic, hint at a broad theme to come.

At bar 112 the ostinato string figure returns in F minor, but with the note C once again exerting a background influence through its presence as a pedal note. The music veers into A flat major, and it is in this key that we hear an inchoate version of the hymn in bars 116–30. It is played by the quartet of horns, traditional bearers of material of this kind.

Free development of the scherzo material supervenes in bar 160. This is its 'final fling' in its pure state. In bar 169, when the pedal note C is abandoned, the music cuts loose from its tonal moorings, and for a while apparent chaos reigns. Tonal order is gradually restored after bar 210, and in bar 224 an E pedal is established.

At bar 231 we finally hear the first strain of the hymn, accompanied by scraps of scherzo material. This moves ambiguously between C major and A

---

[38] See e.g. the trio to the minuet in J. S. Bach's First 'Brandenburg' Concerto (where the parallel thirds of the upper parts become sixths through inversion in many places).

minor in consequence of the oscillation, in the harmony, between A flat (chromatically altered sixth in C) and G sharp (leading note in A). Bars 246–65, notated in 4/4, present the second strain of the hymn. Entrusted to the strings alone, this is block-chordal in texture and recalls similar passages elsewhere in Sibelius's music—for instance, in the 'Ballade' of the *Karelia Suite*. A third strain, growing seamlessly out of the second, occupies bars 266–90. This emphasizes the 'Lydian' fourth, and by modulating to E minor sets up the pedal note (E) for the ensuing variation of the hymn theme.

In bar 291 a continuous quaver movement decorating the pedal note marks the start of the first variation, which follows the same tonal course as the theme itself, though with some abbreviation. Thematic fragments from earlier in the work, notably the 'pentatonic' figure mentioned earlier, invade the texture. A second and final variation arrives in bar 323. This replaces the background of duplet quavers by one of triplet quavers, so restoring the scherzo motion. The movement concludes in a blaze of glory at the end of this variation (bar 375); there is no separate coda.

Sibelius provides no metronomic markings in this symphony, but in performance the third movement, lasting about eight and a half minutes, is slightly shorter than either of the other two. This has no adverse effect on the finale's summative quality, which arises from the complete subordination of its internal form to the task of recalling and then superseding the material of the earlier movements. The composer accomplishes this aim by stealth rather than by overt assertion, clouding the whole process in a mist of uncertainty and ambiguity. But the technique adopted is extraordinarily effective as well as economical, and Sibelius was happy to revisit it in varied form in his later symphonies.

# 6

# The Valedictory Finale

I T WOULD not be wrong to regard the valedictory finale as a 'deviant' variant of the summative finale. Like the latter, it resolves unfinished business rather than initiating new business—and in this important respect it differs from the relaxant finale, which insists (albeit without precluding thematic connections with other movements) on its autonomous status. In an aesthetic sense, however, it could not differ more sharply from both other types. It is slow rather than fast, calm rather than agitated, introverted rather than extroverted, soft rather than loud. It favours regression as against cumulation, simplicity as against artifice.

Historically speaking, the valedictory finale was the last type to emerge in a clear-cut form in instrumental music. We noted earlier the presence of similar features in the final movements (Agnus Dei) of many Masses from the Renaissance onwards. No doubt, such conclusions provided aesthetic preparation of a general kind for the appearance of comparable movements in the instrumental domain, but the link is too indirect to count as a tangible historical connection.

Notwithstanding the presence of at least two somewhat hybridized examples of valedictory finale in the music of Haydn (Haydn's huge productivity and fondness for *jeux d'esprit* made him liable to anticipate almost any subsequent development), the type acquired its *locus classicus* only in the late nineteenth century, with Tchaikovsky's Sixth Symphony ('Pathétique') of 1893. The valedictory finale is associated with the late Romantic age and many of the currents that followed it in the twentieth century (from which one may exclude, for obvious reasons, neo-Classicism).

To simplify the argument, we might say that the relaxant, summative, and valedictory finales correspond to the *Zeitgeist* of the last three centuries respectively. The relaxant type fits in well with the eighteenth-century view of instrumental music as entertainment. The metaphor of music as a banquet, enshrined in the title of Schein's *Banchetto musicale*, illustrates well the discrete nature of the components (hors d'oeuvre, main course, dessert, etc.) as well as the situation of the main components (movements or courses) towards the front of the series.[1] In nineteenth-century society we find an emphasis on the same general qualities (heroism, struggle, progress, plan-

---

[1] The nobler metaphor of the oration (which in any case was normally applied to single movements rather than to whole cycles) never penetrated general public consciousness: it was an object of discourse only among intellectuals and some practitioners.

ning, transformation, affirmation, collective identity) that inform summative finales. Valedictory finales express a range of feelings, running from melancholia to nostalgia, from abstention to exhaustion, from fading out to passing away, that we easily identify with the twentieth-century condition. They represent a retreat from the public into the private sphere and strike a chord with twentieth-century individualism (and post-scientific mysticism). It is no accident that composers marginalized by their minority status (whether through sexuality, religion, or ethnic identity) or by a condition of exile (whether as refugees or as dissidents) have shown an especial liking for this type.[2]

Slowness is a necessary attribute of a valedictory finale. One cannot 'take leave' (as opposed to depart) hastily. In itself, the choice of a slow tempo for a final movement is, seen purely statistically, a historical aberration. It is much less common than the same choice for the introductory movement of a cyclic work in two or more movements. To find a reason is not easy and raises questions about the place of nature and culture in the formation of musical norms.

In a very interesting article whose title reads (in English) 'Fast–Slow–Fast: On the "Classical" Theory of the Instrumental Cycle' Wilhelm Seidel examined how what Koch could still describe in 1793 as a 'tyrannical custom' devoid of discernible reason had become by the middle of the nineteenth century something viewed as entirely natural and reflective of human 'life' itself.[3] The three-movement cycle in the sequence fast–slow–fast was conceived by a succession of German theorists of form and aestheticians running from Forkel via Marx and Hand to Riemann as analogous to such triads as calm–agitation–calm, stability–disruption–stability, and even health—sickness–health. Paradoxically as it might seem, the quick is here seen as calmer, more stable, and healthier than the slow. Against this background it is easy to understand how the view of the finale as a non-literal 'reprise' (Seidel's term) of the opening movement arose—with important consequences for its weight and character.

A twentieth-century sceptic will find little difficulty in interpreting the privileging of the fast–slow–fast triad as a rationalization of musical custom in the early nineteenth century rather than as a universally valid contribution to the aesthetics of music. It has an ideological foundation appropriate to its time and place in that a state of action is considered more 'natural' than one of contemplation. The precariousness of the whole argument is revealed when the movements number more than three. Is a scherzo standing in third place an adjunct to the finale or to the slow movement? Here, the theorists find less common ground and have to resort to ingenious but never very convincing arguments.

[2] Some names: Alkan, Tchaikovsky, Mahler, Prokofiev, Britten, Shostakovich, Bartók, Messiaen, Pärt.

[3] Seidel, 'Schnell–Langsam–Schnell'.

Seidel's account does, however, raise obliquely one question of great importance to the present chapter: is symmetry (in a sequence of tempo relationships) more natural and desirable than asymmetry?

Since, from the eighteenth century onwards, most instrumental cycles begin with a quick movement irrespective of whether they end with a quick or slow one, the question is hard to answer straightforwardly. There is no significant corpus of works on the plan slow–fast–slow (or simple elaborations of this) that one could present as the 'inversion' of fast–slow–fast and therefore use to make a general point. Where it occurred, the introduction of the slow final movement did not bring about any corresponding alteration to the character of the first movement. This fact alone suggests that the resulting asymmetry is only a by-product of the modification of the tempo and character of the finale—it is neither a desideratum nor a problem in its own right. In fact, the unquestioned success of slow finales in such works as the 'Pathétique' Symphony establishes that asymmetrical plans, though less common, are no less intrinsically satisfying than symmetrical ones. More radically, one could argue that asymmetry in one important element (tempo) compels the composer to be more inventive in his use of other elements (tonality, thematic treatment, scoring, etc.) for the purpose of rounding and can therefore exert a positive force.

Because closure of the cycle with a slow movement is unexpected, the composer doing so has to take care to satisfy, at its conclusion, the condition described so aptly by Barbara Herrnstein Smith as 'the expectation of nothing'.[4] Reversion to the home key is an important tool for achieving this state, in the light of the fact that internal slow movements, even when they number more than one (as in Brahms's Third Piano Sonata), customarily offer tonal contrast. When this is not the case—either because the work is homotonal (as in Haydn's String Quartet in C major, Op. 54 No. 2) or because the last movement moves to an entirely new key (as in Mahler's Third Symphony)—there are other means at hand. Any extended movement with an exceptionally high 'stability quotient' (i.e. where the amount of tonal and thematic innovation is low in relation to its length) is likely to be well equipped to serve as a finale. Arnold Whittall makes a similar point when he observes: 'It might well be that a finale can fulfil its function with respect to the harmonic structure of the work as a whole only if it is tonally definite and singular, rather than ambiguous and multiple' (to 'tonally' I would add 'thematically').[5]

The composer also has to ensure that the final slow movement moves into a vacant 'space' in the design of the work. Just as a quick finale has to avoid too close a resemblance—in form, character, etc.—to an opening quick movement (and, for that matter, to any scherzo, if present), so, too, a slow finale has to establish a separate profile, even if, as may happen in its fast

---

[4] Smith, *Poetic Closure*, 34.     [5] Whittall, 'Two of a Kind', 164.

counterpart, elements from earlier in the work reappear in it. If it is a second slow movement, the first must be drastically different. In practice, a valedictory finale is usually the first genuinely slow movement—a fact that strengthens the listener's sense of its finality in the scheme of events, since, in terms of tempo, it fills the only remaining void.[6]

In the interests of historical and analytical precision a clear line must be drawn between slow movements as such and slow epilogues to fast movements. The latter cannot be considered 'slow' in their own right; rather, they apply the brakes to what has until then been interpreted as a fast movement. Where circumstances permit, this braking effect can also be achieved by the use of longer note-values in lieu of an explicit change of tempo. In older music, indeed, this has often been the preferred method. A good example of a written-out *ritenuto* occurs in the coda (so named) of the last of Schumann's *Phantasie-Stücke*, Op. 12. Entitled 'Ende vom Lied' ('End of the Song'), this piece evokes a group of men seated at their *Stammtisch* in an inn and rounding off their evening with a boisterous, sentimental song. The coda halves the harmonic rhythm (the player encounters an unexpected expanse of white notes), and amid enigmatically shifting harmonies the listener hears soft echoes of fragments of the song, as if the drinkers are dispersing unsteadily into the night, humming as they go. The point here, and in countless similar cases, is that the slowness makes sense only in relation to the earlier quick tempo, to which it is subordinate.

A reverse subordination—of quick to slow tempo—occurs in the first valedictory finale we shall discuss, which is that of Haydn's Op. 54 No. 2 (leaving the 'Farewell' Symphony for the next chapter). The first three movements of this quartet—a 'vivace', an 'adagio', and a minuet and trio in 'allegretto' tempo—presage nothing unusual. The governing thematic idea in all of them is the rising fourth (initially and especially from dominant to tonic), and this motif is indeed carried forward into the finale, which mounts it like a pennant at the head of its first two themes. The opening movement is an elaborate but essentially conventional sonata-form movement. Much less usual is the C minor 'adagio' in 3/4 metre, which is hymnic in character and cast in a rounded binary form without repetition of the second section, which ends with a half-close. After the first statement of the opening section the melody of the hymn is transferred from the first to the second violin. This leaves the former free to weave fantastic Gypsy-style arabesques overhead—perhaps the most true-to-life simulation of improvised descant to be found anywhere in Western art music before the twentieth century. The minuet returns to C major and the mood of the first movement, but its trio revisits C minor and reintroduces some of the

---

[6] The 'adagio' finale of Haydn's Op. 54 No. 2 constitutes an exception, since the second movement is also an 'adagio'. However, Haydn observes the more fundamental principle of contrast: the earlier 'adagio' is in a different mode (minor) and metre (triple) from the finale, besides being distinctly slower and wholly different in texture and design.

harmonic asperity that had characterized the 'adagio'. The finale is entrusted with the task of resolving the unsettled contest between C major brightness and C minor gloom.[7]

It starts as if with a conventional slow introduction—again 'adagio', but in C major and 2/4 metre, which ensures adequate contrast with the second movement. This introduction comprises a periodic eight-bar phrase cadencing in the tonic, which, rather unusually, is repeated without alteration (except for a second-time bar). The repetition, which challenges the through-composed tendency of traditional slow introductions, already hints at something unusual.

In bar 9 the music starts again with a different, broader melody introduced by the same 'rising fourth' motto and this time underpinned by a striding cello bass in quavers (which itself also privileges the rising fourth— a good example of the Classical style's habit of distributing the most basic thematic material between melody and accompaniment without distinction). In other circumstances this melody, too, might have served as a slow introduction to a fast movement; its patterned figuration reminds one of the introduction to the finale of Mozart's G minor Quintet, K. 516. But the fact that it is the possessor of its own introduction (bars 1–8 with their repeat) precludes this possibility from the start. Despite the unconventionality of its slow tempo, the melody is recognized immediately as the bearer of the main substance of the finale.

The *Adagio* proceeds fairly conventionally in regular eight-bar periods as follows:

| Bars | Theme | Description |
|------|-------|-------------|
| 9–16 | A1 | Cadencing in the dominant (G major). |
| 17–24 | A1 | The same, repeated with minimal alteration. |
| 25–32 | B1 | Contrasting period, ending with a half-close in the tonic. |
| 33–40 | A2 | Bars 9–16, modified to lead to a perfect cadence in the tonic. |
| 41–8 | A3 | The same in C minor, now modulating to E flat major. |
| 49–56 | B2 | Bars 25–32, modified to lead to a half-close in C (minor). |

Bars 9–40 form a conventional, tonally closed AABA unit. The status of bars 41–8 is less clear, however. Although the turn, at this point, to the tonic minor is a recognized option (and in its context not an unexpected one, since the music re-engages with the 'alternate' key of the work), the retention of the original theme with little alteration is anomalous for a central section and seems to point to some developmental or transitional function. The half-close in bar 56 recalls the ending of the first 'adagio' in preparation for the C major minuet.

---

[7] This quartet and its finale are analysed in some detail in Webster, *Haydn's Farewell Symphony*, 300–11. If my account differs in some of its interpretations from Webster's, this is not because of fundamental disagreement but rather because our analyses serve different larger purposes.

This recollection is not inapt, since what follows is another breezy (though faster) section of music based in C major that is distinct enough in character to come across as a different movement (the contrast is greater than that of the typical trio with its minuet). This 'presto' episode, occupying bars 57–122, resembles the refrain group of a typical Haydn rondo finale. It is in rounded binary form with both sections repeated and a kind of *petite reprise* (bars 113–22) to conclude. Were it not for the preceding 'adagio', one would have expected these bars to form the 'A' of an A–B–A–coda structure such as one encounters in the finale of the 'Lark' Quartet (Op. 64 No. 5).

The 'presto' ends abruptly with a half-close in C that one knows can only herald a return of the 'adagio'. This is very brief, consisting of a restatement of the introduction (bars 123–30) and a new version of period B (bars 131–40) that steers the music, with a light subdominant emphasis, to a gentle but firm cadence in the tonic. In the end, C major triumphs, albeit wearily.

There is no doubt that this is a slow movement with an embedded fast episode rather than a fast movement with an abnormally extended slow introduction and conclusion. All the same, the manifest incompleteness of both the slow and the fast component, considered separately, makes their interdependence a strange affair. The 'presto', a refrain unaccountably deprived of its couplets, fills a void in an 'adagio' that for no apparent reason is unable to generate a central section (or central development) of its own. In other words, their complementarity is predicated on their common mutilated state.

Haydn's inventiveness has to be applauded. At the same time, this finale is not quite as radical or as clear in its intentions as one might have hoped (which may account for its lack of obvious imitations). The 'presto' episode can be viewed as an attempt by Haydn to keep open his lines of communication with the conventional relaxant finale—indeed, as a politic retreat from the idea of a wholly slow finale that the opening of this movement seemed to promise. The opportunity is only half-seized.

Skipping over those Beethoven variation finales which, by virtue of being based on slow themes, arguably qualify as slow valedictory movements (we shall return to them in the next chapter), we arrive at Alkan's 'Grand Sonata' for piano entitled *Les Quatre Âges*, Op. 33 (1848), whose four movements, all in different keys, are conceived programmatically as representations of a man at the ages of 20, 30, 40, and 50 years respectively. The first movement is youthfully energetic in the manner of a finale; the long second movement, headed 'Quasi-Faust', represents the subject in his most heroic phase and adopts a generally fast but varied tempo; the third movement, which depicts the subject as a contented family man ('Un ménage heureux'), has the character of a moderately paced intermezzo; the exceedingly slow finale, combining the characters of prayer and funeral march, shows him as burdened by cares, frustrations, and inexorably advancing old age ('Prométhée enchaîné'). What we have here, in fact, is something resembling the conventional four movements of a sonata in jumbled order: finale–first movement–minuet/scherzo–slow movement. There is no mistaking the valedictory character of the fourth movement, which realizes its allotted function within the programme very effectively.

The musical value of the sonata is debatable, although that is a question concerning Alkan's music in general rather than this single work, which certainly represents him at his best. What is certain, however, is that it exerted minimal influence: its publication was scarcely noticed in the turmoil of the 1848 Revolution, and there is no record of any public performance of it until the 1970s.

The next valedictory finale arrived in 1865: not through composition but through performance; and not by intention but by serendipity. This was the year in which Schubert's 'Unfinished' Symphony, the full score of which is dated 30 October 1822, was finally revealed to the public under the baton of Joseph Herbeck. The vicissitudes of this symphony have recently been re-examined by Maynard Solomon, who argues persuasively that the symphony, in its two-movement state, was not (as many have thought) given by the composer as a personal present to his fellow composer Anselm Hütten-brenner, via the latter's brother Josef, but, using the Hüttenbrenner brothers only as a conduit, was intended to serve as a token of gratitude to the Musikverein of Styria, founded in Graz in 1815, which had elected Schubert to honorary membership in April 1823.[8] Solomon quotes a letter in which Schubert promised to send the society one of his symphonies in score. He makes the very important point that since the concert programmes of the Musikverein, typically for their time, rarely included performances of complete symphonies (only Beethoven's symphonies—occasionally—earned that honour), it would not have been out of order for Schubert to supply it with two symphonic movements from a (still unwritten) larger whole. Less convincing is Solomon's argument that perhaps, in a ground-breaking way, Schubert at some undefined point in time (having abortively sketched most of a minuet and part of a trio) became reconciled to the two-movement format and regarded it *de facto* as definitive. The facts that he himself adduces argue against this notion. Why describe a symphony on its title-page as 'Sinfonia in H moll' if the B minor opening movement was merely a prelude to a second and final movement in E major? Why did Schubert evidently fail to assure Josef Hüttenbrenner that the symphony was not (despite appearances) unfinished when he handed over its score? Significantly, the brothers, for their part, always described it as unfinished. And finally: it is not as if Schubert left no other prematurely abandoned works! My hypothesis, for what it is worth, is that at the point at which Schubert began to copy out the full score (which was before he had completed the

[8] Maynard Solomon, 'Schubert's "Unfinished" Symphony', *19th Century Music*, 21 (1997–8), 111–33.

sketching) he confidently expected to complete the symphony, returning to the work of composition at the point where the score originally ended, which was at bar 20 of the scherzo.[9] This did not happen, either because Schubert had a 'block' (he may have even doubted whether the parts of the scherzo and trio already written were fit to remain) or because he felt he could not leave the Musikverein waiting any longer. Perhaps he decided to bide his time until the performance of, and public reactions to, the completed movements before resuming work. As the evidence unearthed by Solomon shows, the Musikverein did not in the event programme either movement—the score may, indeed, have travelled no further than Anselm himself. This failure, not anticipated by Schubert, to perform the first two movements may have been the underlying reason for the symphony's non-completion.

From the perspective of the symphony's reception after 1865 (it was published two years later), these speculations about the composer's intentions are unimportant. Like the Venus de Milo, the symphony became, in its incomplete (equivalent to mutilated) state, a 'complete' aesthetic object. The architects who designed Greek temples and Roman villas naturally based their aesthetic calculations on the intact structures. Nevertheless, once time, nature, and human hand had done their work, the resulting ruins became regarded, by different people and in a totally different context, as equally perfect. So it was with Schubert's symphony, whose very incompleteness (as Solomon brilliantly describes) was viewed, and still is viewed, as paradigmatic for this artist:

An 'Unfinished' Symphony opens up the connections between Schubert and that aspect of the Romanticism aesthetic that valorizes ruins, fragments, longing, sudden death, and every other idea of incompletion; it is emblematic of an inability to achieve conventional patterns of archetypal transcendence—those bearing on homecoming, triumph, closure, happy ending...The 'Unfinished' Symphony readily turns into a metaphor for Schubert's very existence—his bachelorhood, his disease, his early death, his brief, 'unfinished' life.[10]

From the time of its first performance, the 'Unfinished' has been not only the favourite among Schubert's symphonies but also a favourite among symphonies in general. It would not be unreasonable to argue that the repeated experience of hearing a two-movement work closing with an 'andante con moto' of unusual breadth and beauty 'softened up' audiences for the purpose-written slow finales that were soon to follow.

In 1903 Schubert's 'Unfinished' Symphony acquired a companion-in-arms (or rather, 'without arms') in the shape of Bruckner's Ninth Symphony, left without a finale at the composer's death in 1896. This time, the omission was certainly not wished by the author, who considered allowing

---

[9] The page containing bars 10–20 of the scherzo was removed from the score by Schubert.
[10] Solomon, 'Schubert's "Unfinished" Symphony', 129.

his *Te Deum* to be used as an *ersatz* finale. Concert life, however, has accepted the 'adagio' without demurral as a finale, projecting back on to Bruckner aesthetic values that belong more to the twentieth century than to his own.

The earliest cyclic work in the general repertoire to have a slow finale is Tchaikovsky's Sixth Symphony, the 'Pathétique', which was completed between February and August 1893. It is indisputable that this symphony was the work that put on the map the aesthetic of the valedictory finale and stands as the godfather to most later ones. However, it was narrowly preceded by a work with which it shares several characteristics, including a slow finale: Skryabin's First Piano Sonata, Op. 6. Written in 1892, this sonata remained unpublished for three years, and there is no record of a public performance of it until February 1894, when Tchaikovsky was already dead.[11] Even in the absence of a direct link, however, the parallels are remarkable.

Both Tchaikovsky's 'andante lamentoso' and Skryabin's 'funebre' are dominated by melodic phrases based on the descending minor scale (their openings are shown as Exs. 6.1 and 6.2, respectively). Both are compact movements, uniformly tragic in mood and cast in a simple ABA form (Tchaikovsky's movement has in addition a coda based on its 'B' section). Both restrict themselves—remarkably for their period—to a single alternate key centre for the 'B' section: B flat minor, the subdominant, in Skryabin's case; D major, the relative key, in Tchaikovsky's. (In both cases, the monolithic quality, the 'poverty', of the finale's form produces a remarkable concentration that enables the movement to function all the more effectively as an epilogue to the whole work.) Both works have programmatic associations openly revealed by their composers: Tchaikovsky picked up the idea of a symphony on the theme of mortality from a slightly earlier but abandoned symphony in E flat major that was to have been entitled *Life* (its actual musical material was recycled into other works);[12] Skryabin's finale is a doleful comment on the recent injury to his right hand that threatened his career as a performer. Both works include extra-musical reference: Tchaikovsky quotes a phrase from the Russian Orthodox Requiem in his first movement;[13] Skryabin intones the first four notes of the *Dies irae* in his finale, anticipating his fellow student Rakhmaninov's later obsession.

---

[11] I am grateful to Hugh Macdonald for clarifying, in correspondence, the early performance history of the sonata.

[12] The descending-scale figures in the Sixth Symphony, variously diatonic and chromatic in form, can be interpreted (in the spirit of the old rhetoricians' *catabasis*) as symptoms of decline and death—only presentiments in the case of the first three movements but final actuality in the fourth. The complementary ascending-scale figures, which very significantly occur only in the first three movements, constitute *anabasis*, signifying aspiration and vitality.

[13] This phrase sticks out very prominently since it contains the only use in the whole composition of a 'modally' flattened seventh degree (on trombone 1 in bar 202).

Ex. 6.1. Tchaikovsky, Symphony No. 6 in B minor ('Pathéthique'), Op. 74, last movement, opening

Ex. 6.2. Skryabin, Piano Sonata No. 1 in F minor, Op. 6, last movement, opening

Of course, there are also differences. Skryabin's finale, as its heading suggests, is modelled on the funeral march in Chopin's B flat minor sonata; it features the same chime-like oscillation between tonic and submediant harmony. Tchaikovsky's finale is really a 'romance' displaced from its normal position. In fact, the plan of the Sixth Symphony can be viewed as a revised version of that of the Fifth. Movements 1, 2, 3, 4 in the Fifth become 1, 4, 2, 3 in the Sixth. The 'Valse' in the former re-emerges as a 'quasi-waltz' (in regular 5/4 metre) in the latter. The earlier finale transmutes into a 'scherzo-march' that is far longer and more complex in form than a conventional third-movement scherzo.

The widespread idea that the 'Pathétique' reflects Tchaikovsky's expectation of his own imminent death, or that it even represents a musical suicide note, has been vigorously, and I think effectively, combated in a recent book by Alexander Poznansky.[14] However, all that is in dispute about this symphony is whether the expiring hero is the composer himself or a generalized humanity—and the answer makes precious little difference to the work's reception.

One detail about the finale remains enigmatic. The reduction of the score presented as Ex. 6.1 does not show that the notes of the two parts in the upper stave are taken alternately by first and second violins, and their counterparts in the lower stave are treated similarly by violas and cellos. The bizarrely jagged lines that result from this criss-crossing in bars 1–4 are heard for a second time in bars 19–23 but disappear thereafter, even when the same phrases have a reprise following the 'B' section.

Attempts to find a musical rationale founder. The zigzags are equally ineffective as *Klangfarbenmelodie*, as hocket, or as antiphony. It is doubtful whether most listeners perceive anything unusual when the movement opens; consequently, they also fail to take note of the straightening out later on. The very fact that the technique is not applied consistently even to the same theme leads me to suspect a special hermeneutic significance that remains to be discovered.

After Tchaikovsky came Mahler. His Third Symphony, completed in 1896, contains a lengthy finale whose basic tempo is described as 'Langsam. Ruhevoll. Empfunden' ('Slow. Peaceful. Felt'). Of the six movements in the symphony, this is the second-longest in terms of playing time (about twenty-three minutes as compared with the thirty-four of the first movement), although, typically for an 'adagio', it is rather short in terms of the number of pages (only twenty-two in the Boosey & Hawkes edition of 1944) and, indeed, of musical events.

Paul Bekker identifies this symphony as one of the four Mahler symphonies (Nos. 2, 3, 5, and 7) in which the preceding movements do not lead up to the finale in a straight line of mounting tension but, in his words, 'circle around' ('kreismässig umschreiben') it.[15] This is a needlessly elaborate, and also tendentious, way of describing a perfectly normal symphonic arrangement (such as we know it from Brahms, Dvořák, or Tchaikovsky, for instance) wherein the outer movements form the pillars and the slighter inner movements, two or more, supply contrast and colour.

If we look at this rightly admired finale and compare it with that of the 'Pathétique', we see the same general principles in operation on an expanded scale. Instead of a simple ternary form (ABA), we find a 'doubled' ternary form (ABABA). Once again, the 'B' contrasts remarkably little with the 'A' (and in fact rapidly passes over into development of 'A' material accompanied by a few semi-disguised quotations from earlier movements).

---

[14] Alexander Poznansky, *Tchaikovsky's Last Days: A Documentary Study* (Oxford, 1996).
[15] Bekker, *Gustav Mahlers Sinfonien*, 21.

The neatness of the form is disrupted by Mahler's usual divagations and climaxes, but the punctilious return to D major for each restatement of 'A' lends clarity to the basic formal outline.

Slow this movement certainly is, but can one also speak of it as valedictory? Mahler, who devised a programmatic caption for each movement (for his own private orientation rather than the public's), entitled the sixth movement 'What Love tells me'. Love, in this instance, was meant as divine, not human. In fact, the style of the movement conforms almost throughout to the traditional 'hymn' topos. Consciously or otherwise, Mahler was inclined to dig into his own memory as a conductor and connoisseur of the repertoire when he invented themes for his music, and the 'A' theme closely recalls that of its counterpart in the 'lento assai' (in D flat major) of Beethoven's String Quartet in F major, Op. 135.[16] In the sense that God is apart from this world, the movement is genuinely a leave-taking from the more mundane images that inspire the earlier movements (I: 'Pan awakes. Summer marches in'; II: 'What the wild flowers tell me'; III: 'What the animals of the forest tell me'; IV: 'What Man tells me'; V: 'What the angels tell me'). So here the farewell is not to life but only to worldliness, and the finale is allowed to end in a blaze of glory and even with mock-martial timpani thumps.

The long 'adagio' in D flat major closing Mahler's Ninth Symphony, completed in 1909, is commonly viewed as an instrumental 'remake' (in a broad sense) of the final song, 'Der Abschied', from his recently completed orchestral song cycle *Das Lied von der Erde*. Equally, however, it follows on from the finale of the Third Symphony, with which it shares, at least in its principal theme, the general character of a hymn. Once again, the finale is a counterweight to a substantial first movement, the inner movements (a *Ländler* and a 'Rondo-Burleske') being in comparison mere cameos. However, this is now definitely twentieth-century music: its attenuated orchestration and frequent lack of harmonic or tonal definition lend it a fragility that seems to return us to the theme of mortality, particularly in its closing bars, where, deserted by the other sections, the strings fade away to nothingness.

Not surprisingly, the movement has often been interpreted by commentators as Mahler's own 'farewell' to life: a version of the Tchaikovsky scenario with natural causes replacing suicide. Arguing in ways that parallel Poznansky's, Vera Micznik has recently proposed that this biographical interpretation of the significance of the Ninth Symphony, and of its finale in particular, is quite unfounded and arises from understandable but misconceived wishful thinking.[17] She points out that at the time of its writing

---

[16] The first 'B' theme revisits the 'Frère Jacques' movement of Mahler's own First Symphony (in bars 43–4).

[17] Vera Micznik, 'The Farewell Story of Mahler's Ninth Symphony', *19th Century Music*, 20 (1996–7), 144–66.

Mahler had every reason to suppose that his heart condition was at last under control, that more compositions were to come, and that death was not around the corner. While there is no doubt that he means the final note (marked 'ersterbend'—*morendo*) to signify extinction, it is the general, not the personal, to which Mahler alludes.

The slow finales that we have examined from Skryabin onwards are all relatively autonomous movements: that is, one could perform them separately (as in Mozart's time) without much apparent loss of meaning. In the later twentieth century, when the free-standing Adagio has, so to speak, been reinvented as a genre in its own right—think of the examples by (or attributed to) Albinoni and Barber—for reasons wholly unconnected with valediction, slow movements that conform to the requirements of melodiousness, sensuousness (an important criterion), and moderate length have often been wrenched from their original context and pressed into service as cameos. The slow movement of Borodin's Second String Quartet (later to become 'A Stranger in Paradise') and the irredeemably popular *Canon* of Pachelbel are cases in point.[18]

However, few slow finales of twentieth-century cyclic works have joined this select band, and the main reason is very clear: the modern preference for cyclic unity has tended to bind finales so closely to the preceding movements that their extraction is unthinkable. Some examples will clarify this.

Ernö Dohnányi's Second String Quartet in D flat major, Op. 15 (1906), provides an outstanding demonstration of how, with ingenuity and careful planning, cyclic formal principles can be married to the retention of a strong individual profile for each movement. The composer's basic modus operandi is simple but clever. At the beginning of the opening movement (of three) a set of three motto themes (i.e. themes occupying only a phrase or two) is presented: an 'andante', shown as Ex. 6.3(*a*), characterized by yearning ascents on the tonic chord including an added sixth, with an emphatic descending fourth to close; an 'allegro', Ex. 6.3(*b*), featuring fierce reiterations at different pitch levels of a two-note figure; and an 'adagio', Ex. 6.3(*c*), ending with a sorrowful descending tetrachord.

The preliminaries over, the first movement ('allegro') is allowed to proceed. The thematic substance of its first subject (in a fairly orthodox sonata form) is formed from extensions and reconfigurations of the material in the first motto. Between the exposition and the development section the three mottoes are once again paraded in sequence. During the development elements from all of them are woven into the thematic discourse, counterpointing or linking material from the main part of the movement. Mottoes 2 and 3 in what is close to their original form return to introduce the recapitulation. The movement closes serenely with fragments of motto 1.

---

[18] I have even seen CD compilations of Bruckner Adagios, one piled on top of the other.

Ex. 6.3. Dohnányi, String Quartet No. 2 in D flat major, Op. 15: (*a*) first motto-theme; (*b*) second motto-theme; (*c*) third motto-theme. Reprinted by permission of N. Simrock/Richard Schauer Music Publishers, London-Hamburg

The second movement, in F minor and marked 'presto acciaccato', is as 'bruised and battered' as its heading suggests. It is based relentlessly on motto 2, *moto perpetuo* fashion, with intermittent wails reminiscent of Wagner's Nibelungs. A ghostly, glassy chorale in F major serving as trio provides the only relief. The movement ends defiantly with a half-close and a bitter question mark.

The concluding 'molto adagio' offers balm and solace. Its long opening theme, whose beginning is shown as Ex. 6.4, starts, at last, to develop motto 3, which up to this point has remained only in its primitive state. The rich, chromatic harmony, with its frequent Neapolitan inflections, creates an atmosphere of sustained poignancy. In bar 19 the theme, based in C sharp minor, debouches into a counter-theme, 'poco meno adagio', in the parallel key of C sharp (enharmonically D flat) major. A brief, hushed return to the first theme, translated to E major, ends the outer ('A') section.

The 'B' section is in F minor, key of the second movement (to reach it, Dohnányi 'wrenches' chromatically upwards in the manner familiar from Schubert's Fantasy in F minor for piano duet, D. 940). It is in the same 'Hungarian' style as the central portion of the slow movement of Brahms's Clarinet Quintet. While the first violin rhapsodizes overhead, the cello comments angrily in the bass with ostinato phrases from the second movement; in the middle of the section (beginning at bar 59) the viola reintroduces the longest, most serene version of the derivatives of motto 1 (originally heard in C major, again on viola, in the development section of the first movement).

The return of the first theme is handled masterfully. Sweeping, arpeggiated phrases in semiquavers on the two violins form a dissonant, plangent background to the theme, which is presented by the viola to a cello

Ex. 6.4. Dohnányi, String Quartet No. 2 in D flat major, Op. 15, last movement, opening.
Reprinted by permission of N. Simrock/Richard Schauer Music Publishers, London-Hamburg

accompaniment of plucked chords. Eventually, by the time the counter-
theme arrives, the music has returned to something approaching its original
sweet tranquillity.

The coda begins by revisiting the second-movement theme, now made
almost flaccid by a relaxation of tempo, and mottoes 1 and 2. At bar 142 the
mode changes from minor to major and over a humming drone on the lower
strings the violins present motto 1 in canon: a prolonged celebration of the
added sixth chord that in its naivety recalls, just a little, Dvořák's 'American'
Quartet. The motto finally fragments and the movement ends softly.

This is unquestionably late Romantic music in purely stylistic terms, but it
has a modern 'savvy' and almost a modern aesthetic in its violent mood
swings and confessional intimacy. Where reintroductions of material from
earlier movements in a finale so often appear forced and unconvincing, here
they succeed, partly because the interaction between motto themes and

elaborated themes has been an essential feature of the work right from the start: the end and the beginning, though splendidly contrasted in overall character, play the same games.

If we search for a later counterpart to Dohnányi's motto-into-theme-into-section technique, we can find it, appropriately enough, in a quartet by his compatriot Bartók: No. 6 (1941). Bartók's task is easier, since he is dealing with only one motto theme—the thirteen sinuously chromatic *mesto* bars delivered by the unaccompanied viola as an introduction to the fast opening movement—but, in compensation, his evolution of extended themes is more unilinear and more phased. The main part of the first movement is clearly based on a sonata-form model (including the metrical metamorphosis of recapitulated material so beloved of this composer and, after him, Shostakovich). The two central movements, a 'Marcia' and a 'Burletta', are partly playful, partly aggressive, parodies of generic types (the parallel with the *Ländler* and 'Rondo-Burleske' of Mahler's Ninth Symphony is close). To introduce the first, Bartók places a slightly expanded version of the motto theme in the cello and adds a counterpoint above, each of the three accompanying instruments presenting the same line in a different octave (violin 2 and viola also play *tremolando*). Before the 'Burletta' the theme, expanded still more, is heard in three-part counterpoint, violin 2 and cello accompanying the melody on violin 1.

At the close of the third movement the motto theme is ready to 'take off': it can appear in four-part harmony, and it can expand still further to become an independent movement that needs no sequel. Bartók's choice of first chord, a simple A minor triad with the third on top, already presages that this is to be a movement of resolution, of regression. Gone is the satire; in comes the nostalgia. The structural model for the movement is basically variation form (once again setting a premium on stability rather than contrast); in the later part of the movement Bartók insinuates dreamy wisps of first-movement material, which blend effortlessly into the autumnal mood, thereby augmenting the 'rounding' effect. The ending is deliberately left rather inconclusive in harmonic and tonal terms: it would be difficult to state precisely which of the four notes in the final added-sixth chord (F–A–C–D) is the keynote, even though F is the lowest. As we shall find again, even more strikingly, in a moment, 'calculated inconclusiveness' is a quintessentially twentieth-century contribution to musical rhetoric, and one that naturally affects finales above all.

Having spoken of Bartók's last quartet, one would commit an injustice not to discuss an equally fine valedictory quartet finale by his contemporary Prokofiev: this occurs in the First Quartet, written in 1930 just before the composer's return to Russia.

Prokofiev's music is often difficult to analyse in detail because of the unusually wide (horizontal) span and largely non-modular structure of his melodies. Unlike Bartók and Shostakovich, who (acting on Classical principles) piece together melodies from repeated elements that can be unpacked at will and treated separately, Prokofiev tends to follow a model recognizable from Berlioz (consider, for instance, the *idée fixe* of the *Symphonie fantastique*) in which free extension almost in the manner of a stream of consciousness welds diverse elements indissolubly together. This makes orthodox development based on fragmentation more difficult (the problem is related to Schoenberg's doubts about the structural cogency of symphonies based on folk material). To a large extent, paraphrase and the injection of new material take the place of intensive working-out of short motifs.

The neo-Classical spirit that informed Prokofiev's *Classical Symphony* remains live in his First Quartet, albeit in association with much more astringent harmony. The opening 'allegro', in B minor, is in structural respects almost a parody of the first movement of a middle-period Beethoven quartet. It uses general pauses to separate exposition, development, and recapitulation, and begins the development with a restatement of the first theme in the tonic (the formula of the 'diverted repeat') just as in the first 'Rasumovsky' Quartet.[19]

At a general level, the first movement, although it is more obviously autonomous than its two sequels, establishes firmly the two basic 'ideas' of the work: broken chords (usually in the form of rotations around two or three notes, Alberti-style) and scales. Despite the thematic prolixity, the strong, virtually continuous presence of these two elementary modes of motion (again, indebted to Classical models) helps to make the work cohere.

The main part of the second movement, which moves to C major, is a bustling scherzo (though not so labelled) in rondo (ABACA) form. Preceding it, however, is a concentrated 'andante molto' introduction in which a succession of motto themes to be used and expanded in the second and third movements jostle one another. These fourteen bars constitute the actual fulcrum of the work.

The third movement, marked 'andante', begins in E minor (thus following on well from the end of the scherzo) with desultory statements of one of the mottoes. In bar 9, however, it veers suddenly to B minor and the viola, passing the baton halfway through to the first violin, delivers a romance-like periodic theme to kill for (Ex. 6.5). This theme has in fact grown out of the second part of the first of the mottoes. The rest of the movement is constructed in three ample spans: an 'A' section (bars 1–76) comprising the quoted theme, its continuations, and its subsidiary motifs (which include more motto material from the introduction to the second movement); a slightly more animated 'B' section (bars 77–129), which likewise makes reference to the mottoes; and a drastically abridged restatement of 'A' with a fade-out coda (bars 130–55). The largest of several dynamic and

[19] Prokofiev himself stated that immediately before starting this quartet he had made a study of Beethoven's quartets.

Ex. 6.5.  Prokofiev, String Quartet No. 1 in B minor, Op. 50, last movement, main theme

Ex. 6.6.  Prokofiev, String Quartet No. 1 in B minor, Op. 50, last movement, ending

textural climaxes occurs at the start of the recapitulated 'A', when the first of the mottoes (which is remarkably similar to Beethoven's 'Es muss sein' motto) reappears achingly in the cello, amplified by double-stops, and is seamlessly continued by its derived principal theme.[20] The last five bars are unbearably poignant: a series of riffs, chords, and notes that, although delivered safely back to the tonic, are too drained of energy to persist any longer (Ex. 6.6). This is an early example of a 'farewell through exhaustion': a type of close that Shostakovich was later to make his own.

[20] Shostakovich reproduced this recipe in the finales of his third, sixth, and tenth string quartets, where the theme of the preceding movement (in each case, a passacaglia) returns at the climax with shattering emotional force.

From the abundance of valedictory finales in the music of the second half of the twentieth century, I have selected one for examination: the second movement, individually entitled 'Silentium', of Arvo Pärt's *Tabula rasa*, described not inaptly by the composer as a 'Double Concerto for Two Violins, Strings and Prepared Piano'. In this singular work neo-Classicism (Bachian rather than Haydnesque) and tintinnabulous minimalism come together to produce a powerful and original result.

Like Prokofiev's quartet, this two-movement concerto is based on two primal elements, the scale and the chord: except that here, these elements provide all, not merely a good part, of the material. Moreover, the use of both is governed by mechanical processes similar to ones often employed in late medieval and early Renaissance music: the musical 'clock' is wound up—and it runs.

The first movement, entitled 'Ludus' ('Play'), is in a moderate tempo. Except for a brief, and not very adventurous, excursus at its climax it restricts itself from start to finish to the notes of the 'natural' minor (or 'Aeolian') scale of A.[21] In this movement, the cascades of, or rotations around, notes of the chord (always the tonic chord), decked out as needed with 'inessential' notes drawn from the rest of the scale, predominate over the more slowly moving scale figures, which swing up and down in ever-wider arcs like an acolyte's censer gone wild. The arpeggiated figures, variously in mixed note values, quavers, triplet quavers, and semiquavers (i.e. the 'sewing-machine' patterns familiar from concertos by Vivaldi and Bach), belong only to the two soloists, singly or in counterpoint to each other. The orchestral strings intrude into the solos at intervals with canonic surges up and down the scale (not wholly unlike those referred to in the last chapter in connection with the finale of Sibelius's Third Symphony). Elsewhere, there are the typically Pärtian chimes and slow chants, in which the piano justifies its preparation. The movement ends with a series of hammered A minor chords (accompanied by frenetic activity in arpeggiated semiquaver sextuplets from the soloists) culminating in a triple *forte* sustained A minor chord.

Overall, the effect is one of dynamism, ecstatic abandon (interrupted by enigmatic pauses or incantations), and *Spielfreudigkeit*. Pärt is returning to the original concept of the concerto, described by Johann Mattheson in 1713 as a work 'composed in such a way that at the appropriate moment each part comes into prominence and vies with the other parts'.[22]

What next? With a delicate arpeggiation, the piano introduces a new chord, that of D minor, that will be the 'home' of the music for the duration of the second movement. The tempo, previously 'con moto', becomes (the binary opposition is important) 'senza moto', and the predominantly 4/4

---

[21] Shostakovich, who may here have influenced Pärt, was especially fond of the Aeolian scale; consider, for instance, the start of the slow movement of his Second Piano Concerto.
[22] Johann Mattheson, *Das neu-eröffnete Orchestre* (Hamburg, 1713), 193–4.

metre of the first movement changes to a 6/4 metre that, with hemiola applied in both directions, simultaneously functions as 3/1 and 3/4.

It is immediately apparent that the whole first movement has been nothing more than a prolongation of the dominant chord. The second movement is therefore not a departure but a homecoming. The muting of the strings, the retention of a soft and generally uniform dynamic, the greater prominence of the prepared piano, the unhurried tempo (which, by means of multiple regular speeds produces the sensation of wheels within wheels): all these factors combine to create a glassy, unearthly atmosphere. Pärt's bold intention, grasped intuitively by the listener and confirmed obliquely by his paratexts, is to represent the 'world beyond', after the mortal coil represented by the first movement has been shuffled off.[23]

Once again, broken tonic chords meet ascending and descending Aeolian scales. This time, the priority is reversed. It is the scales, swinging up and down in their ever more extravagant arcs, that predominate. Heedless of harmonic clashes, part-crossing, and limitations of instrumental compass, the lines assigned to each of the two trochaic (long–short) and one dactylic (long–short–medium) formulae wend their unhurried way through the score. These three rhythmic 'modes' (as the thirteenth century would have described them) are shown in Ex. 6.7. We are back in the world of the medieval mensuration canon, and the multiple expressions of threeness (the three rhythmic modes and the employment of triple metre at three different levels) could even hold a Trinitarian significance. The simple chordal shapes and chimes that punctuate the music throughout buttress the already firm sense of periodicity and of rootedness in the tonic.

The ending is remarkable. Each of the three lines eventually descends into the depths and disappears: first, the one in minims and crotchets, on C'; a

Ex. 6.7.  Arvo Pärt, *Tabula rasa, Double Concerto for Two Violins, String Orchestra and Prepared Piano*, second movement: (*a*) theme in 'quick' form; (*b*) theme in 'medium-quick' form; (*c*) theme in 'slow' form

---

[23] Britten achieves a similar effect in the accompanied recitative for tenor, 'It seemed that out of battle I escaped', near the end of his *War Requiem* (1961). The context is, of course, also similar.

little later, the one in semibreves and minims, on $D'$; lastly—played by an unaccompanied solo double bass in triple *piano*—the slowest one, on $E'$. While $E'$ is, historically, the lowest note of the double bass, the modern instrument can descend, as Pärt has already demonstrated, a full octave beneath the cello. So why does he refrain from taking the line down to $D'$, the tonic of the movement, to achieve conventional closure?

The answer is probably to be sought in hermeneutics. At the end of the 'Esurientes' movement of J. S. Bach's *Magnificat*, the composer fails to take the upper parts to their cadential notes (although the continuo part resolves normally) in order to illustrate the sending away 'empty' of the rich. It is possible that Pärt's inconclusive conclusion is intended as an allusion in the same spirit to the ultimate nothingness of even heavenly existence, the *silentium* behind all *silentia*. Alternatively, it might be a reproach to humanity for rashly seeking unattainable perfection. Or does the *Ludus* have the last laugh, after all?

A two-movement scheme in which the movements are in some way complementary opposites is at least no novelty. The paired movements (generally in contrasted tempo and metre) in many Italian keyboard sonatas of the late Baroque and the numerous later examples in Haydn and Beethoven establish the tradition. In the twentieth century two-movement structures regain a little of their lost popularity in such works as Nielsen's Fifth Symphony and Bartók's *Two Portraits*. What is so impressive about Pärt's *Tabula rasa* is the degree of meaningful contrast attained within such forbiddingly circumscribed parameters. But of course: the narrower the boundaries, the more significant each step becomes. Expression is ultimately a matter of relationships, not of quantities.

# 7

# Hybrid Solutions

HYBRIDITY in finales comes in two main forms. One is the movement *di mezzo carattere* that exhibits concurrently features belonging to more than one type of finale. We have already spoken of the many symphonies, concentrated in the second half of the nineteenth century, that are summative by virtue of weight and length but not according to content or hermeneutic import. About some of these it would be possible to debate at length, without certainty of an agreed conclusion, whether the summative or relaxant model was uppermost.

A similar problem is posed by variation finales. The use of variation form for the finales of cyclic works goes back to the chaconnes and passacaglias of the seventeenth century and the minuet variations of the eighteenth. Although lacking the prestige of sonata form, variation form has always been a fairly popular choice for finales. It has the special virtue, in this context, of making multiple returns to the tonic, thus enabling the movement to fulfil especially well its stabilizing role vis-à-vis the whole work. Whether the variations run continuously or form a series of discrete sections, their theme almost never exceeds a moderate tempo. The reason is simple: the classic method of elaborating a theme is to fill in the gaps between its constituent notes and harmonies, for which space is needed. This space is gained most easily by moderating the pace of the theme. Nevertheless, even when the prevailing harmonic rhythm of a variation movement is quite slow (the note values themselves, of course, may in places be very short), it usually qualifies as a 'fast' movement. It becomes the cousin, so to speak, of the *rondo grazioso*.

All this adds up to a 'relaxant' quality (albeit sometimes modified by 'summative' weight). One would not hesitate to place in this category such movements as the finales of Beethoven's 'Harp' Quartet, Op. 74, Brahms's Clarinet Quintet and Second Clarinet Sonata, and the various successors to the passacaglia finale of the same composer's Fourth Symphony by Dohnányi (Second Symphony), Vaughan Williams (Fifth Symphony), Barber (First Symphony), and many others.

Despite this, a few variation finales, by virtue of the abnormally slow tempo of their theme (and the maintenance of a slow harmonic rhythm through most of the movement), verge on, and perhaps deserve to be placed in, the 'valedictory' category. Beethoven's sonatas in E major, Op. 109, and C minor/major, Op. 111, supply the prototypes. It is true that in the first the tempo is significantly increased for several of the variations, but the return of the hymnic theme, unaltered, to close the movement and thus the work confirms the movement's overall identity. One might argue, indeed, that Beethoven's very point in bringing back the theme is to place beyond doubt the valedictory function of the movement. Op. 111 repeats the basic formula, but this time Beethoven eschews tempo change in favour of metrical change (this is the movement with the celebrated variation notated in an extraordinary 12/32 metre), which has the equivalent effect. Since there is a separate coda, no literal reprise of the theme occurs, although echoes of its opening in the final bars are enough to confirm the sense of having come full circle. The variations concluding Prokofiev's two-movement Second Symphony (1925), which offer a soothing respite from a relentlessly percussive first movement, are clearly indebted to Beethoven's model as revealed in these sonatas.

The second sort of hybridity occurs when a finale consists of two contrasted components placed side by side but not otherwise directly related in a thematic or syntactic sense. If each component is formally complete in itself, we may speak (borrowing Webster's term) of a 'double finale'—this concept can even apply when the first component runs into the second, although in such cases care must be taken to distinguish a double finale from a conventional internal movement (slow movement, scherzo, etc.) that leads into a finale proper. Where the contrasted components are both formally incomplete, the second acting as a 'deviant' completion of the first, we may speak instead of a 'divided finale'.

Double finales are at least as old as the tripartite *Tanz–Nachtanz–Tripla* groupings of the Renaissance. In these, the *Nachtanz* and *Tripla* form the dual ending. In Baroque chamber sonatas the gavotte or minuet quite commonly forms the second element in a concluding pair of quick movements, being preceded by an allemande, corrente, or gigue.[1] In such an arrangement the 'first' finale is the weightier, the second the lighter (and shorter). One might even speak of a relaxant sequel to a movement that is already relaxant vis-à-vis the larger work; or, to return to our culinary metaphor, of the cheese and biscuits following the dessert.

The 'Pastorale' in G major that follows without a break (via a second-time bar) the conventional finale in G minor of Corelli's 'Christmas' Concerto (Op. 6 No. 8) is a classic early instance. Here, the 'Pastorale' acts very overtly as an adjunct introduced for a special purpose: a 'bolt-on' addition to a work that would be entirely satisfactory without it (indeed, this movement is marked 'ad libitum', since it is appropriate only during the Christmas season). When we arrive at the Classical period, additional final movements

---

[1] The chamber sonatas of Corelli and Vivaldi furnish many such examples. Each of the twelve works in a collection of violin sonatas published in 1714 as *Allettamenti per camera* by the Roman composer Giuseppe Valentini (1681–1753) has a double finale.

become more common in works of divertimento type, although their presence in the more 'heavyweight' genres remains unusual.[2]

It is thus in the context of a symphony rather than as a basic concept in itself that the double finale of Haydn's 'Farewell' Symphony (No. 45) of 1772 gives cause for surprise. It previous three movements are fairly typical for a passionate minor-key symphony of Haydn's early middle period, although the choice of tonic (F sharp) is highly unusual. The prominence in these movements of two subsidiary keys, A major and F sharp major, has relevance for the structure of the finale, which elevates both of them to a prominent position.

The structure of the finale itself can be summarized as follows:

| Section | Tonality | Bars |
| --- | --- | --- |
| *Presto* | | |
| Exposition | f♯ → A | 1–56 |
| Development | A → b → c♯ → b → A → f♯ᵛ | 57–98 |
| Recapitulation | f♯ → f♯ᵛ | 99–150 |
| | | |
| *Adagio* | | |
| Exposition | A → E | 151–81 |
| Development | E → b → Aᵛ | 182–91 |
| Recapitulation 1 | A → f♯ᵛ | 192–217 |
| Recapitulation 2 | F♯ | 218–57 |

The 'presto' by itself constitutes a complete and conventional sonata structure of a length proportionate to the other movements (see Ex. 7.1(*a*) for the opening theme). It would be simplicity itself to convert the existing half-close with which it ends into a full close on the lines of the 'concert' ending devised for the overture to Mozart's *Don Giovanni*. If the work ended there, we would have a fine but not especially remarkable symphony ending with a relaxant finale.

The 'adagio', of similar length, is less ordinary. For a start, it is placed in end position, which lends it a 'valedictory' character. More to the point, it lacks (in itself) tonal closure. It begins as a movement in A major (see Ex. 7.1(*b*) for the opening theme) and ends as one in F sharp major. What the table calls the first recapitulation is diverted from A major (matching the exposition) to the dominant of F sharp minor—a move that ushers in a slightly longer second recapitulation entirely in that key.

Were it not for the anomalous 'progressive' tonality of the 'adagio', one would be happy to speak of it as a separate movement altogether, especially since no overt thematic links between the two components exist. However, since its linkage to the preceding 'presto' supplies the missing tonal closure (allowing, as one may, for the shift from minor to major), there is merit in

---

[2] The marches ending Boccherini's Guitar Quintet *La ritirata di Madrid* (G. 453) and Michael Haydn's String Quintet in F major (P. 110/P. 59) are typical examples.

Ex. 7.1.   Haydn, Symphony No. 45 in F sharp minor ('Farewell'), last movement: (a) opening;
(b) bars 151–6

the traditional view that the two components form an integrated, albeit
double, movement.

The programme of the symphony, its 'Farewell', belongs exclusively to
the 'adagio'. No departures occur until the end of its exposition, when
second horn and first oboe blow their candles out and leave. The bassoon
leaves in bar 197, and the second oboe and first horn slip away in bars 204
and 205, respectively; this occurs just before the music veers away from A
major towards F sharp minor in preparation for the second recapitulation.
Their departure leaves only the strings, which include a pair of solo violins.
Immediately before the second recapitulation (bar 217) the double-bass
drops out, as do the solo violins (but only temporarily). The cello and the
orchestral violins depart in bars 227 and 235, respectively. In bar 236 the solo
violins, with only the viola remaining as accompaniment, re-enter. The viola
goes in bar 243, leaving the solo violins to snuff out the movement, *pianissimo*.

The extinguishing of the candles and the progressive disappearance of all
the musicians but two before the music has ended are, of course, an enact-
ment of finishing the day's business and retiring to bed. This is, in turn, a
tactful metaphor expressing Haydn's 'political' purpose in writing the
symphony: to remind his employer that the members of the band were
due for their annual vacation. It is a little piece of music theatre that gains
force (as it was doubtless meant to do) from arriving so unexpectedly—not
merely late in the work but also late in the movement. For this reason, I think
that attempts (most recently by Webster) to extend the 'programme' to the
symphony as a whole are unconvincing. At a musical level, of course, the
work coheres magnificently. But its actual programme is only a postscript.

The double-finale device appears not to have survived the Classical
period. Its existence presupposes that each component, in particular the
second, should be light and not over-long, whereas the whole drift of
finale-writing after Beethoven was entirely towards weightier and lengthier
finales, a condition that excluded them. Their place was taken by divided
finales.

The simplest, and doubtless original, form of divided finale is one in which the break in continuity (of the musical material) takes place at the line of division between the recapitulated second subject group and the movement's coda. We see a hint of this in the finale of Beethoven's 'Appassionata' Sonata, Op. 57, whose 'presto' coda opens (in bars 308–25) with a brief, thematically self-contained section in symmetrical binary form, with each half repeated. The material resembles the refrain of a rondo in café-Hungarian style (the finale of Beethoven's String Quartet in C minor, Op. 18 No. 4, provides another such theme) and differs sharply, at surface level, from the rest of the movement. However, Beethoven does not maintain the new idea but reverts in bar 325 (second-time) to the primary material. The 'Hungarian' theme therefore acts only as a diversion, not as the launching pad for a new component.

A fully realized divided finale with its point of separation before the coda occurs in Mendelssohn's 'Scottish' Symphony, whose earliest sketches were made in 1829 but which was finished only in 1842. The first component, in A minor (bars 1–395), is an almost complete sonata-form structure; the second, in A major (bars 396–490), resembles a *Lied ohne Worte* in which the orchestra, like the piano in Op. 19 No. 3 (also in A major and 6/8 metre), acts the part of the singers in addition to supplying their accompaniment. The two components are not thematically related: the first, mildly martial in spirit (the semiquavers slurred to dotted quavers are perhaps intended to evoke the clash of claymores), returns, arguably a little too exactly, to the world of the first movement (Ex. 7.2(*a*) shows the theme's opening); the second reaffirms the symphony's 'Scottish' character, employing as its opening melodic formula the pentatonic 5–6–8 progression (already introduced unobtrusively in the scherzo, initially at bars 10–11) that, together with 'Scotch snaps', enshrined Europe's received idea of Scottishness in music (Ex. 7.2(*b*) shows the beginning).[3]

This movement, and especially its final *Lied*, have come in for much criticism.[4] None of the reservations expressed concerns the actual idea of a double movement; they relate more to generic weaknesses in Mendelssohn's musical language—the poverty of modulation (relative to movement

---

[3] The identical opening formula, followed by a series of 'Scotch snaps', occurs in an 'écossaise' by Telemann that appears as the fifth movement of an *Ouverture* in D major (Dresden, Sächsische Landesbibliothek, Mus. 2392-N-4). The historical connections between Mendelssohn's 5–6–8 motif, Liszt's 'Christus' (or *Vexilla regis*) motto, and the very similar motif with which Mahler prefaces what has been called the *Durchbruch* (breakthrough) in his First Symphony have still to be explored.

[4] See Peter Mercer-Taylor, 'Mendelssohn's "Scottish" Symphony and the Music of German Memory', *19th Century Music*, 19 (1995–6), 68–82. I do not share Mercer-Taylor's view that there is a direct connection between the symphony's *Lied* and the same composer's *Vaterlandlied* (later to be retexted as *Hark, the Herald Angels Sing*) of 1840. While I do not altogether reject his view of the *Lied* as a patriotic gesture (albeit one made, ironically, in ostensibly foreign guise), I find his insistence on its musico-political message—to urge German symphonic music to remain true to its roots—less convincing.

Ex. 7.2.   Mendelssohn, Symphony No. 3 in A minor ('Scottish'), Op. 56, last movement: (*a*) bars 2–6; (*b*) bars 396–401

length), the excessively stereotyped methods of constructing periods, the over-uniform and sometimes flaccid rhythms, etc.

The link between the two components is in fact handled in masterly fashion. At bar 347 Mendelssohn arrives at a six-four chord in A minor that one expects to usher in a series of quickfire alternations of tonic and dominant harmony followed by reiterations of the tonic chord and the end of the movement. But he turns the E in the bass into a pedal note that is prolonged, beneath shifting harmonies, until bar 361, when a tonic pedal, which retains the E as a drone fifth, takes over. The A pedal note remains in place for even longer (thirty bars), while enigmatic, attenuated scraps of second-subject material build up expectancy above. This transitional passage achieves the difficult task of derailing the 'allegro vivacissimo' at the moment calculated to achieve maximum impact while ensuring that the triumphant arrival of the 'allegro maestoso assai' does not sound arbitrary. In purely formal terms, therefore, the movement is successful.

Because a coda is, almost by definition, not only a tonally self-contained area but one for which the thematic substance is freely chosen, its substitution by a new component poses few structural problems for the earlier part of the movement. More radical are the consequences of beginning the substitution at an earlier point in the movement before the existing themes have performed all their usual routines. This is what happens in the finale of Schumann's Second Symphony in C major, one of the most magnificent closing movements in the repertoire but, on account of its great length and unorthodox form, also one of the most problematic and argued over.

The symphony was composed in 1845–6 and first performed, under Mendelssohn's baton, on 5 November 1846. Its writing overlapped with a period (January–November 1845) during which Schumann studied Baroque (Bachian) counterpoint intensively, writing many fugues and canons of his own.[5] An interest in contrapuntal combination, which enters into a natural

---

[5] Compositions from this period include the *Four Fugues* for piano, Op. 72, the *Six Fugues on B–A–C–H* for organ, Op. 60, and the *Six Studies* for pedal piano, Op. 56.

alliance with the drive for cyclic integration, informs the whole symphony, as does the memory of Schubert's 'Great' C major Symphony, whose thematic substance (equally evident in melody, accompaniment, and scoring), lyrical emphasis, and discursive expansion are constantly recalled. Undoubtedly, biographical factors also affected the shape of the symphony, which was completed after a period of poor mental and physical health (the finale can be interpreted as a kind of 'Song of Thanksgiving to the Deity after Recovery from Illness'). Schumann's paraphrase (for a second time) of the 'Nimm sie hin denn, diese Lieder' motif from the sixth song in *An die ferne Geliebte*, which emerges as the principal theme of the finale, and hence of the entire work, hints at a connection not only with Beethoven (the 'great' tune from whose Ninth Symphony also hovers over this movement) but also with Clara Schumann, in bygone years the composer's own 'distant beloved'.

Carl Dahlhaus has interpreted the form of this finale as that of a sonata-rondo movement in which the refrain theme (equivalent to a first subject) is replaced halfway through the movement by a new, lyrical theme (the 'ferne Geliebte' idea) and thereafter forgotten.[6] In fact, the substitution is more drastic than that, since not only the refrain theme but also the episode theme (or second subject) drops out prematurely—the first after its very brief restatement in bars 93–118, and the second following a nominal development in bars 300–15 just after the first appearance of the new theme. John Daverio has described the second half of the movement, running from bar 280 to bar 589, as a set of chorale variations.[7] While the substituted theme certainly has a chorale-like character and appears in varied guises during its many restatements (Dahlhaus quotes a few of the variants), this characterization is inadequate. For a start, the 'basic' version of the theme is neither the one heard on its first (bars 280–99) nor on its second (316–43) outing: these are fragmentary, developmental treatments of a longer theme that in a conventional movement would have been heard in its entirety earlier (during an exposition) but here has to wait for the 'recapitulation'. Indeed, it is arguable that not even the form taken by the theme at the definitive return to C major (the 'recapitulation') in bar 394 is the prime one, since a further version, equally complete but regressive in character, opens the coda at bar 474. A second argument against the chorale-variation interpretation is simply that too much other material—from the movement's own four-bar introduction (an astonishingly rich repository of ideas), from the introduction to the first movement, and (initially) from the earlier episode—is introduced alongside, or in counterpoint to, the new theme. Table 7.1 attempts to describe the structure of the movement, necessarily in very simplified terms.

Up to bar 280 the movement conforms to the pattern of the ebullient, ultra-relaxant finales in Schumann's other symphonies (including the

[6] Dahlhaus, 'Studien zu romantischen Symphonien', 110–15.

[7] John Daverio, *Robert Schumann: Herald of a 'New Poetic Age'* (New York and Oxford, 1997), 320.

TABLE 7.1. *Plan of the finale of Schumann, Second Symphony in C major, Op. 61*

| Bars | Comment |
|------|---------|
| 1–4 | Introduction. This includes a rising octave-long *tirata* and emphasizes the notes C and G (with D as a subsidiary linking note), recalling the fanfare-like motto theme presented in the slow introduction to Movement 1. The *d″-f♯″-g″* progression in bars 3–4 prefigures the opening notes of what will become the finale's main theme. |
| 5–46 | Refrain group (equivalent to a first subject) in C major. Bars 5–8 prolong the dominant harmony reached in bar 4. |
| 47–62 | Transition to G major. |
| 63–92 | Episode, its opening theme based closely on the main theme of the third movement. It continues with contrapuntal development of the theme. |
| 93–118 | Repeat of bars 9–22 from the refrain theme. |
| 119–279 | Development section: bars 119–90 treat material from the introduction, bars 191–280 material from the episode. Freely modulating. The four descending bass minims (*a–g–f–e*) in bars 130–1 are the first of many appearances of the descending tetrachord during this section; these prepare for the substitute opening theme, which uses the tetrachord (sometimes elaborated) as its bass. |
| 280–99 | 'Development' (as if already presented in exposition) of the substitute opening theme, stated successively in E flat major and G major. |
| 300–15 | Resumed development of material from the episode. |
| 316–43 | Further 'development' of the substitute opening theme, stated successively in F minor and C major. This continues as: |
| 344–93 | Resumed development of material from the introduction. Dominant pedal in C major from bar 359 onwards. |
| 394–452 | 'Recapitulation' of the substitute opening theme. A counterstatement of it beginning in bar 418 receives intensification through canonic treatment. The motto theme from Movement 1 makes sporadic appearances. |
| 453–73 | A back-reference to the slow introduction to Movement 1, including the same motto theme. |
| 474–507 | First section of the coda, beginning with the substitute opening theme in its definitive (most diatonic, most quadratic) form. In C major throughout. |
| 508–89 | Second section of the coda (or 'coda proper'). This comprises (a) a fragmented presentation of the same theme (bars 508–15); (b) a tonal digression (516–35); (c) further fragmented presentation of the theme, now transferred, as an ostinato motif, to the bass (536–51); (d) a brief reference to the *tirata* motif of the introduction (552–9); (e) cadential phrases (560–73); and (f) a final affirmation of the tonic chord that works in the *tirata* motif (574–89). |

*Overture, Scherzo, and Finale* of 1841). It would have been very easy to continue in similar vein to the end, especially since bars 119–279 already contain a development section of conventional length that ends in the tonic minor, so making the perfect springboard for a return of the refrain group, to be followed by a transposed version of the episode. Conversely, it would have been almost as easy to reconstruct bars 1–279 so as to create a conventional antecedent to bars 280–589 (although the anomaly of the jettisoned episode would have had to be resolved in some way).

But this is not what Schumann wants. He has opted for a non-symmetrical structure in which the listener's expectations are thwarted halfway through. He has grafted a summative ending on to a relaxant beginning. This has not happened through a surrender, on the composer's part, to an erratic stream of consciousness: it is the consequence of a bold and rational strategy that takes an established principle—the subordination of the parts to the whole—further than ever before (and perhaps also since). The finale has become 'deformed' in the interests of the cycle as a whole. Freed from any need to recapitulate material from earlier in the movement, the second part of the finale can devote its full energies to becoming a 'super-coda' for all four movements.

Parenthetically, one may add that it is the tragedy of Schumann reception that his early piano works, notable for their episodic, sometimes haphazard, structure and bizarre flights of fancy, have coloured our general approach to his music, tempting many commentators to regard his later application of contrapuntal devices and cultivation of large-scale forms as ill-considered deviations from a natural Romantic spontaneity. Only half a century ago Mosco Carner could, incredibly, describe the C major Symphony as 'laborious, dull, often mediocre in thematic invention, plodding and repetitive in argument'.[8] Even today, Schumann's departures from the conventional plans that he was supposed to have been following all too often inspire excuses instead of the justifications they deserve.

The claim has recently been made by James Buhler that the finale of Mahler's First Symphony is also a divided movement—but divided in a very original manner.[9] Its two components, based, respectively, in F minor and D major, interlock in such a way that the recapitulation (Buhler prefers the term 'reprise') of the first (bars 458–630) functions simultaneously as the development section of the second; conversely, the 'exposition' of the second (bars 370–427) is a premature irruption (a 'false' coda) occurring near the end of the development section of the first, while its return and extended continuation (bars 631–731) constitute the 'true' coda, which, although

---

[8] Mosco Carner, 'The Orchestral Music', in Gerald Abraham (ed.), *Schumann: A Symposium* (London, 1952), 176–244 at 221.

[9] James Buhler, '"Breakthrough" as Critique of Form: The Finale of Mahler's First Symphony', *19th Century Music*, 20 (1996–7), 125–43. Buhler does not himself use the term 'divided', but the sense of his argument points in that direction.

contradicting the tonality of the movement's opening (F minor), restores that of the first movement (D major) and thereby provides overall tonal closure.[10] Buhler describes the structure of both components as sonata form. This is unarguably true in the case of the F minor component, which has a 'mirror' recapitulation, whereby the second subject group, originally appearing in D flat major (bars 175–237) after the first group, returns in an F major paraphrase (bars 458–532) before the first group. The sonata-form model is more problematic, however, for the D major component, which has no second theme or second key in its exposition. But for present purposes, it is unimportant whether the D major component is regarded as a full-blown sonata structure or (as I prefer) as a coda preceded at some remove by a 'false' coda. Either way, it constitutes one part of a divided whole.

There are some very interesting aspects of this symphony that deserve separate comment:

1. Mahler's peculiarly 'modular' method of constructing themes. These can be described as provisional assemblies of short units, usually motivically related among themselves, which are formed into new horizontal (melodic) or vertical (contrapuntal) combinations as the movement progresses. 'Theme' and 'motive' are hard to separate, and both have a highly fluid nature. In these circumstances, it can often be an arbitrary decision to consider a given passage as restatement or development.

2. Mahler's unusual treatment of modulation, which hardly distinguishes between the processes applied in non-developmental sections (expositions, recapitulations, codas) and those found in development sections proper. In the First Symphony Mahler anchors all sections and larger subsections in a single tonality, regardless of their position and function. Routines traditionally favoured in development sections such as the modulating sequence, in which a single idea is taken through a number of keys in turn, simply fail to materialize.

3. The richness of inter-movement relationships. Since the whole symphony, and in particular the first movement, has a common thematic and tonal basis, there is constant 'leakage' from one movement into another. The outer movements of the First Symphony are so similar—indeed, the last part (bars 574–630) of the varied restatement of the F minor first subject in the finale simply 'cannibalizes' the last part of the development section in the first movement (bars 305–51)—that the finale could aptly be described as an enlarged and intensified new version (or a 'summative transformation') of the first movement.[11]

[10] Bars 428–57 are developmental in relation to both structures; they recapitulate in D minor the material of the slow introduction to the first movement, which, although notated from the start in D minor, with one flat in the key signature, remains effectively in A minor until it gives way to the opening theme of the first subject (initially in D major) in bar 63.
[11] Their relationship resembles that of the outer movements in Schumann's Fourth Symphony, except that in Mahler's case there is a pronounced end-weighting altogether absent in the earlier work.

The first and last movements are both based rigorously on a set of six keys, around which the music circulates (these are also the keys represented by the pedal notes that dominate both movements). They form two subsets: one consists of D, F, and A (the distinction between major and minor will be ignored, since Mahler shifts at will between the two modes); the other consists of D flat, F (common to both subsets), and C.[12]

How the keys circulate can be shown by a simple outline (the bars given are those in which the new tonality first appears clearly):

*Movement 1*
A (1) – D (63) – A (71) – D (207) – Db (243) – C (275) – F (281) – D (352)

*Movement 4*
F (1) – Db (175) – C (290) – D (375) – F (436) – D (623)

Each movement contains one example of a striking 'wrench'. The shift from D major down to D flat major in the first movement occurs during the development section, which opens, highly unusually, with a prolonged passage in the tonic (bars 207–42).[13] In the finale the dramatic tonal event is the abrupt upward motion from C major to D major at bar 375—the 'rupture', as Buhler terms it, since it occurs on the cadential chord of an important motto theme that earlier was heard entirely in C major (in bars 297–305) and later will be heard entirely in D major (in bars 631–9).

The thematic substance of the four movements is equally tightly controlled. The basic set of notes from which all the main motifs and themes derive comprises degrees 1–3–5–6–8 in either their major-key or minor-key version. This pentatonic substructure, underpinned by drone fifths or octaves, contributes more than any other feature to the naively rustic mood of the entire symphony. The ascending fifth (1–5) and its 'filled-in' variants (1–3–5 and 1–2–3–4–5) and the descending fourth 8–5 (expanded as 8–7–6–5) are too obvious to need illustration. More interesting is the unwonted prominence of degree 6 and its ability to move directly to any of the other degrees making up the set. Example 7.3(*a*) illustrates its conventional, suspension-like resolution on degree 5.[14] Examples 7.3(*b*) and (*c*) show progressions to degrees 3 and 1 respectively. Least orthodox is the progression to degree 8 seen in Ex. 7.3(*d*), the motto theme of the last movement; this is shown in its 'ruptured' version, where a second melodic kink is produced at the point of fissure—2–3–5 (in D) being a transposition of the earlier 5–6–8 (in C). The 5–6–8 (2–3–5) progression is not, like its counterpart in Mendelssohn's 'Scottish' Symphony, a blatant attempt at local colour: it is a condensed, elliptical version of the sequential 2–3–4,

---

[12] D minor and D flat major are related in a special way described in German terminology as *terzgleich*: having the same third (but a different tonic).

[13] The unusualness is only increased by the fact that the entire exposition, including the introduction (bars 1–162), has already been repeated.

[14] All examples are taken from the finale.

Ex. 7.3. Mahler, Symphony No. 1 in D major, last movement: (*a*) bars 327–32; (*b*) bars 450–4; (*c*) bars 574–7; (*d*) bars 368–74

3–4–5 progression first encountered in bars 307–8 of the first movement, which itself goes back to a similarly upwards-groping sequence (this time, mostly by chromatic steps) introduced in bars 47–55 of the same movement. The diatonic form of the progression makes an appearance in the second half of Ex. 7.3(*c*).

Stepwise ascent is probably equatable, in terms of the work's hermeneutics, with human endeavour. In this context, the 'saltation' between degrees 6 and 8 (and similarly between degrees 3 and 5), which unexpectedly accelerates the ascent, perhaps represents heroic achievement. In a letter of 1894 to Richard Strauss, quoted by Buhler, Mahler interpreted the 'rupture' as a false victory that required further struggle for its consolidation (i.e. the 'breakthrough' initiated by its pure D major statement).[15]

This may be a good idea for a programme, but its musical realization is weak. The problem is that the supposed climactic struggle, in bars 428–630, consists almost entirely of the recapitulation (sometimes virtually literal) of material already heard either in the finale or in the first movement. Almost by definition, a recapitulation of familiar material cannot communicate struggle convincingly. The novel concept of a premature coda was not in itself unsound, but it would have been better first to allow it to follow the recapitulation and then (in order to represent the 'struggle') to insert a dynamic, developmental section containing new material between the two motto statements, the result being something closer to the asymmetrical

[15] Buhler, ' "Breakthrough" as a Critique of Form', 126. Both Strauss and, more recently, Henri-Louis de La Grange have cast doubt on the effectiveness of the D major peroration following the 'rupture'.

finale of Schumann's Second Symphony. A separate weakness is that the 'breakthrough' motto theme loses much of its lustre by being too similar to its counterpart in the first movement, the D major 'hunting' theme first heard in muted tones during the development section (bars 209–18) and then at full throttle to open the recapitulation (bars 358–63). Indeed, at least half of the problem lies not in the actual shape of the finale itself but in its dangerously close relationship to the first movement, with which it shares metre, basic tempo, and (eventually) also key. If pursued too relentlessly, especially at the surface level, cyclic unity soon ends up by subverting the *raison d'être* of the individual movement and weakening its internal logic.

Never common, divided finales have survived into the twentieth century. In his *Concerto for Orchestra* Lutosławski begins the finale with a passacaglia and follows this with a toccata and finally a chorale. The neo-Classical—in fact, neo-Baroque—titles of the components typify the kind of situation in which a composite movement is likely to thrive. The old forms and styles have become motifs to play with in a game of novel juxtapositions. Needless to say, the twentieth-century composer, mindful of organic principles, is unlikely to allow each component to go its separate way: their thematic relationship has to be made overt so that the progress from one to the other seems logical (naturally, the paratexts contributed by the composer in the form of a title, and either by him or by a sympathetic commentator in the form of programme or sleeve notes, also help to guide the listener along the desired path). In fact, the great difference between this music and (in their own age) Haydn's or Schumann's is that the possibility of surprise has to all intents and purposes been removed: long before the music takes its new turn, the listener is ready and waiting.

# 8

# *Patterns of Development*

U P TILL now, our discussion of finales has been taxonomic rather than chronological, and chronological rather than genre-related. The time has come to investigate how and where the three basic types of finale have been employed in each of the main multimovement genres of Western instrumental music between 1700 (with occasional backward glances) and 1900 (with occasional forward glances). Examining the genres separately reveals that each, in any given period, has its characteristic preference for a type of finale—modified but rarely altogether overridden by the individual preferences of 'schools' and composers—and that these preferences are sometimes strikingly divergent. Some of them persist for a surprisingly long time, while elsewhere new tendencies emerge.

We start with the suite, which is undoubtedly the oldest multimovement genre in the instrumental realm, even if its creation occurred slowly and haphazardly. We then move on to the sonata in its various manifestations: works labelled 'sonata' for one or two instruments as well as their equivalents for upwards of three instruments, which since the middle of the eighteenth century have generally gone by the name of 'trio', 'quartet', 'quintet', etc.[1] Next comes the symphony (such genres as the divertimento or the serenade will be regarded as lighter variants of the symphony or of the equivalent chamber genre as appropriate). Lastly, we will look at the concerto, to which (for reasons that will soon become evident) comparatively little reference has been made so far.

It goes without saying that this account will not aspire to the dutiful inclusiveness of a *Konzertführer*. It will, of course, try to get the broad picture right, but the composers and works singled out for special discussion will, as before, reflect their usefulness for the general argument rather than their familiarity or even their musical importance. Inevitably, some material first introduced in earlier chapters will be revisited in this new perspective, but I hope not redundantly.

---

[1] The change in nomenclature from 'sonata a tre' and 'sonata a quattro' to 'trio' and 'quartetto' seems to have occurred first in Germany. From there the new forms of title rapidly spread (probably via Lombardy) to the rest of Europe. The 'trios' by Telemann published in Frankfurt in 1718 must be among the earliest instances of this usage.

## The Suite

It is important to distinguish between 'suite' as a historical or analytical concept and 'Suite' as a title prefaced to a work. Historians and analysts like to group and then label works according to their actual characteristics, regardless of title.[2] The title is, of course, not discounted absolutely—it is what usually brings the work to the scholar's attention in the first place—but it does not have the ultimate say. When composers choose titles for their compositions, however, they do so for a range of paratextual reasons, some of which may ignore or even negate historical continuities and analytical realities. But if it remains true that nearly all works labelled 'Suite' by their composers possess the properties we associate with the genre, these are probably outnumbered (giving due weight to compositions written before 1700) by comparable groups of works with different collective titles or no title whatever.

The first suites were informal groups of dances. The earliest examples, from the early fourteenth century, consist of pairs on the *Tanz–Nachtanz* pattern.[3] For instrumental music, the impulse towards cyclic grouping came from without: from practice on the dance floor. In its power to coax music into forms larger than the individual piece, at a time (the late medieval period) when no internal mechanism for doing this existed, the institution of dancing could be compared with the Christian liturgy in the vocal sphere.

A price was paid for this informality. Right from the beginning, the suite has respected the integrity of the individual dance (or character) movement. This has meant that although individual pieces have often been based on shared material—the earliest examples in fact anticipate the variation suite in this respect—no piece has been made subordinate to another. Until the modern period, the way has nearly always been left open to remove or add movements, and sometimes even to arrange them in different order. Longer suites such as one finds notably in the music of the French organists and harpsichordists of the late Baroque period not infrequently have the character of anthologies rather than of multi-pieces in Dunsby's sense. One symptom of this relatively loose association is that run-on relationships between adjacent movements are non-existent in early suites and today still very rare. Another—very familiar to performers of suites by Bach and Handel—is that difficult and easy pieces mingle freely: where omission is sanctioned, it is not so vital to maintain a uniform technical level.

---

[2] Famously, William S. Newman's four-volume history of the 'sonata idea' rejects this modus operandi in favour of what the author calls a 'semantic' approach: anything called a sonata by its composer is treated as one; conversely, anything not so called does not belong in the study by right. This criterion has the virtue of being simple to apply in a consistent way, but it leads to some surprising omissions and tends to seal off the sonata tradition too neatly from the cognate traditions.

[3] I must here acknowledge my debt to David Fuller's masterly article 'Suite' in *The New Grove* (xviii. 333–50), which leaves few corners of the suite tradition unexplored.

A further important shared characteristic of suites throughout the ages is that they are designed for entertainment, not edification. This is obviously true when the component movements are all dances and the music accompanies actual dancing; it remains largely true when the dances are listened to as wholly 'abstract' music or when character pieces take their place. Even a set of *Three Piano Pieces* by Schoenberg (his Op. 11), whose individual pieces are headed by nothing more evocative than the appropriate roman numeral followed by a tempo marking, already conveys by its choice of title (of which the avoidance of 'Sonata' is the most conspicuous feature) the promise, in the event unfulfilled, that heavy demands will not be made on the listener.

Consistent with this looser, lighter character is the suite's preference, never once challenged throughout its history, for a relaxant finale. Whether short or long (this feature, at least, varies considerably), the finale of a suite tends towards liveliness, not to say cheerfulness. Summative intentions are discouraged by the self-contained nature of each movement, while valediction is difficult when the tradition of a slow movement—lying in any position—is so weak.[4] One inheritance from the world of the dance that the suite has never quite shed is its avoidance of the very slow movement. It is true that Corelli, who in his Op. 2 (1685) was apparently the first composer to label a cycle of dance movements as a whole (rather than an initial movement) a *sonata da camera*, imports a few abstract 'adagio' or 'grave' movements from the church sonata, but the fact that these stand out as elements borrowed from a different tradition only emphasizes the point. Even Schumann's many sets of character pieces, which in terms of the suite tradition exhibit many idiosyncratic features (for instance, run-on relationships between movements), almost never end with a genuinely slow movement.[5]

Another surprisingly consistent feature is the avoidance of grandiosity, even to some extent in opening movements.[6] The long variation movements, normally chaconnes or passacaglias, that close some late Baroque suites are certainly weighty movements, as we observed earlier, but their emphasis on virtuosity, the constant changes in their figuration, and their inability to spend long periods away from the tonic help to keep their temper relatively light. Sparkle, not gravity, is the quality usually sought in a suite finale.

---

[4] Alban Berg's *Lyric Suite* for string quartet (1926), the last of whose six movements is an 'adagio desolato', constitutes the obvious exception, but one cannot help feeling that its description as a suite in the first place is arbitrary; nothing would have been lost by giving it the title *Lyric Quartet* or *Six Movements for String Quartet*.

[5] This observation applies to the following sets for piano: *Papillons* (Op. 2), *Davidsbündlertänze* (Op. 6), *Carnaval* (Op. 9), *Phantasie-Stücke* (Opp. 12 and 111), *Kreisleriana* (Op. 16), *Novelletten* (Op. 21), *Nachtstücke* (Op. 23), and *Faschingsschwank aus Wien* (Op. 26). The one exception is the aptly named 'Abschied' ('Farewell') closing the *Waldscenen*, Op. 82.

[6] The long, elaborate preludes that open J. S. Bach's 'English' Suites are an anomaly in the history of the genre. Impressive though they are in themselves, they have not escaped criticism on grounds of their disproportionate length and weight.

The informality with which dance movements were originally grouped together, sometimes in a very ad hoc manner, is reflected in the casualness with which the cycle as a whole was named during most of the second half of the seventeenth century (before then, it seems not to have been named at all). There were two approaches, both of which operated on the *pars pro toto* principle. One was to appropriate the name of the first movement and apply it to the whole group. Thus we find suites described variously as *ouvertures, balletti, intrade, introduzioni, sonate,* etc.[7] Of these, the terms *ouverture* and *sonata* (as in *sonata da camera*) managed to survive into the next century.[8] The second approach was to name the group after the sequence of movements that followed the introductory one. This produced, in French, *suite;* whence its Italian and English cognates *seguita* and *sett,* respectively.[9] The fact that *suite* prevailed as the generic term used by later composers and theorists probably had many causes, but one of them was presumably that other genres had already staked a claim to the names *ouverture* and *sonata.* The term took a long time to become established (outside Italy, which continued to prefer *sonata*); well into the eighteenth century we find *Livres de clavecin,* such as Rameau's second (1724) and third (c.1729) books, in which the only way to identify the boundaries of the suites they contain is to ascertain where the keynote changes. Key unity, incidentally, was more restrictively observed in Baroque suites than in other instrumental genres of the time (conversely and ironically, the post-Baroque suite has applied it less restrictively). In Italian chamber sonatas the movements (except for inserted slow movements) were usually both homotonal and homomodal;[10] in French and German suites and their imitations in other northern countries major–minor contrast within the same *ton* was not merely allowed but often specially cultivated as an attractive effect.

The conception of the cycle as a head-movement plus various sequels placed in a descending order of rank brings to mind a more general meaning of 'suite', which is 'retinue'. The subordination of the later movements to the first is expressed verbally in some seventeenth-century sequences of dances, in which a 'Corrente' and 'Sarabanda' following an 'Allemanda' are

[7] 'Sonata' was the general-purpose term applied to single instrumental movements of any kind, but in a context where each dance was named according to its specific type, the only remaining 'sonata' was usually the abstract introductory movement—which was therefore in a position to lend its name to the whole group. See Talbot, 'The *Taiheg,* the *Pira* and Other Curiosities', for a more extended discussion.

[8] To call an *ouverture* an 'orchestral suite' is not a misnomer provided that one accepts that the label is not original and is inspired by analytical rather than philological considerations.

[9] *Seguita* is very rare. It appears, however, in the Op. 1 of Giuseppe Baldini (c.1740), entitled *III Seguite e III Sonate per flauto traversiere e basso continuo.*

[10] The only exceptions I know are the twelve chamber sonatas in Benedetto Vinaccesi's Op. 1 (1687), whose eleven or twelve movements include a central group of three or four dances in a different, though related, key. The impulse behind the key change was probably the quite extraordinarily large number of movements in each sonata.

preceded by the possessive adjective 'sua' ('its').[11] Right from the start, the suite was front-weighted by intention.

David Fuller regards the addition of the gigue to the cycle of movements normally encountered in a suite as a decisive watershed; in fact, two consecutive sections of his *New Grove* article are entitled 'The classical suite before the addition of the gigue' and 'The classical suite after the addition of the gigue'. Before 1650 a basic three-movement core of dances consisting of allemande, courante, and sarabande had been established as a norm in suites for keyboard and plucked instruments. They were joined after 1650 by the gigue, which initially did not displace the sarabande as final movement (in the Italian *sonata da camera*, indeed, the sarabande remained common as a closing movement well into the eighteenth century). The first known suites to place the gigue after the sarabande were those of Dietrich Becker (*Musicalische Frühlings-Früchte*, 1668), and by the end of the century the gigue had established itself as the final member of the core group. In keyboard music it could be either preceded or followed by lighter dances mostly taken from the ballet rather than the ballroom (gavotte, bourrée, etc.) or by character pieces. In the second case, of course, it ceased to be the actual finale, although, when the final movement is short and light, the gigue can sometimes be regarded as the first component of a double finale.[12]

Why the gigue emerged so quickly, by a process akin to natural selection, as the 'normal' finale is not surprising when one considers the general principles applying to relaxant finales that have already been discussed in this book. It is in a quick tempo, normally faster than that of any of the other dances, and its compound metre distinguishes it clearly from the allemande. Its playful character comes out in its fondness for wide leaps (inherited from the dance steps themselves), for fugal openings to sections (sometimes with inversion of the subject at the start of the second section), and for either *moto perpetuo* figuration in even notes or for jagged rhythms. It is amenable to a wide range of stylizations (of tempo, rhythm, etc.), which means that it can be tailored very precisely to its context. In fact, its relationship to the first movement (whether an allemande or a prelude) mirrors that of a sonata finale from the same period.

All this is very evident from J. S. Bach's suites. Although Bach can hardly be taken as a 'representative' suite composer of the late Baroque (if such a person exists), even within the German orbit, his choice of dance types or character pieces to serve as last movements has great historical importance, given the close links between the revival of the suite in the nineteenth century (after nearly 100 years of oblivion) and the Bach revival. In fact, Bach and Handel were the only two composers whose suites were available

---

[11] As in Pietro Degli Antoni's *Balletti, correnti, e arie diverse*, Op. 3 (1671).

[12] It is noticeable that when the gigue is the penultimate movement, the movement following it tends either to be clearly weightier (as in a chaconne) or clearly lighter (as in a gavotte); a movement of equivalent weight is rarely chosen.

in published editions during most of that century; the rediscovery of the *clavecinistes* and of Corelli arrived too late to make much of an impact on the revival.

In Bach's suites the hegemony of the gigue as a finale is marked to a degree rarely encountered in the music of his contemporaries. The 'English' and 'French' Suites for keyboard and the six suites for cello employ nothing else as their finales, while only the second of the partitas for keyboard (No. 2, with its 'Capriccio') departs from the pattern. The three partitas for violin are admittedly more varied, ending, respectively, with a 'Tempo di bourrée' plus *double*, a chaconne (following a gigue), and a gigue. As one would expect, the four orchestral *ouvertures* are also less uniform (this is true of French overtures in general): the first ends with a pair of passepieds, the second with the well-known 'Badinerie', the third with a gigue, and the fourth with a 'Réjouissance'. The *Ouverture in B minor* for keyboard (partner to the 'Italian' Concerto), appends to its gigue a short character piece called 'Echo' that was probably inspired by similarly titled movements by Bonporti and Valentini.

Bach's gigues are probably the most varied in character ever to have been penned by a single composer. For him, the gigue is not a simple 'topic' but an entire recipe book. The six gigues from the 'French' Suites illustrate the range of possible stylizations (Ex. 8.1 gives their openings). Not a single rhythmic formula is duplicated—which one could not say about comparable sets by Corelli, Vivaldi, or even Handel. All this, of course, is typical of Bach's desire to be encyclopedic, a feature that manifests itself throughout his oeuvre.

The suite based on dance movements was the only Baroque instrumental genre to peter out completely (as opposed to becoming transformed according to new stylistic paradigms) in the Classical period. *Ipso facto*, it was the only Baroque instrumental genre eligible for revival in the nineteenth century (since only what is dead or moribund can be revived). What happened to it parallels the fate of the madrigal one and a half centuries previously; this genre came into being in the 1530s, rose rapidly to a dominant position, then declined abruptly and virtually disappeared in the mid-seventeenth century, ending up as a 'revived' genre, whose features were deliberately kept archaic, in the late Baroque period.

Fuller distinguishes, among post-Baroque examples, between the antique suite, the characteristic suite, and the extract suite. The first is the 'revived' type, initially modelled on Bach and/or Handel but later becoming more eclectic. The second replaces the dances (with the possible exception of up-to-date dances such as the waltz and the galop) by character pieces; the defining factor, which marks such a suite off from other kinds of multi-piece, is that each movement type is represented only once—hence Beethoven's sets of *Bagatelles* and Schubert's *Moments musicaux* do not qualify. The third converts wholly instrumental extracts from a longer, more

Ex. 8.1. The opening of the 'Gigue' in J. S. Bach's 'French' Suites: (a) Suite No. 1 in D minor; (b) Suite No. 2 in C minor; (c) Suite No. 3 in B minor; (d) Suite No. 4 in E flat major; (e) Suite No. 5 in G major; (f) Suite No. 6 in E major

heterogeneous work (such as an opera or ballet) into a sequence of movements for concert or recreational use. This operation, which need not be
carried out by the composer himself, began already in the later seventeenth
century with Lully and Purcell. In an extract suite the order of the movements
is essentially pragmatic in that it need not correspond to the original order:
what works best as a finale according to the usual criteria is placed last.

The antique suite almost came into being via Mozart's enthusiasm for
Bach, which resulted in his composition in 1782 of an *ouverture* and allemande in C minor followed by a courante in E flat major for piano (K. 399/
385i); these were followed seven years later by a gigue ('Eine kleine Gigue')
in G major, K. 574, which may or may not be an intended continuation. If we
ignore this possible precursor, whose lack of tonal unity argues against
regarding it as a suite in the ordinary sense, the earliest known post-
Baroque suite is the one in six movements published by William Sterndale
Bennett in 1841 as *Suite de pièces*, Op. 24. Further examples by Joachim Raff,
Woldemar Bargiel, and Franz Paul Lachner soon followed. The earliest
works in the 'antique' category to have survived in the general repertoire
(it has to be emphasized here that to describe a suite as 'antique' does not
preclude an admixture of character movements or of dance types unknown
to the Baroque) are the first three of Tchaikovsky, composed between 1879
and 1884, which are for full orchestra.[13] Admittedly, the low incidence in
them of genuinely 'neo-Baroque' movements makes their claim to the
description a little tenuous: Suite 1, for example, comprises an 'Introduzione
e Fuga', a 'Scherzo', an 'Intermezzo', a 'Marche miniature', and a
'Gavotte'.[14] A better early representative of the type is Grieg's commem-
orative suite *From Holberg's Time*, which exists in dual piano (1884) and
string orchestra (1885) versions. Here, the movements are 'Prelude', 'Sarabande', 'Gavotte' (with a 'Musette' as alternate movement), 'Air', and
'Rigaudon'. Grieg's version for string orchestra exemplifies the close association of the genre with this medium, another child of the Bach revival and
therefore the ideal vehicle for a backward-looking genre. All the movement
types are authentically Bachian (even if their realization owes as much to
Handel) except for the rigaudon, which proves an excellent substitute for
the gigue in its role as a relaxant finale.

Alongside the antique suite, the two other types emerged and flourished
in the later nineteenth century. To attempt to cite them all would produce a
mere catalogue without relevance for the argument of this book, so it must
suffice to mention, in order to clarify definitions, a few examples familiar
from the concert repertoire. For the characteristic suite, we have Saint-Saëns'

---

[13] These are: Suite 1 in D major (1879), Suite 2 in C major (1883), and Suite 3 in G major (1884).
A fourth suite, subtitled 'Mozartiana' (1887), consists of free arrangements of Mozart movements.
[14] Similarly eclectic suites were composed soon afterwards by Tchaikovsky's compatriots
Arensky (1885) and Rakhmaninov (1893, 1900–1).

*Suite algérienne* (1880), precursor of a long line of such suites whose titles add a suitable adjective to the word 'suite', and Bizet's *Jeux d'enfants* (1871). For the extract suite, we have the same composer's two suites from *L'Arlésienne* (1872–6), the second of which was arranged as a complement to the first by Ernest Guiraud, and Sibelius's *Karelia Suite* (1893). For obvious reasons, the gigue is not a movement type to expect in suites of either kind, but it finds many valid counterparts, many of which adopt the 'poem of speed' formula (as in the 'Galop' closing *Jeux d'enfants* and the 'Farandole' ending the second suite from *L'Arlésienne*).

One oddity among nineteenth-century suites is Nielsen's *Little Suite for String Orchestra*, Op. 1 (1888)—perhaps one of the most endearing first publications ever produced. Its three movements are prosaically entitled 'Prelude', 'Intermezzo', and 'Finale', which is to say no more than beginning, middle, and end (although the central movement has the lilt of a waltz). Unusually, the 'Finale', which is by far the longest movement, is summative in character, absorbing the main material from the 'Prelude', which is presented both at its beginning and at its end. This pronounced end-weighting coupled with inter-movement reference is intrinsically foreign to the spirit of the suite tradition. Naturally, the fault (if fault it be) lies not in the music but in the title. The composition contains enough reminiscences of Dvořák's *Serenade in E major*, Op. 22 (1875), also for string orchestra, to suggest what a better choice of title might have been.

Certain general trends are apparent in the twentieth century. Although the neo-Classicism of the inter-war period, in its flight from late Romantic subjectivity, privileged matter-of-fact titles connecting a new work with the pre-Romantic past (in his Op. 25 Schoenberg saw nothing amiss with combining the most radical musical language with the most traditional morphology and nomenclature), a contradictory tendency—the flight from genre identification altogether—operated concurrently and in the later part of the century became dominant, at least among 'serious' composers. For lack of a better alternative, one would place Messiaen's vast movement cycles (*Visions de l'Amen*, *Vingt Regards sur l'enfant Jésus*, *Catalogue d'oiseaux*, etc.) in the analytical pigeon-hole marked 'suite', but one knows immediately that such a term does no justice to the complexity, coherence, and, above all, poetic vision of such works. For the same reason, it would demean Holst's *The Planets* (1916), a more conventional work in terms of length, to insist too strongly on its classification as a suite.[15] Similarly with Janáček's *On an Overgrown Path* (1901–8) or Bartók's *Contrasts* (1938). As a rule of thumb, one can say that any cyclic work from the twentieth century that includes 'suite' in its title is likely to be backward-looking and none too adventurous. Conversely, the absence of this word invites the listener or commentator to approach the work with fewer preconceptions.

[15] The concluding movement of *The Planets*, 'Neptune, the Mystic', is a rare instance of a valedictory finale in a suite-like work (Messiaen provides other examples).

## The Sonata

We left the general discussion of the sonata, in Chapter 2, with some observations on how the change of cultural style between the seventeenth and eighteenth centuries reflected itself in a reduction of the number of movements and a concomitant increase in their average length. This process can be traced back to the first flourishing of the Bolognese school around 1660. Many north Italian composers of the time favour a five-movement (F–S–F–S–F) plan, even if we are talking here of a 'typical', not a 'standard', layout.[16] In the generation of Corelli (1653–1713), whose church sonatas for the trio combination published as Op. 1 (1681) and Op. 3 (1689) exerted enormous influence for some decades to come, the most common plan became one of four movements: S–F–S–F. In his solo violin sonatas (Op. 5, 1700) Corelli experimented with a new kind of five-movement plan (S–F–S–F–F), probably devised in order to give the violinist an opportunity to show off, at the end of the work, both his mastery of passage-work and his ability at polyphonic playing, but this gained little currency.

Under the influence of the concerto and perhaps also the orchestral sinfonia, the sonata soon underwent a further reduction: to three movements, arranged in the pattern F–S–F. We may note here that this shift from four to three movements parallels a similar one occurring in the solo cantata during the same period. Isolated examples exist before 1720, and by 1730 the new three-movement plan had become dominant. Some Italian composers working in the middle decades of the century (G. B. Somis, Locatelli, Tartini) experimented with a S–F–F plan, but this failed to take root.[17] Remembering Corelli's five-movement plan mentioned earlier, one is tempted to propose as a general rule that arrangements in which slow and fast movements do not alternate strictly prove less acceptable in the long run.

The F–S–F scheme thus consolidated itself several decades before the advent of the Classical style, or (to put it more exactly) the maturity of sonata form, which so many writers have regarded, I think one-sidedly, as the defining criterion for the periodicization of eighteenth-century music. From the Classical period onwards, three movements have constituted the 'baseline', as it were, of the sonata. The addition of the minuet and its successors (scherzo, intermezzo, etc.) to make a four-movement scheme has since then been common, but far from mandatory. Indeed, there briefly flourished, up to the time of Beethoven, a more radical practice of reducing the sonata to two movements on the lines of the late Baroque Italian keyboard sonata (D. Scarlatti, Paradies, Durante). As many as eleven out of the sixty-odd keyboard sonatas of Haydn have only two movements, as do six

---

[16] There is often some room for dispute over how many movements a sonata has, especially when a run-on relationship links one putative movement to the next. The criteria for distinguishing a movement from a mere introduction or conclusion were discussed in Ch. 2.

[17] A curious late example of the S–F–F plan is Mozart's Piano Sonata in E flat, K. 282/189g, composed in 1775.

of Beethoven's thirty-two.[18] The fashion for two movements extended briefly to duos and ensemble works: Mozart's Violin Sonata in E minor, K. 304/300c, Haydn's Piano Trio in G major, Hob. XV/25, and Boccherini's String Quartet in E minor, Op. 33 No. 5, all exemplify the trend. For aesthetic reasons too obvious to need discussion, the nineteenth century favoured the four-movement over the two-movement 'variant', and it is only in the twentieth century that a two-movement structure has reappeared on the agenda of sonata composers.

From Corelli's time onwards most sonatas have had two fast movements, and the question has been how to style them and how to differentiate them according to their position and function in the cycle. Before 1700 most fast movements, irrespective of other considerations, were fugal or at least imitative in texture and unitary (through-composed) in structure, with the possibility of a reprise of the opening at the point of return to the tonic. Differentiation between the first and second allegros was achieved primarily through metre, gradations of tempo, and rhythmic style (sometimes, textural features reinforced the 'lightness' of a finale). The influence of the faster dance types (*giga, gavotta, corrente, sarabanda*, etc.), all in 'short' or compound metre, is clearly perceptible in many finales—and occasionally receives acknowledgement in the shape of a heading such as 'Tempo di gavotta'.

Even before 1700 a few sonata finales were cast in binary form, imitating in this not only dance movements but also the wholly 'abstract', one-movement chamber sonatas that one finds in a collection such as Legrenzi's Op. 4 (1656). The importance of the initially very limited adoption of binary form at this stage is not that it is ancestral to sonata form and in that respect 'looks forward' but that it signals a shift of emphasis from form as process (the free evolution of a subject) to form as design (the juxtaposition of complementary elements).

There is a 'classic' type of Baroque sonata poised mid-way between old and new approaches to style and structure. Its essential characteristic is that the first allegro is rigorously fugal on the traditional pattern, while the second, no less substantial, explores the architectural possibilities of binary form. This type is exemplified to perfection by the Trio Sonata in C major, BWV 1037, today attributed, as mentioned earlier, to Bach's pupil Goldberg. The fugue is a hefty, well-worked-out *allabreve* on two subjects, recalling, in its almost comical rhythmic rigidity, the ritornello theme opening the second aria of Bach's cantata *Widerstehe doch der Sünde* (BWV 54); the finale is a 'Gique' in 12/8 metre developing on a more ample scale, and with a more calculated approach to thematic development and repetition (the reprise is very clearly signposted), the stereotyped gestures of the Corellian dance movement. The dissimilarity of structure between the two fast movements

---

[18] In contrast, Mozart's keyboard sonatas stick religiously to a three-movement plan.

means that little effort needs to be made to differentiate them in other respects.

From the 1720s onwards, binary form becomes employed increasingly for all fast movements (and not infrequently for all three or four movements). As a result, texture, tempo, style, and metre return as the principal agents of contrast between the first and last allegros. Northern Europe experimented briefly, in its first flush of enthusiasm for the concerto, with ritornello form in the first movements (but only rarely in the finales) of sonatas. Bach's Flute Sonata in B minor, BWV 1030, and Zelenka's Trio Sonata in F major, ZWV 181/5, offer good examples.[19] This fashion, which Italy never followed, petered out by the 1740s. On the other hand, more durable substitutes were found for the binary form normally used in finales. The popularity of variation form (initially nearly always on a minuet theme) and the rondo (*rondeau*) dates from the 1720s (it is not directly connected, therefore, with the advent of the Classical style, even though the incidence of both forms tended to increase as the century wore on). Early examples of variation movements in sonatas occur in the Op. 2 (for flute and bass) of Locatelli (1729), while the finale of Zelenka's Trio Sonata in C minor (ZWV 181/6), dating (like its companion) from c.1721–2, is an imposing rondo.

By the time Haydn started to write his keyboard sonatas, in the early 1760s at latest, the structural options available for finales—sonata form, binary form (rounded or otherwise), minuet and trio form, variations, and rondo—had all taken on their specifically 'Classical' shape, acquiring such features as transitions, contrasting subjects, modulations to remote keys, and codas.[20] It is interesting to see how Haydn's preferences change in the course of his career. In his earliest sonatas (Nos. 1–31 in the Wiener Urtext edition), all of which were composed before 1768, sonata form, minuet and trio form, and simple rondo form (first or second rondo) mingle on an approximately equal footing and without any obvious relationship to the number or character of the other movements. In No. 32 (1768–70) the first variation movement appears, and up to No. 53 (1781–2) eight further variation finales (either 'single' or 'double') occur. In the early and mid-1770s, in fact, the variation becomes the favoured option, displacing the minuet and trio (though sometimes adopting minuet tempo and character, as in Nos. 44 and 45). In the later sonatas (Nos. 54–62) only sonata and rondo forms remain. Rather surprisingly, sonata-rondo form makes only one appearance in the whole of Haydn's sonatas: in the finale of No. 58. The reason for its rarity may be that in the late eighteenth century the sonata was regarded as a less significant genre than either the symphony and the string quartet (its close association with female performers would have been enough to cause

---

[19] Telemann was especially fond of ritornello form for opening allegros.

[20] In theory, fugal form was also available, but the introduction of fugue occurred much earlier in chamber genres and the symphony than in the piano sonata or the duet sonata, where Beethoven was its pioneer.

this), and therefore more tolerant of lightness and looseness of structure in finales.

Simple or complex, many of Haydn's sonata finales display one of his most endearing and enduring qualities: wit. Before the Classical period, musical wit, as opposed to gross humour, is quite rare: its strong presence in Domenico Scarlatti's sonatas (whose 'ingenious jesting with art'—a phrase found in the preface of his *Essercizi per gravicembalo* of 1738— becomes a motto for Haydn in Gretchen Wheelock's book) shows merely how in so many respects Scarlatti is a Classical composer *ante diem*. Musical wit depends heavily on uncertainties of continuation, which are not the same thing as surprises. In Vivaldi there are plenty of unexpected turns for which the listener is unprepared and which have to be legitimized after the event. But these rarely express wit since all the time the composer remains manifestly in charge. Very different is the case in Haydn (and in all those who have followed his lead), where the composer himself appears to fall victim to uncertainty, sharing the indecision with his listeners. Under such conditions, even a relatively orthodox continuation can sound witty simply by solving the riddle and relieving the tension.

The basic materials out of which to create witty effects are many. A familiar resource is the juxtaposition of opposites. The contrasts can here be of register, of dynamics, of texture, of harmony, of key, or of mode; regular phrase structure can be counterposed to irregular; compressed statement to expanded. Ambiguities of all kinds (tonal, syntactic, etc.) can be exploited, as can obsessive repetition. How some of these elements combine to create wit may be studied in the finale of the first of the three sonatas Haydn published with a dedication to Therese Jansen on his second visit to London (1794–5). Both this sonata (No. 60, Hob. XVI/50) and the one following it have finales in an unusual form: the first section (repeated) follows the concise plan of a binary-form minuet with a modulation to the dominant but no proper second subject group (i.e. a first—and only—subject leads directly to a brief closing section in the new key); the much longer second section (likewise repeated) proceeds, however, in a conventional sonata-form manner, with not only a development section but also a newly invented second subject inserted between the first subject and the closing group.[21]

Example 8.2 shows the opening of the movement, taking it up to the point where the closing section in G major begins. Bars 1–4 reproduce a favourite topos of Haydn: the basic, undecorated melodic outline is $c''-d''-b'-c''$, harmonized in the expected manner with $I-II^6-V^7-I$. However, these

---

[21] Beethoven imitated this form with notable success in the toccata-like finale of his two-movement sonata in F major, Op. 54. In this movement the first section (or 'quasi-exposition') is unbelievably short—only twenty bars out of 188. Its brevity may have been one reason why Hugo Leichtentritt mistook it for a rondo refrain (see p. 62, earlier), although the return of the opening theme at the head of an extended coda was perhaps another factor.

Ex. 8.2.  Haydn, Piano Sonata in C major, Hob. XVI/50, last movement, opening

decorations, besides contributing essential material for later development, are themselves witty in conception. In the melody we have the 'stuttering' figure of three repeated notes followed by a 'twittering' figure, while the bass has a fussily energetic figure of thirds rising by step. The first surprise comes in bar 4, where the expected resolution to a root-position tonic chord does not happen on account of the telescoping of a four-bar consequent (bars 3–7), in which the four-note scale-figure appears not only in parallel but also in contrary motion. An opening eight-bar phrase has thus been compressed ingeniously into seven bars. The theme resumes one octave higher but is derailed in its third bar by the chromatic alteration of the two bass notes, which sound especially deviant because of the false relations made with the previous chord. The fermata in the next bar feigns puzzlement over how to proceed. Will the next chord be one of E minor? Of E major? Of F sharp major?

These enticing possibilities are forgone in favour of a resumption of the phrase (the accompaniment taken down an octave) and its continuation via a normal process of modulation (via tonicized VI) to the dominant. The effect is of a false start corrected. In the process, the $f\sharp'$ is left dangling: the errant chord is abandoned as hopeless instead of being resolved conventionally.

The false start, the resolution of ambiguity in an unexpected way, the ever-changing registers and textures, and the elision or expansion of phrase endings are the principal mechanisms both for Haydn's development of his material and for the maintenance of a consistently witty demeanour until the end. It is a remarkable fact that the first full close in the tonic employing root-position dominant and tonic chords occurs as late as bar 88, four bars from the final double bar.[22] Restlessness due to the avoidance of strong cadences is another important ingredient of the total effect.

It would be hard to overstate the long-term impact of Haydn's 'revolution of wit'. Of course, not only finales were its beneficiaries: examples abound in minuets or scherzos and in the 'scherzando' variety of slow movement. But ever since Haydn, relaxant finales have been the main locus of a composer's most extravagant humorous effects. One cannot imagine the half-speed reappearance of the main theme at the start of the recapitulation of the fourth movement of Shostakovich's Tenth Symphony or the dislocation by a semitone of the 'barrel organ' theme at bar 711 of the finale of Bartók's Fifth String Quartet in any other type of movement.

In comparison, Mozart's sonata finales are more staid, though no less effective in their context. His earliest sonatas (K. 279–283/189d–h) betray the influence of the symphony in their preference for sonata form. From K. 309/ 284b onwards, however, sonata-rondo form (in many ingeniously formed variants) predominates. Mozart's ideal in such movements is a vivacious elegance that smiles rather than chuckles.

In Beethoven's hands sonata-rondo form becomes the near-automatic choice for those finales not in sonata form. As against ten sonata-form movements in his piano sonatas, there are sixteen in sonata-rondo form, three simple rondos, two variation movements (Opp. 109, 111), and a fugue (Op. 110). Over half the sonata-rondo movements are in moderate tempo, conforming to the *rondo grazioso* model.

From a structural point of view, it is notable how close to ordinary sonata-form movements most of Beethoven's sonata-rondo finales are. They have elaborate transitions and developments, and without exception feature a substantial coda that replaces, or continues forward from, the last statement

---

[22] This bar number assumes that each section is written out only once, using repeat signs and second-time bars (the Wiener Urtext edition writes them out twice).

of the refrain. The multiple statements in the tonic of their refrain theme and the absence of repeat signs at the end of the exposition mark off these finales quite clearly from movements in sonata form proper, but their 'tone' is not necessarily lighter or their developments any less thorough.

Few sonata finales since Beethoven have strayed from the structural options he himself moved between. Variation form and fugue, encountered only in his last group of sonatas, have attracted the more ambitious, but in the case of some of the fugues—for instance, the ones in Hindemith's Third Piano Sonata (1936) and Barber's Piano Sonata (1949)—one detects a fondness for the form over and above any compelling need to use it at that point in the work. In general, the sonata-rondo or 'light' sonata form models have remained supreme. This is especially evident in the nine completed piano sonatas of Prokofiev, over all of which (except the first: a one-movement work after the manner of Skryabin, the obvious influence standing behind it) the spirit of Beethoven hovers. In fact, the most interesting developments in the sonata after 1830 have concerned large-scale single-movement form, about which more will be said in Chapter 9.

## The Quartet

By 'Quartet' one means, of course, the string quartet, which, in respect of quantity and prestige, ranks highest among the genres of chamber music without piano. If the duet sonata and the piano trio both reveal their distant origins as 'accompanied' sonatas by conforming in broad terms to the model of the piano sonata, the string trio, the string quintet, the wind quintet, and the various '-ets' from sextet onwards gravitate towards the string quartet.[23]

One striking fact differentiates the quartet tradition from the sonata tradition. Right from the start, four rather than three movements have constituted the 'average'. The *divertimenti* (a title applied fairly indiscriminately in the 1760s and 1770s to recreational works in several movements for any sub-orchestral medium) making up Haydn's quartets Opp. 1 and 2 regularly include a fifth movement in the shape of a second minuet/trio pair. But from Op. 9 (1771) onwards the four-movement norm, with the minuet placed either second or third, becomes operative.[24] String trios and

---

[23] The piano quartet and quintet constitute a special case. Because three or more melody instruments (most often strings, but occasionally wind, as in Mozart's Quintet in E flat major, K. 452) can form a 'complete' harmony unaided, the temptation exists to model the style of such works (though not their first-movement form) on that of the piano concerto. In the above-mentioned quintet, as also in his two piano quartets with strings, K. 478 and K. 493, Mozart willingly succumbs. Nineteenth-century piano quartets and quintets such as those by Schumann, Brahms, Franck, and Dvořák tend to avoid any allusion to the concerto in their quest for more serious utterance.

[24] It is worth observing that Boccherini, whose string quartets were valued second only to Haydn's in the late 18th c., oscillates between two and four movements throughout his career, following in this the 'sonata' model. However, these works can safely be placed outside the main tradition since their historical resonance was so slight.

quintets are similar, but if we turn to works for larger forces such as Beethoven's Septet, Op. 20, and Schubert's Octet, D. 803, we see that the number of movements tends to increase; those two works (the second is in fact a reworking of the motivic substance of the first, centred on the palindromic progression 8–7–(7)–8) both have two slow movements and a scherzo in addition to a minuet.

It is common to explain the fact that the '-ets' have supernumerary movements (taking four as the norm) by pointing to their light, 'divertimento' character. However, this is probably to confuse cause and effect. The reason for the general increase in a work's length (resulting, all other things being equal, in more movements) as the number of its players climbs may rest on nothing more profound than the ordinary conditions of music-making as experienced by those who practise it as a recreation rather than a duty. At one extreme we have the piano sonata, which has a value as private music enjoyed by the player even before it acquires any non-playing listeners. Here, short length can be a positive advantage, since it increases flexibility and eases the task of learning a new work. When four players come together to form a quartet—and here one must remember that until the public concert became the dominant forum of professional music-making quartets were ordinarily convened on an ad hoc basis by the leader)—it is essential to justify the effort by providing more substantial fare. This applies with even greater force to septets, octets, and nonets, which may require a unique line-up of players—in which case, having played through one composition, they cannot simply take out another.

Once the number of movements exceeds four, the problem of giving them sufficient variety of character arises. The easiest way is to make some of them 'light' (the Beethoven Septet and Schubert Octet both achieve this by turning one of the two slow movements into an undemanding set of variations). And once lightness gains a foothold, it is liable to infect the whole work; even Beethoven's Op. 130 (with its six movements) is not uniformly a 'heavy' work—which is one reason why the removal of the *Grosse Fuge* was well advised.

There are purely musical reasons, of course, why the string quartet emerged so quickly and, as it turned out, definitively as the main bearer of serious thoughts in the realm of chamber music. Writing in four parts, whether for voices or for instruments from the same family, represents a point of intersection where all vital musical desiderata can be achieved and none need be sacrificed: harmonic fullness or contrapuntal complexity can go hand in hand with transparency of texture; homogeneity of timbre with contrast of register; *concertante* individualism with blended sound.

Writing for a quartet of solo instruments, initially with continuo, first became common in the early eighteenth century. There are plenty of individual examples of four-part writing in the sonata literature of the seventeenth century, but these never coalesced into a recognizable practice. The early eighteenth-century quartet, which bore a multitude of titles (*sonata a quattro, quartetto, quadro*, etc.), came in two varieties, only one of which is truly ancestral to the modern string quartet. In the first, pioneered in France and cultivated there and also in Germany (where Quantz named it *quadro*) only up to the end of the Baroque period, the spirit and technique of the trio sonata are retained but the 'upper' instruments (i.e. those normally playing above the continuo bass) increase to become three instead of two. Most *quadri* use obbligato instruments chosen for their timbral and technical contrast (e.g. flute, violin, and bass viol). Good examples are by Dornel, Boismortier, and Guillemain in France, and, most notably, by Telemann in Germany.[25] Generally, *quadri* were styled as sonatas, although some take the form of chamber concertos or of *ouvertures*, as in the first of Telemann's three published collections (Hamburg, 1730), in which two examples of each 'genre' appear.

Telemann produced at least thirty-eight compositions of this type, but another twenty-seven quartets by him are for four-part strings including viola. The vital difference here is that the fourth part is not an equal-ranking obbligato part but a 'filler' that participates only rarely in the thematic discourse. This kind of quartet was taken up by other German (including Austrian) and Lombardic composers in the middle of the century and, with the continuo dropped and a minuet (or two) added, leads on to Haydn.

It was Haydn's quartets, with their superior artistry and greater clarity of style and purpose, which supplied the formative influence transmitted to later generations of composers and earned him the reputation of being the founder of the genre. There are some interesting and significant parallels between his choices of structural options in his quartets and his sonatas. Up to Op. 20 sonata form, usually on a smaller scale and with simpler methods of treatment than in first movements, dominates in finales. Then in Op. 33 (1781), the quartets claimed in Haydn's letter inviting subscriptions to be composed 'in a quite new, special manner', rondo (or sonata-rondo) and variation form suddenly topple sonata form from its pedestal.[26] In these movements lightness becomes a vehicle not for triviality but for wit, 'popular' elements, and special effects of all kinds. Arguments about what Haydn meant by his 'new manner' will doubtless continue, but the novel style of the Op. 33 finales would have been sufficient justification for the description.

In retrospect, this can be seen as a case of *reculer pour mieux sauter*. Variation form thereafter disappears from the menu (perhaps because it is required for slow movements and some opening movements). Rondo and

---

[25] The history of this genre is summarized in Michael Talbot, 'Vivaldi's *Quadro*? The Case of RV Anh. 66 Reconsidered', *Analecta musicologica*, forthcoming. The earliest *quadri* known to me are those of the Parisian organist Louis-Antoine Dornel (Op. 1, 1706, and the lost Op. 4, *c*.1715).

[26] Only the first quartet retains it; Nos. 2, 3, and 4 are rondos, while Nos. 5 and 6 are variation movements.

sonata-rondo form remain, but in a position subservient to sonata form. The experience of Op. 33 is not wasted, since in the later quartets there is considerable interchange between the traditional constituents of sonata-form and rondo-form movements. A rondo such as the finale of the Quartet in A major, Op. 55 No. 1, borrows from sonata form the idea of a fugal development (in lieu of a second couplet). A sonata-form movement such as the finale of the Quartet in D minor, Op. 76 No. 2 ('Fifths' Quartet), begins, like a rondo, with a self-contained refrain theme in binary form before proceeding normally. Such *rapprochement* would be better described as convergence than as hybridization since there is so little musical resistance to the combination of elements: through Haydn's genius, taxonomic affiliation is made to appear a pedantic detail irrelevant to meaning and effect.

Mozart's quartets are conventionally divided into two groups: the thirteen 'early' quartets stretching from K. 80/73f (1770) to K. 173 (1773) and the ten 'mature' quartets comprising the set of six published in 1785 with a dedication to Haydn as his Op. 10, the three 'King of Prussia' quartets, and the singleton, K. 499 ('Hoffmeister' Quartet). The finales of the first group are diverse, including short sonata-form movements, rondos, and even a couple of fugues (in K. 168 and K. 173) paying homage to the older composer's Op. 20. None is especially remarkable or meritorious, although some provide the first outings for motivic ideas taken up with more success later. On those of the second group the effect of age and experience is evident. Except for the variation movement in K. 428 (the D minor quartet from Op. 10), all are extended movements in sonata or sonata-rondo form. Whereas in the earlier group learned and 'popular' (*buffo* or folk-like) elements are kept apart—with the result that the first tends to dryness and the second to triviality—in the mature quartets they usually appear not separately but in juxtaposition and even in combination, as if each were intended by Mozart to keep in check the excesses of the other. The *buffo* humanizes the learned, which in turn civilizes it. The successful marriage of the two styles in the finale of K. 387 is universally acknowledged, but in a less overt manner the same felicitous combination occurs in those of K. 464, K. 499, and K. 575. On first hearing the two bars of the singing main theme of the K. 575 finale, shown as Ex. 8.3(*a*), it is hard to anticipate their intensive treatment as a contrapuntal *soggetto*, which begins in the exposition and reaches fever pitch in the development section, from which Ex. 8.3(*b*) is drawn (dynamics and marks of phrasing and articulation are omitted for greater clarity).

In the finales of Beethoven's sixteen quartets (not counting the separately published *Grosse Fuge*) every lesson offered by Haydn and Mozart is absorbed. But Beethoven invents a number of new ways of treating finales that deserve special mention.

The finale of the last Op. 18 quartet, in B flat major, is headed 'La Malinconia' ('Melancholy'). The label applies in particular to its long 'adagio' introduction, characterized by chromatic side-steps and an inverted-

Ex. 8.3. Mozart, String Quartet in D major, K. 575, last movement: (a) opening; (b) bars 136–43

turn figure, written out in grace notes, that presumably expresses gnawing disquiet. The main section, marked 'allegretto quasi allegro', is so bland and lacking in drama as to be a parody of the *rondo grazioso* tradition. But its banality works well in the programmatic context as the depiction of a cheerfulness that is merely external and mechanical. Inevitably, the 'adagio' returns, this time enclosing an abortive attempt to resuscitate the 'allegretto'. When the 'allegretto' finally breaks free, it is in the wrong key (G major) and has to struggle back to the tonic, which is symptomatic of the movement's tragicomic mood. The only problem with this finale is that the staged banality of the 'allegretto' theme is hard to distinguish from the artless banality that a Dittersdorf or a Diabelli might innocently have produced; Beethoven fails (perhaps he does not even try) to convince the listener of his critical distance from the material. Very different is the case of the two mottoes, respectively slow and fast, in the finale of the Quartet in F major, Op. 135. Both of them ('Muss es sein?' and 'Es muss sein!') are pithily comic, but they are carefully woven into a sonata-form movement of great sophistication, where they function as ornaments, not as prime substance. In this way, Beethoven preserves the mock-profound programmatic quality while conceding nothing as regards compositional finesse.

Each of the finales in Op. 59, the 'Rasumovsky' set, brings something special to the repertoire. In No. 1 (F major) it is the successful integration in a complex sonata-form movement of genuinely folkloristic material—the *thème russe*, which is the 'reference theme' for the whole quartet.[27] In No. 2 (E minor) it is the sustained off-tonic opening in C major of the refrain theme, whose return is always prepared as if this were indeed its key. (One might add here that the avoidance of the tonic or dominant chord at the start of a finale, whether or not the substituted chord is tonicized, plunges the listener *in medias res* and thereby connects the finale more firmly to whatever has preceded it. A similar, if less dramatic, effect is produced by the G in bare octaves opening the finale of the E flat quartet, Op. 127.) The fugato forming the first subject of the sonata-form finale of No. 3 (C major) introduces us to a new use of the fugal topos: not as an emblem of learning but as a vehicle for heroic (if garrulous) energy; the reduplicative nature of Beethoven's long-spun-out subject already prefigures, in miniature, the rhetorical *élan* that the passing of the theme through the instruments in turn will augment.

The initially understated, almost diffident, character of the variations closing the 'Harp' Quartet in E flat major, Op. 74, almost leads one to expect a 'valedictory' movement. However, Beethoven builds up speed by stages, and the end is more conventional than the beginning. Where the variations do break new ground is in their total renunciation of traditional virtuosic gestures: everything is subordinated to mood and expression. It is perhaps regrettable that this is the only variation finale in all the Beethoven quartets. Three more examples of the form having the same poetic emphasis (in Opp. 127, 131, and 135) are to follow—but these are all internal movements.

The finale of the 'Quartetto serioso' in F minor (Op. 95) seems planned to cock a snook at this august designation. Everything goes well up to the coda, since all the main themes are in the minor mode and uniformly elegiac in cast. Then the genie is suddenly let out of the box: the tempo is ratcheted up

---

[27] Appropriately, this movement (whose main theme begins on the submediant) provides a splendid early example of the 'Russian Sixth' identified by Mark DeVoto.

from 'allegretto agitato' to 'allegro', the mode switches to major, and with a gossamer lightness prophetic of Mendelssohn's scherzos the music races breezily to its close. The effect is totally subversive. One could invent a new label for this type of ending and call it a 'transformational coda'. The main point is not the increase in speed, which is common enough in Beethoven's codas, but the unanticipated reversal of mood. Only one other coda to a finale in the Beethoven quartets, that of Op. 132, seeks a comparable effect (again from elegiac minor to ebullient major): the speeded-up versions of principal thematic material in Op. 18 Nos. 4 and 6, Op. 59 No. 2, Op. 74, and Op. 127 intensify rather than negate the prevailing affect.

The finale of the C sharp minor quartet, Op. 131, is perhaps the most unusual, although its peculiarity is an aspect of the seven-movement cycle as a whole rather than of the individual movement. To explain why this is so, one has to refer to general principles governing the tonal 'circuit' of a movement as they operated between 1700 and 1900 (to draw these boundaries conservatively). Irrespective of whether a movement is placed in the home key of a work or in a foreign key, it normally sits at the 'hub' of its own tonal universe. That is, it visits the dominant, the relative major or minor key, the subdominant, and any other foreign keys in accordance with general custom or with its special needs. There is no reason in principle why the scale degrees visited in an internal movement in a foreign key should be different from those visited in an outer movement in the tonic.

Before the seventeenth century, during which the changeover occurred, the principles governing tonal relationships were different. The six alternative finals (equivalent to tonics) for any given key signature were all situated on the circumference, as it were, of a ring of modes. A movement in the Lydian mode could make cadences on scale degrees II, III, V, VI, and VII only; in the case of the Mixolydian mode, these became II, IV, V, VI, and VII. In modern language, one would say that a movement in one of these two modes has an inbuilt bias towards the 'sharp' or the 'flat' side, respectively (the Ionian mode would represent an intermediate, neutral setting).

In Op. 131 Beethoven resurrects the idea of a fixed group of primary tonal centres (we have already encountered this concept in the discussion of Mahler's First Symphony) that dominates each movement, regardless of the changing tonic. These centres are co-extensive with the keys that function as tonics for the movements, namely C sharp minor (movements 1 and 7), D major (movement 2), B minor and F sharp minor (movement 3), A major (movement 4), E major (movement 5), and G sharp minor (movement 6). Accordingly, the finale is severely biased towards the 'flat' side, reserving a prominent place for D major, B minor, and F sharp minor, which in a normally configured movement would be only marginal areas. The plagal cadence in C sharp minor (with *tierce de Picardie*) that ends the movement is strangely, and movingly, inconclusive, despite the vigour of its assertion:

there has simply been too much F sharp minor (and too little G sharp minor) for equilibrium to have been established. It would almost (but not quite) be appropriate to classify this movement as 'summative' on the grounds that it is by far the longest and most elaborately worked out of the seven and makes fullest use of the keys in the group.

Beethoven doubtless proceeded intuitively in making the tonal designs of the several movements so interdependent. The result is an unusually cohesive, inter-referenced work that looks forward not only to the 'cyclic' principle as applied in the later nineteenth century and subsequently but also to the concept of a large-scale work in a single movement.

The finale of Op. 131 makes clear allusions to the fugue subject of the opening movement—most appropriately, in view of their rounding effect, which is needed in such a long work. However, Beethoven's quartets, unlike his piano sonatas and symphonies, contain no unaltered 'flashbacks' to earlier movements in their finales. This step is first taken by Mendelssohn in his pair of early quartets, Op. 13 (A minor, 1824) and Op. 12 (E flat major, 1826). The first has a saccharine motto theme in A major based on one of the composer's own songs that provides both an introduction to the first movement and, slightly extended, a coda to the finale. The second reintroduces the main theme of the opening movement in the coda of a rather scrappy finale that veers puzzlingly between C minor and the tonic. In the next generation it becomes almost *de rigueur* for a quartet to refer back to first-movement material overtly or covertly. These references are subtle in Brahms's first two quartets, but in the third he very ingeniously brings back the 'hunting' theme from the first movement not at the very end but in the penultimate variation. This leaves time for the first-movement material to soak thoroughly into the finale, where it appears finally and fittingly as a counterpoint to the variation theme. Smetana, in his first, autobiographical, string quartet, reintroduces the lyrical second subject of his first movement in the tragic coda of his fourth movement (representing the effects of deafness). Perhaps with a little wisdom after the event, the same theme on its first outing is described in the composer's programme for the work as offering 'a presentiment of approaching misfortune'.

The ultimate realization of the recall of the opening as ending is a pure arch form such as ABCBA. One nineteenth-century quartet, the third (1849) by the Swedish composer Franz Berwald, exhibits precisely this form, where 'A' has first-movement character, 'B' slow-movement character, and 'C' scherzo character. Because of the run-on relationship between all of its movements, this concise work is arguably a one-movement structure—and its long-drawn-out transitional passages (which unfortunately overshadow the primary material) would support such a contention—but as an exercise in overall symmetry it certainly looks forward to the many similar essays in the twentieth century, among them Bartók's Fourth and Fifth String Quartets.

In the course of the twentieth century the string quartet has trodden many different paths. One of them has been miniaturization, either for the sake of concentration and extreme refinement (Webern, String Quartet, Op. 28, 1938) or in a deliberate attempt to 'decanonize' the genre (Stravinsky, *Three Pieces for String Quartet*, 1914). By and large, however, composers opting for the genre (a gesture towards tradition in itself) have stuck by the structural patterns established in the later nineteenth century. This will become clearer when we examine Shostakovich's fifteen quartets in Chapter 10.

## The Symphony

The crucial fact in the early history of the symphony was that it originated not as an autonomous instrumental genre but as a piece of instrumental music placed in front of a long vocal piece, usually an opera but sometimes an oratorio or a cantata. From the generation of Alessandro Scarlatti (1660–1725) onwards, it adopted the fast–slow–fast structure that soon became normative also for the concerto and, a little later, the sonata. Because it was not autonomous, ordinary considerations of balance did not apply. If the third movement was markedly shorter and lighter than the other two, this was in one respect a benefit, since it accelerated progress towards the start of the drama proper.

Reinhard Strohm has pointed out that although the *sinfonia avanti l'opera* did not—until the advent of Gluck and the gradual implementation of reforms that various commentators, including Johann Mattheson and Francesco Algarotti, had been advocating for several decades—seek to reflect or prepare for the peculiarities of the drama that it preceded, it was by no means insensitive to the general context in which it found itself. As Strohm puts it:

It is probably transparent that the three composers Pergolesi, Hasse and Vinci have similar conceptions of an opera sinfonia. What they all want to express is a generalized image of the most important subject matter and characters of the drama, hierarchically differentiated. The first movement presents the royal and male subject, the second a suffering female or a conflict with her or within her, and the third catches a glimpse of further characters and their backgrounds ... If the functions of the three movements were to be identified with dramaturgical terms, the first would be dedicated to the *soggetto* and the *ethos* of the leading character(s), the second to *pathos* and probably also *ethos* of the *prima donna*, and the third would mix *soggetto* and perhaps aspects of setting, *decorazione*; it might have a physical connection with the beginning of the drama itself. The first and last arias of certain characters, the beginnings and ends of Acts as well as of the opera, will be consciously placed to respond to the sinfonia.[28]

---

[28] Reinhard Strohm, *Dramma per musica: Italian Opera Seria of the Eighteenth Century* (New Haven and London, 1997), 246–7.

This is perhaps more elaborately described than it need be. The typical first movement (in addition to being a 'noise-killer' that quietens the audience) gives a foretaste of the noble, heroic affects that will be represented in the main body of the opera; the second movement expresses the pains, and perhaps the pleasures, of love, which is equally certain to be an ingredient of the plot; the last movement prefigures the mandatory *lieto fine*—in fact, its tonality, form, instrumentation, and melodic character often resemble those of the final *coro* in striking fashion, although Strohm is right also to speak of a possible link to the opening of the first act.

Sinfonias were valued for their own sake by opera-goers. This is evident from the large number of them that were purchased as separate items from Italian music copyists and survive today in libraries all over Europe and beyond. Once acquired independently, they could be performed independently as de facto 'chamber' symphonies (to use the term 'chamber' in its original, wide sense, which embraced virtually any music heard outside the church or the theatre). Composers were not slow to respond to the demand and supply free-standing sinfonias directly to their customers.[29] Doubtless, in the early days many were simply borrowed from existing dramatic works, but the purpose-written chamber symphony was certainly in existence in Lombardy and the Veneto by the 1730s.

The chamber symphony and the operatic sinfonia parted company definitively when the latter became, in the second half of the century, a one-movement form. Cut adrift from its old moorings, the symphony now became subject to the same criteria of balance and proportion as the instrumental genres that had always been independent. This meant, among other things, that the short, cheerful finale anticipating the opera's happy ending had instead to look back on the two preceding movements. Although it did not lose its 'light' character until the nineteenth century (and, in so far as the relaxant finale has never been off the agenda, has never lost it completely), the finale moved gradually to the position of near-equality with the first movement that the symphonies of Haydn and Mozart exhibit from the 1780s onwards. This trend towards equalization was initially accelerated, in the decades immediately preceding the 'rondomania' of the 1770s, by the adoption of binary form (evolving in due course into sonata form) by both movements.[30]

It was probably the chamber symphony, among the triad of 'three-movement' genres (symphony, sonata, concerto), that pioneered the insertion of a fourth movement, the minuet and trio.[31] This innovation took root first in

[29] Such are the five sinfonias by Benedetto Marcello inscribed to a certain 'Monsieur Drex' (perhaps a reference to a member of the landowning Drax family) in the British Library, Add. MS 31579.

[30] The original first-movement form of sinfonias had been similar to that of the *concerto a quattro*: a series of periods headed by statements of a motto presented successively in various keys. In contrast, finales always preferred binary form, symmetrical or rounded.

[31] The word 'insertion' is here essential, since the minuet, as a rondo or a variation movement, was from much earlier times a legitimate option as a third and final movement.

Austria. Italy and its musical satellites resisted it for some time, although, as one sees in Boccherini's later symphonies, it quite soon came round. North German critics and such composers as C. P. E. Bach also initially resented the minuet as an interloper that threatened to detract from the symphony's serious tone.[32] Indeed, the minuet did exactly that, but through Haydn's brilliant example the public was easily persuaded that such detraction had compensating virtues. Haydn himself produced no symphonies without minuets after 1765, and Mozart's 'Paris' (1778) and 'Prague' (1786) symphonies are isolated examples in his maturity. By the end of the century the symphonic minuet was triumphant internationally—perhaps the first feature invented in the German-speaking lands ever to become part of the universal language of Western music. From that time onwards, it is the three-movement symphony (of which those by César Franck, Rakhmaninov (No. 3), and Shostakovich (No. 6) spring to mind) that has to explain itself. Stravinsky's *Symphony in Three Movements* proves the point by drawing attention to the peculiarity in its title.

What was not quite settled was the position of the minuet. Should it come second or third? Third position was more normal, but in Haydn's case minuets in second place persist up to No. 68 (1779) before disappearing for good. In his four-movement chamber symphonies, Mozart only once (in K. 75) placed the minuet second (unlike his father Leopold, who frequently did this).[33] Beethoven followed the example of late Haydn (normally with scherzo substituted for minuet) until the Ninth Symphony, where the scherzo comes second.

The relocation of the minuet or scherzo to second position, and the slow movement to third, proved a popular option among composers of the Romantic symphony. It is not always easy to decide whether the composer of a given symphony determined the 'slot' for his scherzo first and then tailored the movement he wrote in accordance with the need to provide sufficient contrast (especially in relation to the basic pulse) to each of the movements, one slow and one fast, that flanked it, or whether the scherzo was written first and its position then determined pragmatically. If a useful rule of thumb can be formulated, it is that the faster the scherzo, the more likely it is to come second; minuets and similarly slowish movements (including some labelled 'scherzo') tend to come third. This principle clearly operates in Mendelssohn's five symphonies and also in Schumann's four, making allowance for the fact that in the latter's five-movement 'Rhenish' Symphony (No. 3) the so-called 'Scherzo', in second position, is a gentle *Ländler* that, together with a slow movement marked 'feierlich' (solemn), encloses an 'adagio espressivo' which is more animated than either.[34] Other

[32] See Wheelock, *Haydn's Ingenious Jesting with Art*, 45–6.

[33] Zaslaw, *Mozart's Symphonies*, 208–9, where the author points out that Mozart's string quartets and quintets (K. 464, 499, 515, and 516) are more flexible in this respect.

[34] Mendelssohn's chamber music follows the same pattern, with the notable exception of the Octet, in which the unfortunate similarity of pulse between scherzo and finale (highlighted

composers, however, are creatures of habit. Brahms and Gounod like to have the scherzo third, while several of the Russians (Borodin, Balakirev, Rakhmaninov) always place it second. Bruckner started out as a 'scherzo third' composer but deserted to the other camp in his last two symphonies. What one can definitely say is that having the extra movement and the choice of placing it in two alternative positions gives the composer greater flexibility in his choice of a basic pulse for the finale, which can, according to circumstances, be either slower or faster than that of the preceding movement.

Like the sonata and the quartet, the symphony passed through a phase, centring on the 1770s, in which alternatives to a sonata-form finale (rondo, variations, fugue) were very frequently employed. It is significant that the two variation movements in pre-1770 Haydn symphonies—in Nos. 72 and 31—are both finales. However, following the introduction of variation form to slow movements, which occurs first in No. 47 (1772), it is these rather than finales that come to be regarded by Haydn in his later symphonies as the form's natural locus. The rondo remains—albeit increasingly in a form rich in transitions, developments, and recapitulations that borders on sonata form. Fugue enjoys an initial vogue—Haydn is only one of several composers (the list includes Dittersdorf, Míča, Monn, Richter, Wagenseil, and Haydn's brother Michael) to cultivate it in finales—but after No. 70 (c.1779) it appears only in the guise of developmental fugal episodes (fugatos) embedded in larger sonata-form or rondo structures. By the time of the 'London' Symphonies, written in the first half of the 1790s, sonata and sonata-rondo forms are triumphant.

Mozart's symphonies follow Haydn's lead. There is, however, a special quality about his late symphonic finales that is missing in his older mentor. This is the similarity of their 'tone' (expressed concretely in tempo, metre, motivic and figurational design, patterns of orchestration, and many other features) to that of *opera buffa* overtures. No one can mistake the kinship between the overture to *Le nozze di Figaro* and the finale of his Symphony No. 35 in D major ('Haffner'), or between the main section of the overture to *Die Zauberflöte* and the finale of Symphony No. 39 in E flat major.[35] What is interesting here is that although the one-movement operatic overture is by origin a symphonic first movement bereft of its original sequels, it has

rather than redeemed by the quotation) shows by negative example why the principle of sufficient contrast is so important.

[35] Wheelock (*Haydn's Ingenious Jesting with Art*, 117–25) examines the case of a Haydn overture in D major (Hob. Ia/7) that was pressed into service both as an opening movement of a symphony (to No. 62) and as the finale of one version of another (No. 53, the 'Imperial'). The author argues (p. 117) that the use of basically the same material in two different symphonic contexts suggests 'that in function and style there was little to distinguish an opening from a closing movement'. This is put a little too radically. What is important is that in its actual context the movement is 'weighty' vis-à-vis the finale in the first, 'light' vis-à-vis the first movement in the second. Its *mezzo carattere* allows it to serve both purposes successfully.

acquired, in an *opera buffa* (not, however, *opera seria*) context, the stylistic attributes of a symphonic finale. It marries first-movement form to finale content.[36] Or (looking at the similarity from the other perspective): the symphonic finale has taken on operatic traits. In Mozart's case, this was obviously a natural process of convergence in which neither side (symphonic or operatic) dominated.

It is a truism to say that Beethoven's symphonies begin where Haydn's leave off. His first two symphonies are distinctive for their scale and 'tone' rather than their overall conception and use of form. Even some of the subsequent symphonies (Nos. 4, 7, and 8) can be said to 'play' with the Haydn model (especially through applying extremes of compression and expansion to individual components of the forms) rather than to alter it fundamentally. This group of five relatively normal symphonies, which includes both 'light' (Nos. 1, 4, and 8) and 'heavy' (Nos. 2 and 7) finales, provided models for the more conservative nineteenth-century symphonists, beginning with Spohr and Weber, and continuing with Mendelssohn and the Leipzig school.

As we have seen, the 'Eroica' presents both an unusual form (variations 'beefed up' with connective and developmental passages) and an unusual scale. Neither factor takes away its relaxant character in the context of the whole work, and this symphony can be regarded as the godparent of all later symphonies (Brahms's Fourth is one example) that attempt to differentiate the form of the outer movements to the maximum extent, while giving them similar weight and scale.

Although not often regarded as among the most seminal of Beethoven's symphonies, the 'Pastoral' (No. 6) can claim to have opened up several new vistas in the symphonic tradition. It has a programme (of the 'set of tableaux' variety) and evokes the outdoor world with a new-found Romantic sensibility. Its finale is probably the most uniformly lyrical movement of its type composed up to then (1808) and on that account is a precursor of the valedictory finale, in which lyricism is inevitably a major ingredient. Perhaps the most interesting feature of the Sixth Symphony is the concentration of local colour (we need not distinguish here between 'national' and 'exotic') in its finale. This colour is anticipated in the alternate section in 2/4 of the scherzo-like third movement ('Joyous Meeting of Peasants'), not only in the yodels of the main theme but also in its counter-motif (beginning on first flute in bar 173), which seems to be based on a fragment from a *Ranz des vaches* different from the one on which the finale theme is based.[37] Only in the finale, however, is the folk material absolutely dominant. There is

[36] Significantly, however, there are usually no repeats in the overture—a structural feature more common at the time in finales than in first movements.

[37] This *Ranz* (from a print of 1710 ) is reproduced in A. H. King, 'Mountains, Music and Musicians', *Musical Quarterly*, 31 (1945), 395–419, opposite p. 401. To my knowledge, the borrowing has not been noticed before, even by King.

undeniably an implicit hermeneutic message when a composer introduces borrowed material in a last movement: he utilizes the property of regression (the creation of, or reversion to, simpler shapes and processes ), found to some degree in almost any finale, in order to reveal a naive primal source that latently supports the whole edifice of art music and can even be regarded as superior to it in the sense that it appears, in retrospect, to be its precondition. This hermeneutic effect is naturally magnified if this primal material has social, religious, or national affiliations. As its children the 'Pastoral' Symphony can count such works as Mendelssohn's 'Reformation' Symphony (1832), Tchaikovsky's Second Symphony ('Little Russian', 1872), Dvořák's Ninth Symphony ('From the New World', 1893), Nielsen's Third Symphony (*Sinfonia espansiva*, 1911: its songlike finale evokes the world of patriotic Danish art song, as exemplified by the composer's own *Den danske sang*), and Schulhoff's Third Symphony (1935: here, the finale recalls the 'mass song' of the Communist movement).

Most influential of all Beethoven's symphonies was, of course, the Ninth. Its choral finale has always been the most discussed of its movements, from both an aesthetic and an analytical point of view. Recent analytical inspection has yielded contradictory results. For some commentators, it conforms freely to a sonata-form pattern.[38] For others, it reproduces within a single movement an entire four-movement plan.[39] For James Webster, its form is 'polyvalent': that is, its structure appears different according to the parameter studied.[40] I remain convinced, however, that the best model for mapping it is variation form. It is, in fact, a reincarnation of the 'Eroica' finale, with even more introductory, developmental, and episodic material, and, of course, the complication of added solo and choral voices. In saying this, I am restating the position taken in 1947 by Dika Newlin, whose remarks on the Ninth Symphony finale I find very convincing. Newlin wrote:

Beethoven's conception, which it is most important to establish correctly here since it has often been misapprehended, is a rigidly and abstractly musical one. The formal principles and thematic material of the Finale of the Ninth Symphony are laid down along instrumental symphonic lines before the voices appear; we are presented with a finale in variation-form which (with the exception of the recitative) would be of

[38] See e.g. Ernest H. Sanders, 'Form and Content in the Finale of Beethoven's Ninth Symphony', *Musical Quarterly*, 50 (1964), 59–76, and Leo Treitler, 'History, Criticism, and Beethoven's Ninth Symphony', *19th Century Music*, 3 (1979–80), 193–210.

[39] This interpretation is made in Ernest F. Livingstone (1971), 'Das Formproblem des 4. Satzes in Beethovens 9. Symphonie', in *Bericht über den Internationalen Musikwissenschaftlichen Kongress Bonn 1970*, ed. Carl Dahlhaus *et al.* (Kassel, 1971), 494–7. Treitler offers the four-movement model as an alternative to that of a single sonata-form movement (see preceding footnote), and the four-movement scheme is upheld in David B. Levy, *Beethoven: The Ninth Symphony* (New York, c.1995).

[40] James Webster, 'The Form of the Finale of Beethoven's Ninth Symphony', *Beethoven Forum*, 1 (1992), 25–62.

equal validity as a purely instrumental piece. The way in which the voices are handled can be explained logically in this way alone... Beethoven did not approach the problems of this movement from the vocal viewpoint; had he done so, the history of the Ninth Symphony and of its subsequent influence would have been a far different one.[41]

What Newlin seems to be saying is that this is almost a case of music set to words, rather than the other way round. Although Schiller's text is not irrelevant or inapposite, it is more important for what it represents in the abstract (exalted, liberating thoughts) than for what it consists of concretely in terms of a series of stanzas forming a poem that contains an argument. It could be likened, as a cumulative device, to the piccolo, double-bassoon, and trombones that emerge unexpectedly in the finale of the Fifth Symphony.

As Newlin observed, not all the composers who believed they were following the precedent set by Beethoven in their symphonic works using voices in fact did so. Mendelssohn's *Lobgesang* is a genuine cantata (in itself no more symphonic than his *Die erste Walpurgisnacht*) that happens to have three purely orchestral movements as an extended prelude. Similarly with Berlioz's 'dramatic symphony' *Roméo et Juliette*, which, notwithstanding its interspersed instrumental movements, resembles a real symphony no more closely than his 'dramatic legend' *La Damnation de Faust*. Newlin makes a partial exception for Mahler, whose writing for chorus in the finale of the 'Resurrection' Symphony shows the same subordination to symphonic form as Beethoven's movement.

If more evidence were needed that the finale of the Ninth Symphony remains, in a fundamental way, 'instrumental', it could be found in those many summative finales without vocal participation that it inspired, starting with Bruckner's Third Symphony. Although we have argued that the finale of Beethoven's Fifth Symphony is also summative, the relatively compact dimensions of this work in all its movements and the concentration of the finale's summative elements in its coda make it a less potent model for the future than the Ninth. Undoubtedly, the 'untidiness', the episodic character, of the Ninth Symphony's finale (a feature that we have identified earlier, in another context, with the sacrifice of movement-level objectives to work-level ones) is its most forward-looking quality—not the inclusion of voices *per se*.

The perceived failure of Beethoven to solve the finale 'problem', even when he so conspicuously addressed it in his Ninth Symphony, was the starting point for Paul Bekker's identification of a distinct 'Austrian' school of symphonists (Schubert–Bruckner–Mahler) in the post-Beethoven era. His chapter 'Der symphonische Stil' (from *Gustav Mahlers Sinfonien*) makes curious reading today; its dogmatism, excessively teleological outlook,

---

[41] Newlin, *Bruckner, Mahler, Schoenberg*, 157.

ethnocentricity, extravagant language, and willingness to contort facts in order to make them fit the grand simplicities of a handful of governing ideas are all repellent.[42] Nevertheless, Bekker's ideas, which have remained influential in some quarters up to more recent times, contain many useful insights.

Bekker's first postulate is that Beethoven's symphonies represented not a starting point but a dead end. He distinguishes three schools of symphonists in the German *Kulturraum* (no other is taken into account) active in the decades following Beethoven. The first, described as Central German, Romantic, and bourgeois, embraces Mendelssohn, Schumann, Brahms, and unnamed *Akademiker*. Bekker taxes this group with having diminished and trivialized the symphony with pictorial and literary accretions; he labels their work 'unsymphonic'. The second group, that of the programme symphonists, comprises principally Liszt and Strauss. Bekker notes approvingly that this group developed the monumental aspect of the symphony but accuses it of allowing the genre too easily to degenerate into illustrative music. He views the predilection for one-movement forms as an evasion rather than a solution of the symphonic problem. Salvation arrives, however, in the third group, the Austrian symphonists, who are identified as the triad Schubert–Bruckner–Mahler. These symphonists reject programmes in favour of a simple expression of feeling. In their hands the symphony becomes a vehicle neither for humanism (as in Beethoven) nor for a 'speculative ethic' (as in the Central Germans) but for a pantheistic nature worship. In successive stages they transfer the weight of the symphony from the front to the end, so achieving the genuine *Finalsymphonie* that had eluded—despite their best efforts and clear signs of awareness of the problem—the Central Germans. Bekker describes Schubert as the 'herald', Bruckner as the 'strongest elemental power', and Mahler as the 'achiever' (*Vollender*).

Schubert is praised for his freedom and boldness (with reference to his last two symphonies); he 'storms past' Beethoven instead of treading in his footsteps. Bekker highlights Schubert's simple joy in music (*Musikfreudigkeit*) and the popular (*volkstümlich*) elements in his style. This, he argues, is a non-logical music: a symphonic manner of becoming and germinating ('eine Symphonik des Werdens und Keimens') in which the final goal is not predetermined but discovered as the music proceeds. In Bruckner's hands, the first movement takes on a preparatory (therefore non-prescriptive) character, which is a step in the right direction, but the composer's intention to achieve a grand climax in the finale founders for two reasons: first, the 'adagio' (Bekker is thinking in particular of the last two symphonies, where this movement comes third) is treated so monumentally that it cannot but overshadow any sequel; second, the finale is too repetitive of the spirit and material of the first movement.

[42] Bekker, *Gustav Mahlers Sinfonien*, 11–34.

In this author's eyes, Mahler creates a successful *Finalsymphonie* on each of the nine occasions. Bekker divides the symphonies into three categories. Those in category 1, comprising symphonies 1, 6, and 8, evince a straight-line progression towards a climactic finale. Category 2 contains the four symphonies (Nos. 2, 3, 5, and 7) in which there is no ascent to the finale: instead, the diverse middle movements, suite-like in their relative brevity and lightness, are 'camped around' the focal finale ('um das Finalzentrum gelagert'). The symphonies in category 3 (Nos. 4 and 9) occupy a middle position; here, the finale offers an empirical resolution without constituting an actual climax.

To pick holes in Bekker's argument and entire system of classification is only too easy. He asserts, without arguing the case, that there was a single 'necessary' direction for the post-Beethoven symphony to follow—their failure to choose this path is the only criticism of substance he levels against the Central Germans and the programme symphonists. He places the three groups in absurdly watertight compartments: who could deny Schubert's indebtedness to Beethoven (consider, for instance, the links between Beethoven's Seventh Symphony and Schubert's Ninth) or that of Mendelssohn, Schumann, and Brahms to the Austrian composer? And can one really discount Bruckner's and Mahler's direct indebtedness to Beethoven? Bekker's typology of Mahler symphonies is tendentious, to say the least. For a writer who insists on process (a quintessentially temporal feature), what sense does it make to introduce the purely spatial imagery of a circle of encamped movements, as if a second and a fourth movement were placed on different sides of a finale? How can Mahler's Fourth Symphony be a *Finalsymphonie* when its sunny last movement takes at most half as long to play as either its first or its third movement?[43]

Nevertheless, some of Bekker's points strike home, particularly if interpreted less exclusively and dogmatically. He is right to detect a special 'tone' (*volkstümlich*, expansive, open-air) in the Austrian—provincial rather than Viennese—tradition. It is also undeniable that the three members of the Austrian group treat formal schemata with unusual freedom (I would relate this freedom in particular to the blurring of lines of demarcation between expository (or recapitulatory) and developmental sections). Finally, there is no doubt that the incidence of end-weighting, and of summative finales, is generally higher in Bruckner and Mahler (if not yet in Schubert) than in their Central German counterparts. Twentieth-century developments in the symphony are harder to summarize on account of the individualism, responsiveness to passing fashion, and eclecticism that characterizes all artistic production in more recent times. Three trends, perhaps, can be singled out. The first is organicism: the attempt to make of the symphony

---

[43] Our standard typology of finales works very well for Mahler's symphonies. The finales in Nos. 4, 5, and 7 are relaxant; those in Nos. 1, 2, 6, and 8, summative; those in Nos. 3 and 9, valedictory.

an exemplary demonstration of 'profound logic'. Sibelius stands as father-figure to this tendency, one of whose symptoms is a preference for single-movement form (or at any rate a reduction in the number of movements). The second is neo-Classicism. No significant composer has created an entire corpus of neo-Classical symphonies, but several have visited the terrain at least once: Prokofiev (No. 1, 'Classical', 1917, and arguably also No. 7, 1952); Nielsen (No. 6, *Sinfonia semplice*, 1925); Stravinsky (*Symphony in C*, 1940, and *Symphony in Three Movements*, 1945); Kodály (1961). The largest, and in historical terms most important, tendency could be described as 'na-tionalistic-humanistic' or 'humanistic-populistic'. It includes symphonies by Americans (Chávez, Copland, Harris, Piston), Britons (Vaughan Wil-liams), Central Europeans (Henze, Honegger, Martinů, Schulhoff, Weill), and, of course, Russians (Myaskovsky, Prokofiev, Shostakovich). As far as the treatment of finales is concerned, the first camp inclines to the summa-tive, the second to the relaxant (almost a *sine qua non*), and the third to no particular type.

## The Concerto

The concerto shares with the suite the position of having opted for a particular kind of finale (again, the relaxant) early on in its history and having remained faithful to it ever since. Indeed, the formula for a relaxant finale that crystallized only a few decades after the concerto came into existence not only served the same genre as a model right up to modern times but also prefigured the kind of finale adopted half a century later in the sonata, quartet, and symphony. Similarly, the concerto adopted a three-movement plan sooner than any other genre, and thereafter adhered to it more rigidly.

By origin, the instrumental concerto was a specialized, progressive var-iety of sonata. Initially, its only point of distinction was that it was designed especially for performance with many instruments (normally, strings) to a part: an 'orchestral' performance, as we would call it today. Specifically orchestral music was being written from at least the 1660s onwards in Italy and France; the first works identified as concertos on which a date (at least, a date of publication) can be set are those published in the Op. 5 (*Sinfonie a tre e concerti a quattro*, 1692) and Op. 6 (*Concerti musicali*, 1698) of Giuseppe Torelli (1658–1708), a composer active in Bologna and for a time in Ansbach, whose historical importance for the emergent genre was attested by Johann Joachim Quantz.[44]

What strikes one about these pioneering concertos is the relative weak-ness of the differentiation between the finale and the one (or sometimes two)

---

[44] According to Quantz, Torelli was reputed to have written the first concertos (*Versuch einer Anweisung, die Flöte traversière zu spielen* (Berlin, 1789[3]), 294).

earlier quick movements.[45] All employ the same structural principle (the 'motto' form mentioned earlier), but the finales tend to be on a more generous scale, developing their material more extensively, than the preceding quick movement or movements—Torelli's fast first movements, in particular, often have a pithy, breathless character, and a less continuous manner of musical development. In other words, these early Torelli concertos show a slight end-weighting. As yet, solo passages are rare (*concerto a quattro* is the name typically given at this time to a work for orchestral strings in four parts without soloist), and where they occur, for colouristic purposes or in order to demonstrate virtuosity, such episodes make minimal impact on the chosen structure.

However, pressures for the adoption of a more obviously relaxant type of finale soon made themselves felt in the concerto, drawing inspiration from the chamber sonata and even more strongly from the operatic sinfonia. The symptoms of this evolution are a preference for 'short' metre, binary form, dance rhythm, and compact dimensions. The first clear sign of these influences appears in the six concertos included in the Op. 2 of Tomaso Albinoni (*Sinfonie e concerti a cinque*, 1700).[46] This composer had, by the turn of the century, established himself as a member of the leading group of operatic composers active in Venice, and the references to the idiom of the sinfonia were doubtless a conscious stylistic allusion. In the finales concerned, 'motto' form is abandoned in favour of a concise binary form. This form remains, for the rest of the Baroque period, an available option for a concerto finale. Albinoni himself does not employ it again until Op. 10 (*c.*1735), but many composers in Italy and elsewhere turn to it on occasion, especially in *concerti a quattro*, where no need to separate *solo* and *tutti* arises. (We saw, however, that binary form can be adapted very successfully to produce alternate *solo* and *tutti* passages, as concertos by Vivaldi and many other composers show.)

Albinoni becomes a pioneer again in his Op. 5 (*Concerti a cinque*, 1707), where each of the twelve finales is a fugue with *concertante* episodes for the principal violin. I am drawing a rigorous distinction here between the use of fugato in *tutti* sections, which is a common occurrence in the early concerto and remains so even after the adoption of fully-fledged ritornello form, and the casting of the movement as a fugue *per se*. The compatibility of fugue with the relaxant model has been explained in Chapter 4, and the argument does not need repetition, but it is worth noting that these finales are perhaps the first examples in musical history of the use of this form as a specific 'marker' for a finale. Albinoni himself, Vivaldi, Valentini, J. S. Bach, Handel,

---

[45] The three-movement plan (F–S–F) is occasionally encountered in the first generation of concertos but becomes normative in north Italian concertos (i.e. excluding those of Corelli, his Roman colleagues, and his foreign imitators) only after *c.*1700.

[46] Albinoni's concertos are discussed in greater detail in my *Tomaso Albinoni: The Venetian Composer and his World* (Oxford, 1990).

Telemann, and Leclair were among the composers of concertos subsequently to cultivate the fugal finale, but the practice did not persist past the end of the Baroque period.

The 'classic' Baroque concerto was created by Vivaldi, who is central to our discussion in view of his key position in the history of the concerto and vast and varied output of these works. Despite his readiness to experiment and produce, on occasion, the unexpected, Vivaldi's basic conception of the finale in relation to the first fast movement (which is normally the opening movement) is very clear and consistent. The two movements almost always share a form, ritornello form, in which (to simplify greatly) tonally closed *tutti* sections based on a common fund of thematic material alternate with tonally open *solo* sections where one or more soloists develop new or loosely derived material. As a rule, the finale almost matches the first movement for weight, complexity of construction, and duration—but not quite. The average difference is less than one would encounter between the first and last movements of a late Haydn symphony, but is nevertheless perceptible.[47] A good sample of concertos to examine in relation to this question is provided by the forty-two works contained in the five published collections running from Op. 8 (1725) to Op. 12 (1729), which represent Vivaldi during the period of his maximum productivity and greatest stability of style. The choice of metres already expresses the general tendency. Eleven concertos—over a quarter—cast the two fast movements in common time and 3/4 metre respectively; nine have common time followed by 2/4 metre; eight have common time followed by 3/8 metre. Of the other nine combinations, only common time plus common time, with three examples, and common time plus 12/8 metre and 2/4 metre plus 3/4 metre, both with two examples, occur more than once.

The disparity of weight between the outer movements is actually no greater than was the case in Torelli's early concertos, but now operates in favour of the first movement. The fact that it is not pronounced allows Vivaldi, when he so wishes, to 'mirror' in the finale tonal or other processes adopted in the finale.[48] Imitators of Vivaldi active during the second, third, and fourth decades of the century largely followed his formula. We find it again in Bach, Leclair, Telemann, and a host of minor composers. The range of structural options for a finale widens during these years. Ritornello form

[47] That Vivaldi considered last and first movements to be fundamentally different in kind is shown by the fact that, although he was an inveterate self-borrower who often 'cannibalized' one work to use individual movements from it in another, first movements are always substituted for other first movements, and finales for finales. Conversely, when a first movement and a finale open with the same theme—this applies to the sinfonia RV 147 (finale) and the *concerto a quattro* RV 150 (first movement)—the continuation is always different. See also Ch. 4 n. 41.

[48] In his minor-key works Vivaldi sometimes 'inverts' the tonal curve so that the subdominant stands in place of the usual dominant. Where this occurs in the first movement, it is quite likely to recur in the finale.

remains the clear favourite, but in addition to binary form and fugue we now occasionally encounter variation form (either sectional or continuous, as in the chaconne) and also—in the German, if not yet the Italian, concerto—the rondo. Bach, eccentrically, uses a da capo form derived from vocal models in a few finales, including that of the Sixth 'Brandenburg' Concerto.

In the 1740s, however, the disparity of weight begins to widen noticeably, marking a change of aesthetic that will reach fruition in the Classical concerto. The relative enlargement of the sinfonia finale and the relative reduction of the concerto finale produce an interesting phenomenon of convergence in the middle of the century. Quantz's recommended timings for the movements of a concerto, which prescribe five minutes for the first movement, five to six for the slow movement, and three to four for the finale, correspond well to the new approach taken by the *galant* age. It is difficult to divine precisely what the motor of this change was. It may be simply that the more expansive treatment now generally applied to ritornello form (requiring, for example, a greatly enlarged opening *tutti*) could not be reproduced twice in one work without increasing the total duration unacceptably.

As noted earlier, the rise of Paris as a publishing and concert-giving centre in the mid-eighteenth century had a general 'gallicizing' effect, one consequence of which was to confirm the new-found desire for a more pronounced lightness in the finale by substituting rondo form—the French form par excellence—for the traditional ritornello form.[49] In the violin concerto, which until Mozart was the dominant species of concerto, the fashion for rondo finales dates from around 1770.[50] From the Classical period onwards, the concerto adheres not only more consistently but also more exactly than the symphony to the relaxant model. There have hardly ever been concerto finales that storm the heights in the fashion of Beethoven's Fifth and Ninth Symphonies (Brahms perhaps comes closest, in his First Piano Concerto) or that fade away gently like Tchaikovsky's *Symphonie pathétique* (but Berg's Violin Concerto, conceived as a Requiem for Manon Gropius, is the outstanding example to the contrary).

We should pause at this point to consider why a relaxant—indeed, often ultra-relaxant—type of finale should have become so normative in concertos from the Classical period onwards. The obvious answer is probably a sufficient one: the guiding principle of a solo concerto is the demonstration of individual virtuosity, which is predominantly elaborative, not developmental, in nature. This is enough to rule out the summative option.

[49] A few German concertos of the late Baroque period already substitute rondo for ritornello form in their finales. The best-known example is the third movement of Bach's Violin Concerto in E major, BWV 1042.

[50] See Chappell White, *From Vivaldi to Viotti: A History of the Early Classical Violin Concerto* (Philadelphia, 1992), 83–7. White names François Barthélemon in Paris and Felice Giardini in London as pioneers of the change.

Although lyrical expression is also part of the virtuoso's equipment and has its necessary place in the concerto (primarily, of course, in the slow movement), it is not a defining characteristic and cannot be allowed to prevail at the work's close, so removing the valedictory option. *Faute de mieux*, the relaxant option alone remains.

Its traditionally light finale, most often in some kind of rondo form, has in the past sometimes proved an obstacle to the aesthetic appreciation of the concerto among serious music-lovers. The objection is that the finale 'lets the side down'. Even Cuthbert Girdlestone, whose book on Mozart's piano concertos is a classic of taxonomic clarity and musical insight, regrets that this composer did not go even more against the trend of his time. He first makes a rather sweeping general point (which is really only a restatement of received opinion on the finale 'problem' as this was conceived in the mid-twentieth century):

It is seldom that the finale of a work is the equal of the andante and the opening allegro. How often are we obliged to own that the last movements of works whose first movements had pleased us have left us dissatisfied! This does not apply to one single age; it is common to all, and to all composers from the 17th century to our own days...Generally speaking, it remains true that a composer, for one reason or another, does not reach in his finales the height of his andantes and allegros.[51]

Next, he considers the Classical period in particular:

At the time of Mozart and Beethoven the inferiority of the finale was deliberate. A *galant* public must have listened with difficulty to music whose character was unremittingly serious; it felt more than we do the need for contrast, and two serious movements on end were no doubt enough...The frankly superficial character of the finale is therefore intentional with *galant* composers.[52]

A tension becomes evident here between Girdlestone's *persona* as a historian, who wishes to understand why things had to be as they were, and his *persona* as a critic, who adopts the aesthetic values of his own age. The two approaches remain compartmentalized and unreconciled. One benefit of the move towards, and eventual privileging of, 'historically informed' performance in the late twentieth century has been to stimulate 'historically informed' reception. Today, we do not in any way deny the possibility of a trivial or over-light finale, but we at least make the effort to empathize with the *Zeitgeist* of an earlier age and to adjust our aesthetic lenses accordingly. We would no longer attempt, as Girdlestone did, to make a tally, among the instrumental works of Mozart's 'great' (i.e. Viennese) period, of finales that were 'merely recreative', ones which 'rose above' this basic level, and ones which were 'in no wise inferior to the opening allegros'.[53]

---

[51] Cuthbert M. Girdlestone, *Mozart's Piano Concertos* (London, 1958²), 47.
[52] Ibid.
[53] Girdlestone (p. 48) counts 111 works in all, of which 'about forty' are placed in the second category and 'a score' (including the piano concertos K. 453, 466, 488, 491, and 503) in the third.

Whatever his ultimate aesthetic reservations, Girdlestone at least grants Mozart's rondos credit for giving their composer occasion to show himself 'at his greatest as master of form'.[54] Focusing on the piano concertos, he points out the complexity and variety of their structure, mentioning poly-thematic refrains and couplets, contrapuntal episodes, genuine development of material, couplets and codas in contrasting tempo or metre, suppression of the refrain (especially between the second and third couplet), unusual dispositions of *solo* and *tutti*, quiet endings, and many other notable things.

In a way, both the first movements, which retain the ritornello form inherited from the Baroque concerto but little by little are steering it in the direction of sonata form, and the rondo finales are alike in that they are clearly sectionalized forms in which development takes second place to statement.[55] This is a simple consequence of the need to keep dialogue (or even opposition) between soloist and orchestra to the fore. Development is too integrated a musical process to maintain a strong presence in a concerto, although Mozart usually does his best to maximize it within the constraints.

One might even argue that by employing artifice of many kinds to raise his concerto finales above triviality, Mozart achieves a greater effect than if they had been 'naturally' elevated. This is the obverse of the situation of the 'Turkish military band' variation in the finale of Beethoven's Ninth Sym-phony (or, less drastically, of its counterpart in the 'Eroica' Symphony, the G minor variation), where the unprepared coarsening of tone makes the sham-banality more evident and more powerful in its effect. If nothing else, Mozart's concerto finales show that a choice of 'tone' is not in itself a passport to musical greatness or insignificance: it is merely a background against which the real determining factors, the composer's musical imagin-ation and mastery of his material, come into play.

One interesting feature of the finales of Mozart's piano concertos (and of those by his contemporaries, including Haydn) is their preference for open-ing with the soloist, either entirely unaccompanied or (less often) lightly accompanied.[56] The choice is significant, since neither rondo nor variation form makes this normative—if anything, the rondo favours a *tutti* opening,

---

Predictably, both minor-key concertos (K. 466 and 491) and both concertos with variation finales (K. 453 and 491) belong to the last category. The 111 finales comprise, according to Girdlestone, seventy-six in rondo (including sonata-rondo) form, eighteen in sonata-form, and seventeen in variation or minuet form.

[54] Ibid.

[55] What used to be called (according to a sonata-form schema) the 'first', 'preliminary', or 'orchestral' exposition is simply the opening ritornello, which in scale and complexity dwarfs all subsequent ritornello statements—as is seen already happening in Vivaldi's last concertos and in those of his immediate successors, such as Locatelli and Tartini.

[56] The finales to Mozart's twenty-three original piano concertos comprise ten that open with the orchestra (the soloist acting only as continuo accompanist), ten that open with the unac-companied soloist, and three in which the soloist is lightly accompanied by the orchestra. Each type occurs throughout Mozart's career, but there is a preponderance of 'unaccompanied solo' openings from No. 14 (K. 456) onwards.

since the traditional home for extended solos was the couplets. The rationale for a solo opening is probably to be found in the most general principles governing final movements, which were discussed in the opening chapter of this book. To open with the soloist confers immediacy—the sense of continuing, rather than initiating, something. It is the absence of preceding music that makes this option so rare in a first movement: Beethoven's solo opening in his Fourth Piano Concerto in G major, Op. 58, is striking and unsettling precisely because it thrusts intimacy on us *ex nihilo*.

Resisting the temptation to dwell on some particular finale in a Mozart concerto (of which a few examples have been mentioned in earlier pages), we turn now to Beethoven.

Beethoven's importance for the concerto in general is undisputed—for one thing, his last three piano concertos complete the transmutation of ritornello form into sonata form—but as far as finales are concerned, there is not so much to say. All are well-developed sonata-rondo movements that brilliantly express Beethoven's temperament and technical prowess (especially in relation to the use of the left hand) in a structure left unaltered from Mozart. One sign of things to come, however, is the run-on relationship between the last two movements in the same three concertos. In the Third Concerto, although there is no formal link, an immediate transition is needed to connect the G sharp at the end of the slow movement with its enharmonic equivalent, A flat, at the start of the third. Similarly in the Fourth Concerto, where E acts as the pivotal note between the last chord of the 'andante con moto' and the first chord (on the subdominant degree) of the 'vivace'. In the Fifth Concerto the link is made explicit and combined with the 'false starts' device employed in the First Symphony.

It is an observable fact that the concerto has from the time of Beethoven onwards been more hospitable to run-on relationships between movements (whether between the last two movements alone or between all of them) than the symphony: one need think only of Mendelssohn's two piano concertos and his Violin Concerto, or of Schumann's Piano Concerto, to appreciate the point. One may ask: why the difference?

The idea that there is a deep structural significance in these joins can be discounted immediately. Although the dovetailing is often very neat, with one movement 'emerging' out of its predecessor, it hardly ever affects our perception of the form decisively. A better reason can be sought in what one might term the 'rhetoric' of the concerto. The soloist, acting as the protagonist of a narrative, demands our focused attention in a way that a musical argument diffused among the community of orchestral instruments does not. To preserve this attention and keep the narrative running as continuously as possible is obviously a prime objective that may well account for the popularity of inter-movement links in the concerto.

A by-product of this linkage between movements is the possibility of miniaturizing scale without making the individual units appear excessively fragmentary. The typical duration of a concerto in late Mozart and Beethoven is between twenty and thirty minutes. This order of length, which corresponds closely to that of a four-movement symphony of the same period, is about the most a three-movement plan can sustain without tiring the soloist. During the nineteenth century the average length of symphonies increased considerably. A few composers of concertos chose to follow the same path. The four-movement 'symphonic' concertos of Henry Litolff (1818–91), complete with scherzos, are genuine 'symphonies with a principal piano part' (to borrow Spohr's epithet for Mozart's concertos). Cast somewhat in the same mould are the two piano concertos of Brahms (the second of which also has a scherzo) and similar works by his successors D'Albert, Dohnányi, Busoni, and Pfitzner.[57] But the symphonicizing urge was foredoomed. For a start, a 'genre' movement such as a scherzo can find it hard to achieve sufficient contrast with both of its neighbours if it is made subject to an identical *concertante* mode of treatment (a simple F–S–F plan runs less risk of this). And the problem of physical or aural fatigue remains.

In contrast, miniaturization—de-symphonicization, one might call it—allows the composer more easily to increase the number of movements or relatively autonomous sections and thereby gain variety. Weber's *Konzertstück* in F minor for piano and orchestra (J. 282, 1821), which has four linked movements (with a slow transition between the last two), and his even earlier concertinos for clarinet (J. 109, 1811) and horn (J. 188, 1806/1815) are pioneering examples of this species of miniature concerto. They draw more than a little on the older tradition of the Classical fantasia, whose maturest examples, Schubert's 'Wanderer' Fantasy for piano (D. 760, 1822) and his similar fantasies for piano and violin (D. 934, 1827) and piano duet (D. 940, 1828), provide excellent models of cycles in which individual movements sacrifice a little of their formal roundedness in order to lead via a transition into their successors. Weber's essays in compression were followed by others from Spohr (Violin Concerto No. 8, 'in modo di scena cantante', 1816), Kreutzer (Second Piano Concerto, 1824), and Alkan (*Concerti da camera*, Op. 10, Nos. 1 and 2, 1832–3). Liszt's two piano concertos are the most interesting products of this tradition. Of the E flat concerto, completed in 1849 but subsequently revised twice, Dahlhaus writes: 'Liszt's happy amalgam of pianistic paraphrase, the character piece (a central tradition in piano music), thematic transformation (suggested by Schubert's *Wanderer* Fantasy), and monumental quadruple variation has formed a bridge between the virtuoso manner and the symphonic style.'[58] In effect, Liszt's concerto consists of a fairly recognizable opening movement, a tripartite central movement—comprising a cantabile–recitative–pastorale medley

[57] Busoni's five-movement Piano Concerto, Op. 39 (1904), which employs a male chorus in its finale, takes up to eighty minutes to perform. This is surely a record for any concerto.

[58] Dahlhaus, *Nineteenth-Century Music*, 142.

(bars 1–76), a 'scherzando' (bars 77–183), a link passage based on the first movement (bars 184–251)—and a finale that serves up metamorphosed variants of the four main themes of the central movement, presented in the original order, with a return of first-movement material for the *stretta* conclusion. After Liszt, the miniature concerto—sometimes now expressly in a single-movement structure divided, medley-fashion, into successive sections, survives, but increasingly as a 'débutant's' concerto or as one for a type of solo instrument that cannot convincingly spread itself over three movements of conventional size.

Whether in symphonic or miniature format, the concerto likes to end with relaxant jollity. However, one can detect a general change in the stylization of the concerto finale from the 1920s onwards as a result of the wave of neo-Classicism that broke over music after the First World War. Whereas for the symphony neo-Classicism entailed a return (of some kind) to the Viennese Classical symphony, for the concerto it signalled instead a return to the Baroque, and specifically to Bach. The Baroque influence has manifested itself in two main ways.

The first is the distribution of solo interest among more members of the orchestra than the soloist proper, taking its cue from the type of composition with multiple soloists (often misnamed, with sublime disregard for actual historical usage, the 'concerto grosso') represented by Bach's 'Brandenburg' Concertos. In Nielsen's Flute Concerto (1926) and Clarinet Concerto (1928) the co-soloists (or 'counter-soloists') are the trombone and side-drum respectively. Berg's *Chamber Concerto* (1925) has joint piano and violin soloists, performing mostly alone in the first two movements, respectively, but combining in the third. In Bartók's *Concerto for Orchestra* (1943) and its many imitations all the instruments become, from time to time, soloists. In Stravinsky's *Concerto in D for String Orchestra* (1946), the soloist-less state of the primitive concerto around 1700 is recalled, and with it, Mattheson's description of the concerto quoted earlier in Chapter 6.

The other legacy of the Baroque concerto is a fondness, particularly evident in finales, for motor rhythms. Bach, who developed his concerto style during the 1710s on the basis of the Vivaldian models current at the time (i.e. before the rhythmic innovations of the 'Neapolitan' style, introduced in the mid-1720s, had arrived on the scene), is especially fond of repetitive rhythmic stereotypes (the finales of his two solo violin concertos offer good instances). Hence the non-stop agitation in the finales of such concertos as Martinů's for double string orchestra, piano, and timpani (1938), Barber's for violin (1940), and John Adams's for the same instrument (1993).

In conclusion, I offer a quick, slightly malicious, observation on modern concertos in general. Even more rapidly than the symphony, the concerto has become a profoundly retrospective genre. It exists today above all to fill a prescribed niche in a concert repertoire still dominated by music of the last century and governed by a traditional system of professional stratification that divides instrumentalists into soloists and non-soloists. Concertos belong quintessentially to the world of official commissions and engagements. For that reason, to compose a concerto in the modern age—even to use the mere word in the title—is publicly to signal one's return to the fold after a period, sometimes a lifetime, of wandering. After *Eight Songs for a Mad King*...a *Strathclyde Concerto* (or ten). After *Chromochromie*...a *Concert à quatre*.

# 9

# Codas and Finales

ARE finales simply codas writ large? Are codas simply finales writ small? The questions are not idle, since in this study parallels have repeatedly been drawn between the two. Both strive for closure, for balance, and for the resolution of tensions. Both use the powerful effects of cumulation and regression to these ends. Both are partial to humorous or extravagant effects and easily accommodate modal shifts. The two even have a common origin (albeit in the finale's case not a unique origin) in the closing sections of multisectional instrumental works composed during the Renaissance and early Baroque periods.

Yet we should take care not to fall into the fallacy of hierarchic uniformity, against which Leonard Meyer warns us. Some important differences are also apparent. Most finales are literally detachable and when performed separately are able to make a rounded and even satisfying whole. In contrast, even the most extended and thematically independent coda would make an unsatisfactory piece on its own. Moreover, nearly all finales have well-defined beginnings—even if the preceding movement runs into the finale, the composer will normally interpose a double bar and provide some clear indication (be it only a numeral) that a new movement has begun—whereas in codas so a sharp a delineation is unusual. A coda is concerned almost exclusively with closure, whereas even the most summative finale cannot altogether forgo the processes of exposition and development.

There is little consensus among commentators on the criteria by which the start of a coda can be identified (which is why different analysts often locate it at different points within a given movement). The problem is that the coda is only the last of a series of sections (or, for structures on a smaller scale, phrases) that cumulatively stabilize the tonality at the end of the movement. In a simple sonata-form movement this process begins at the start of the recapitulation, intensifies after second-subject material arrives in the tonic, and moves to a culmination in the later stages, when the material becomes progressively more quadratically phrased, broken up into small fragments, and oriented around dominant and tonic (and finally perhaps just tonic) harmony. All these events also have to occur, if not necessarily at such length, in the exposition, which gives the composer the option to have no coda at all or (expressing it another way) to use a simple transposition of the 'closing section' of the exposition—a term generally preferred nowadays to 'codetta'—for the recapitulation. This is what happens in many sonata-form movements in Mozart's works—for example the opening 'allegro' of the Piano Sonata in G major, K. 283/189h.[1] In fact, unless the recapitulation has been reduced in length in some way (for instance, by the excision of a bridge passage linking the two subject groups), a coda may be redundant in strict structural terms. This does not mean that having one is unwarranted, but it places an onus on the composer to justify its presence, which usually entails inventing new things for the primary material to do.

I should add here that my notion of redundancy runs counter to the mainstream of modern analytical thought, according to which great composers do only what they absolutely need to do. Thus if a coda exists, it must have some vital function that requires its presence. Rosen writes without hesitation: 'The classical coda is closely related to an anomaly in the main body of the work.'[2] Similar, if slightly more cautious, is the view advanced by Joseph Kerman when he observes: 'Again and again there seems to be some sort of instability, discontinuity, or thrust in the first theme which is removed in the coda ... In addition to [the coda's] harmonic function it has a thematic function that can be described as or, rather, suggested by words such as "normalisation", "resolution", "expansion", "release", "completion," and "fulfillment" '.[3] For Jonathan Dunsby, 'the function of a coda in extended forms is to resolve tonal processes, to collect and concentrate melodic and rhythmic figures from the word and—in Schoenberg's terminology—"liquidate" them by reducing their characteristic features, and perhaps to provide a dynamic and usually also a registral resolution'.[4] All these factors are, in their context, possible and even quite probable reasons for a coda. What I am arguing is only that they are not sufficient reasons, since a composer, acting on the impulse of his imagination, may always opt to do more than is strictly necessary.

A coda may be a simple addendum to the original closing group, in which case its opening is easy to determine.[5] Very often, however, it 'takes off' from an earlier point, substituting itself for the continuation that occurred on the first occasion (i.e. in the exposition). In such cases, the coda can be said to grow out of the second subject or the closing section and

---

[1] For Haydn the situation is less clear-cut. Haimo (*Haydn's Symphonic Forms*, 92) states that 'codas are rare events in Haydn's works in general, and in his early symphonies in particular', while Rosen (*The Classical Style*, 394) offers a corrective to this oversimplified view by pointing out that 'Haydn's codas, at least in his later years, are inextricably fused, even tangled[,] with his recapitulations.' Beethoven uses the coda more regularly; Zilkens (*Beethovens Finalsätze in den Klaviersonaten*, 120) finds it absent only once in the finales of the piano sonatas (in the F minor sonata, Op. 2 No. 1).

[2] Rosen, *Sonata Forms* (1988²), 301. This statement occurs only in the second, revised edition of Rosen's book, in which an extra chapter, 'Codas' (pp. 297–352), has been inserted (appropriately) after the chapter entitled 'Recapitulation'.

[3] Kerman, 'Notes on Beethoven's Codas', 149.

[4] Dunsby, 'The Multi-Piece in Brahms', 187.

[5] Such is often the case when the combined development and recapitulation are repeated and the coda follows the repeat sign, as in the finale of Mozart's 'Jupiter' Symphony.

consequently begins during, rather than at the head of, a musical period.[6]
More radically, a coda can take the form of an interpolation placed entirely
within the original closing group so that, in the strictest sense, it cannot be
counted as an independent section at all.

Codas are not peculiar to sonata-form movements, of course. In Classical
rondos their incidence is in fact higher than in sonata-form movements, if
only because an unvaried, unextended quotation of the refrain group would
seem inadequate and unimaginative.[7] For variation movements, the situation is more fluid. In its own right, a concluding variation, whether extro-
vert in style (as in the minuet variations ending Haydn's Piano Sonata in A
major, Hob. XVI/30) or reflectively simple (as in the finale of Beethoven's
Op. 109), may be perfectly adequate to round off the movement, especially
when there have been periodic returns to the tonic all the way through. In
many instances, however, a composer will seize on the opportunity to
escape the trammels of the repetitive structure and allow his imagination
to run riot. A *locus classicus* of such a coda (and apparently not part of the
work's initial conception) occurs in Haydn's independent set of variations
in F minor, Hob. XVII/6. It is enough to transform a pretty work into a
demonic, devastating one.

Codas of any considerable length are an invention of the Classical period.
No form used in late Baroque music requires them. In through-composed
movements (which include fugues as well as movements in 'motto' form)
the concept of a coda is fairly meaningless because there is no relevant
previous material to be extended or from which to deviate. In symmetrical
binary-form movements the two sections are usually 'end-matched'; that is,
at some point the material in the tonic used to close the second section
becomes a transposed version of what earlier ended the first section. (This is
the ancestor of the type of Classical sonata-form movement in which the
coda is a perfect reproduction of the codetta.) On the rare occasions when
such end-matching is irregular, there is usually a reason connected with the
movement's proportions.[8] In the 'Allemande' opening the sixth of J. S.
Bach's 'French' Suites, for instance, bars 9–12 concluding the first section
correspond to bars 22–5 in the second; but in order to correct the untidiness
of the phrase structure (the second section has already 'overshot' the point
of perfect symmetry, which is twenty-four bars), Bach has to append three
further bars, which function as a coda. The result is a 12:16 relationship
between the two sections, which, although a clear departure from the
symmetrical norm, at least looks planned and rational. In the 'Gigue' of

---

[6] In principle, a coda can replace material from as far back as the opening of the recapitulation, as we have already (in Ch. 7) seen occur in the finale of Schumann's Second Symphony.

[7] Girdlestone (*Mozart's Piano Concertos*, 55) remarks accurately that for Mozart codas are
more normal in finales than in first movements.

[8] We leave aside here the special case of minor-key movements, in which, for technical
reasons (the impossibility of satisfactorily converting material from major to minor merely by
adjusting accidentals), end-matching tends to be much looser than in major-key ones.

the same suite, whose opening was illustrated in Ex. 8.1( $f$ ), Bach's desire for symmetry brings about a modification in the other direction: the bars corresponding to bars 19–22 in the closing period of the first section are simply excised in order to preserve a 24:24 relationship. In other words, the coda is an occasional corrective device rather than a feature valued in its own right. The same is true in ritornello-form movements, where the opening theme normally comes back unaltered (or abridged, as in dal segno repeats) to close the movement, even if, by later standards, the ending can sound abrupt.[9]

In one type of extension, however, the Baroque period anticipates Classical usage. It has a fondness for echoed repeats of final cadential phrases. These may amount to a *petite reprise* of the complete closing phrase (as in some binary-form movements), or they may merely restate the final cadence (as in the closing ritornellos of concertos). In both cases, the regressive intention is clear: simple cadential repetition takes over from conventional processes of continuation such as sequential *Fortspinnung* as a method of signalling the imminence of the movement's end.

In codas of the Classical period such repetitions usually become multiple and even multi-stage. A common formula is to begin by restating a complete phrase, then to repeat (once or more) only its second portion, then only its cadential phrase, then only the two cadential chords, and finally, perhaps, the tonic chord alone. There is no standard musical term to describe this process of progressive reduction, but I would propose 'tapered repetition', a concept that emphasizes the idea that the repeated portion becomes ever smaller. The more 'tapered' a restatement becomes, the more plasticity it acquires, so that at the composer's bidding any significant theme or motif from the earlier part of the movement can be recalled (with whatever adjustment to its interval structure or rhythm is needed) against a background of alternating tonic and dominant.[10] A famous example of this is the passage beginning at bar 631 in the first movement of Beethoven's 'Eroica' Symphony, where the horns give out a perfectly diatonic, perfectly quadratic, version of the movement's opening theme, which was originally chromatically inflected and non-symmetrical in phrase structure. The illusion is created that the coda's version is the 'reference theme', of which the initial version is a purposeful deformation whose eventual rectification is the movement's main objective. Of course, this is too simple a description— it is as if one said that the purpose of a sentence was to arrive at a full stop.

---

[9] A case in point is the truncated ritornello at the end of the first movement of Bach's Harpsichord Concerto in D minor, BWV 1052, which is really too brief to bear the load of an ending.

[10] It is significant, however, that, as their sketches reveal, composers often conceive the codal versions of their themes at an early stage in the compositional process, thus endowing them with far more than 'afterthought' status. Peter Cahn examines this interesting point in 'Aspekte der Schlussgestaltung in Beethovens Instrumentalwerken', *Archiv für Musikwissenschaft*, 39 (1982), 19–31.

What has happened is that Beethoven has used the normal feature, for codas, of regularly alternating dominant and tonic harmony as scaffolding over which to erect a recall of this theme (and, in fact, also of other themes).

Tapered repetition accounts for the complete substance of many classical and later codas, even quite long ones. But there is another important device that can be used in codas to introduce or appear in alternation with it. This is the type of temporary disruption (especially in relation to tonality, though other factors may be involved) that in a literary context goes by the name of 'terminal modification'. Barbara Herrnstein Smith, writing with special reference to William Blake's *Auguries of Innocence*, explains that the device is used to create closure. In her words: 'A disruption occurs just before the end. The re-establishment of regularity is the cue for ending.'[11] The main function of such a disruption is to provoke a counter-reaction that establishes regularity more firmly—to set up, whether teasingly or with dramatic ferocity, an artificial instability against which the final stability is all the more strongly profiled. It announces closure even as it staves it off. The *stretta* of nineteenth-century operatic numbers is a favourite place for employing the device. Berlioz's overture *Le Carnaval romain*, based on material salvaged from his opera *Benvenuto Cellini*, offers a brilliant demonstration of the *stretta* in purely instrumental terms. This section (bars 356–450) has no fewer than four separate disruptions, each of which is before long slapped down by reassertion of the tonic, A major. The first, beginning in bar 367, makes a sudden transition to E flat major (diametrically opposite A major in the circle of fifths). The laborious return to the tonic, which is regained in bar 381, is achieved by progressive alteration of the notes of a broken-chord phrase that, used as an ostinato, underpins a recall of the overture's slow theme originally given out by cor anglais (it is the same technique that can transform the word 'pear' into 'cart' via the intermediate stages 'peat', 'pert', and 'part'). During bars 381–91 strings in A major battle, in a quickfire exchange of cadential phrases, with wind in D flat major.[12] In bar 397 simple metre (2/4) rudely interrupts the saltarello (6/8) metre, and a series of erratically zigzagging unisons strays into E flat major (visited for a second time) before being equally brusquely reined back to A major and the original metre. Between bars 407 and 421 the tonic reigns supreme, as the saltarello theme is delivered in a special codal version that anchors it more firmly than before in a single key. In bar 422, just when the listener expects a flurry of concluding dominant and tonic chords, Berlioz pulls his final rabbit out of the hat: a roaring G natural on the trombones ushers in a cascade of modulations down the circle of fifths that is wrenched back to A major just in time.

[11] Smith, *Poetic Closure*, 77.

[12] This 'clash of remote keys' is similar to the well-known instance just before the end of the fourth movement ('March to the Scaffold') of Berlioz's *Symphonie fantastique*, where G minor and D flat major battle for supremacy.

It is not uncommon for commentators to refer to long codas (notably Beethoven's) in which modulation appears as 'second developments'. Kerman deplores the practice, and rightly so.[13] A development section connecting an exposition to a recapitulation has as its tonal function to bridge a tonal gap, be it only that between dominant and tonic. In fact, as many overtures (and some slow movements in Classical sonatas and symphonies) show, this hiatus does not require bridging in any absolute sense: any tonic chord of the dominant key concluding an exposition can be interpreted immediately, without or without prolongation, as the dominant of the home key and thereby act as a springboard for the recapitulation. A development section is a highly artificial creation, a means of delaying the return to the tonic by making it indirect. Its artificiality, its studied 'inventiveness', is the very reason why it enjoys such latitude in relation to length and complexity. A coda, in contrast, has to walk on the spot. Its tonal divagations may be striking, but even as he introduces them, the composer employs every device to reassure the listener that they are impermanent.

In all other respects than the tonal, however, codas can deploy the full repertory of developmental devices: fragmentation, augmentation, diminution, contrapuntal combination, dialogue, and the rest. Kerman's objection to the use of the word 'development' should in no sense be taken as a denial of the many correspondences between development section and coda (sometimes manifested overtly as parallelisms) that may exist in a given movement.

Some idea of the variety and scope of codas can be gained by examining the outer movements of three Beethoven piano sonatas from the early part of his middle period: the Op. 31 set.

1. *Sonata in G major, Op. 31 No. 1.*   First movement, bars 280–325. The coda begins with a return to the movement's opening three-bar motif, prolonged so that the original descent from $g''$ (with tied upbeat) to $g'$ is reproduced in two successive lower octaves; this three-octave descent is then balanced by an ascent (which likewise places tonic and dominant on alternate strong beats) and an arpeggiated decoration of the dominant chord. The second part of the coda, starting in bar 296, plays with the original consequent phrase (syncopated chords in the right hand against on-the-beat chords in the left), exploiting the strict alternation of tonic and dominant harmony for humorous effect, intensified by placing extra rests between the phrases. The entire coda 'composes out' the first eleven bars of the movement, replacing the original modulation to the dominant (which immediately leads to more adventurous tonal forays) by an insistence on tonic and dominant so unrelieved as to become comical.

Third movement, bars 225–75. This is a sonata-rondo movement which, in the absence of a strong separate idea for the first couplet (recapitulated as

[13] Kerman, 'Notes on Beethoven's Codas', 152–3.

the third couplet), could be termed monothematic. The coda leads on from the final statement of the refrain, which, in a spirit of mock pathos, is performed in slow motion ('adagio'), its phrases being separated by rests. The dominant chord of its final cadence is prolonged with a pedal note (from bar 241), the tempo increasing to 'presto'. With the resolution to a tonic chord in bar 248 the coda proper begins. This short coda uses and repeats intensively the turn-figure with which the refrain theme opened, always in conjunction with a dominant or tonic quasi-pedal ('quasi', because of the decoration of the harmony note that the turn-figure entails). Beethoven makes great play with the alternation of E♭ and E♮ as alternative appoggiaturas to D. The first note introduces, by its chromaticism, an element of disruption that its diatonic counterpart assuages. (Terminal modification need consist of no more than that.)

2. *Sonata in D minor ('Tempest'), Op. 31 No. 2.*   First movement, bars 219–28. The exposition of the first movement is unusual for a minor-key work in that its second subject group (including the closing group, if one insists on distinguishing one) lies entirely in the dominant minor rather than the relative major. This enables its recapitulation, occupying bars 171–218, to be little more than a straightforward transposition of bars 41–88 in the exposition. The ten-bar coda, marked 'pianissimo', is a mere prolongation of tonic harmony; broken-chord figuration deep in the bass eventually subsides into two quiet final chords. A more minimalistic coda is hard to imagine.

Third movement, bars 323–99. This is a sonata-form movement that, like the first movement, uses the dominant for its second subject group. Once again, the recapitulation of the latter goes over familiar territory. It even reproduces in transposed form the chord (a diminished seventh chord on C♯) that was used in the exposition both to introduce the repeat of the exposition and to launch the development. However, its reappearance a fourth higher than before (over F♯) gives the coda an opportunity to have an off-tonic (subdominant) opening. Starting in G minor (the 'disruption'), the coda, based on the same broken-chord shape shared between the hands from which the first subject is formed, works its way unhurriedly to D minor, which it reaches in bar 351. There follows a complete restatement of the first subject, initially amplified by chime-like syncopated pedal notes in the right hand, which leads via a short extension to the third and final phase of the coda, beginning in bar 385. This takes the form of a fourfold alternation of tonic and dominant chords (still using the same motivic material), succeeded by seven bars of tonic arpeggiation.

3. *Sonata in E flat major, Op. 31 No. 3.*   First movement, bars 220–53. Transposition of the lead back to the repeat of the exposition gives Beethoven another opportunity to begin the coda out of key. Since the opening chord of the movement is a first-inversion supertonic chord (a six-five chord over

A♭), the bass note at the opening of the coda, D♭, seems very remote. However, an extension of the rising progression first heard in bars 3–6 allows Beethoven to wriggle back to the home key, so that from bars 234 to 245 he is able to repeat the material of bars 7–17 unaltered except for a short cadential extension. Bars 246–53 initially play with a version of the linking phrase first heard in bar 8 alternating between tonic (left hand) and dominant (right hand) harmony, proceeding in bar 250 to simple elaboration of the tonic chord.

Third movement, bars 263–333. The opportunity to do something spectacular in this coda is precluded by the unusual manner of its introduction. The main portion of the recapitulated second subject, which runs from bar 209 to bar 250, is a transposition of bars 34–75 in the exposition—not, however, in the tonic, E flat major, but instead in the flattened submediant, G flat major. Between bars 250 and 262 the music works its way back sequentially, via E flat minor, to the dominant seventh chord, over which, in thin wisps of accompanimental figuration, the coda begins in bar 263. The opening phrase of the first subject duly arrives in bar 281, and the major form of the tonic chord is heard for the first time in bar 282. Beethoven plays with the same phrase sequentially, taking it via F minor into the subdominant, A flat major (subdominant emphasis just before the close is almost a dogma in Beethoven, though not so to the same degree in either Haydn or Mozart). An A♭ chord pounds away in bars 303–6, and leads, via a diminished seventh on A♮, to a regular cadence in E flat in bar 312. Bars 303–12 are then restated in a lower register in the manner of a *petite reprise*. From bar 323 to the end we have the usual game of oscillating tonic and dominant harmonies; the dominant chords are given extra piquancy by including the ninth, alternately in its more dissonant (C♭) and more euphonious (C♮) versions. In this movement the coda includes a couple of effective 'lower-level' disruptions (the subdominant emphasis and the dominant minor ninth), but the 'higher-level' disruption (the modulation to G flat major) has already occurred before it arrives.

Between them, these six movements offer a good conspectus of what to expect in a normal coda, which in the examples studied accounts for between about 4 and 21 per cent of the movement's total length. Some codas, especially in Beethoven, are exceptionally long and complex, and it will be useful to examine one of them that has achieved a certain notoriety among analysts on account of its considerable length and puzzlingly close relationship to the part of the movement—only slightly longer—that precedes it. This is the finale of the Eighth Symphony, Op. 93 (1812).

The movement starts conventionally enough. Bars 1–27 form a first subject in F major; bars 28–47 a transition; bars 48–67 a second subject in C major based on a contrasting lyrical theme and with an out-of-key start (bars 48–59) in A flat major; bars 68–90 a closing section, which at its conclusion returns to F major. In bar 91 the opening comes back in the original key but veers off along a different path in bar 105. This return, coupled with the absence of a repeat, has been enough to suggest rondo form to some commentators.[14] However, the first movement of the String Quartet in F major, Op. 59 No. 1, which no one has yet thought to describe as a rondo despite the return of the opening theme at the head of its coda, launches its development section in an identical way, so the sonata-form model remains valid. From bar 111 to bar 150 there is a long, modulating passage in which a motif extracted from the first-subject theme is treated exhaustively in near-canonic imitation by inversion. The roots of the chords underpinning this passage progress in a chain of twenty-four rising fourths from A in bar 112 to D in bar 147; modulation to remote keys is skilfully averted by making two of the fourths augmented (Bb–E and F–B) instead of perfect.[15] The first fourth (A–D) is reached after eight bars, the next eight at regular two-bar intervals, and the final fifteen at one-bar intervals. This produces an exhilarating, typically Beethovenian effect of acceleration. Bars 148–57 have dominant preparation in A; the mode changes from minor to major in bar 151, when the opening of the first subject is heard *fortissimo*. Mid-way through bar 157 the pedal note (E) resolves to F, and four bars later the recapitulation begins.

Three things are unusual about this development section: its brevity; the simplicity of its structure (it effectively consists of just one main element and two subsidiary ones); and the complete absence of wide-ranging modulation, which is the reason why no retransition is needed. Actually, it possesses general characteristics that are observed more often in Beethoven's codas than in his development sections. This fact is important for the later course of the movement.

The first subject, transition, second subject, and closing section are recapitulated almost without alteration (the transition is amended and slightly extended). By retaining the modulation one degree to the flat side with which the closing section ended, Beethoven finds himself in the subdominant in bar 266. The coda therefore starts in that key, a procedure we observed earlier in the finale of Op. 31 No. 2 and the first movement of Op. 31 No. 3.

The first part of the coda (bars 267–354) mimics the entire development section, paraphrasing a fifth lower both its scheme of modulation and its style of thematic treatment. We hear first the opening theme, transposed to B flat major; then (in bar 282) the sequence modulating by fourths, which is varied by transforming the motif treated in imitation into striding *Pfundnoten* and including rising as well as falling intervallic patterns; and finally, the

---

[14] The first may have been Sir George Grove, in *Beethoven and his Nine Symphonies* (London, 1896²), 301.

[15] The octaves in which the notes making up the chain of fourths appear, and the instruments on which they are played, are continually varied throughout.

Ex. 9.1.   Beethoven, Symphony No. 8 in F major, Op. 93, last movement, bars 356–94

Ex. 9.1.   *(contd.)*

scrap of opening theme in D major over an A pedal note. In bar 351 the A is exchanged for F, and we are back in the home key.

In the second phase of the coda (bars 355–437) the recapitulation itself is the object of mimicry. The first subject is presented with a 'twist'; in bars 372–8 the loud unison D♭, originally treated as a chromatic note within the home key, is first tonicized and then turned (with the help of enharmonic alteration) into the dominant of F sharp minor, the *terzgleich* key.[16] The music does not remain long in this unexpected region; Beethoven slips back into F major via the note A, which is common to the two keys. This passage, which illustrates perfectly the nature of disruption in codas (and the inevitable restoration of stability that soon follows), is shown as Ex. 9.1. A short transitional passage in typically energetic coda style leads to the re-emergence of the second subject, now presented wholly in F major, in bar 408; on its repeat, the melody is even taken into the bass for the first time (bars 420–8).

The third phase, the 'conventional' coda, opens with a *fortissimo* tonic seventh chord in bar 432.[17] Thereafter, until the close of the movement in bar 502, its course is normal; snippets of the main theme are profiled against tonic and dominant (or simply tonic) harmonies. The barefaced procession of F–A dyads up and down the octave registers in bars 458–69 is perhaps the most radical (as well as the most hilarious) act of musical simplification Beethoven ever countenanced.

In a recent article Robert Hopkins argues that the coda of this movement should be understood as beginning only in bar 438 (he does not include the introductory tonic seventh chord, but that is an unimportant detail).[18] What precedes it he identifies as a 'second' development and 'second' recapitulation. On the basis of this classification, he even visualizes the movement as a kind of 'grand' rondo in which the exposition, 'first' recapitulation, and 'second' recapitulation are the refrain, and the 'first' and 'second' developments the two couplets.

Most of the dispute is about the use of words, not about actual musical relationships. In defence of my description, I would argue that the extreme length of the coda is no barrier to considering it as forming a unity; nor is its complex structure, since other sections, too, are subdivided. The concept of mimicry is useful here, since it highlights the fact that, without negating their essential nature and function, sections may be able to draw extensively on material used with a different function elsewhere in the movement. The

---

[16] See Ch. 7 n. 12 for an explanation of *terzgleich*.

[17] The tonic chord with flattened seventh is a topos of Classical and Romantic codas (it introduces the last of the four 'disruptions' in the coda of Berlioz's *Carnaval romain* overture). Its virtue is to draw the music towards the flat side, compensating for any earlier sharpward bias, and to provide a simple form of instability that it will be the business of the coda to correct.

[18] Robert G. Hopkins, 'When a Coda is More than a Coda: Reflections on Beethoven', in Eugene Narmour and Ruth A. Solie (eds.), *Explorations in Music, the Arts and Ideas: Essays in Honor of Leonard B. Meyer* (Stuyvesant, NY, 1988), 393–410. Rosen (*Sonata Forms* (1988²), 330–51) also gives an analytical account of this coda, from which mine differs only in detail and emphasis.

coda of the finale of the Eighth Symphony is able to appropriate in whole-sale fashion the material and processes of the earlier development section only because, exceptionally, the music of this section is weak in 'development-specific' elements. The material of the recapitulation can be similarly used because it already possesses features (e.g. fragmented texture) that are highly compatible with a coda. A comparable case would be that of the first movement of Beethoven's String Quartet in A minor, Op. 132, where the development section mimics the exposition, progressing from the first sub-ject (in E minor) to the second subject (in C major). This, too, is enabled by special circumstances: the unfolding of the exposition itself in an almost developmental manner.

During the entire course of its 236 bars this coda keeps its eye firmly on closure. Even in its first two phases it contains not one gesture that hints at a new theme to come or a new tonal region to probe. If the 'mimicking' passages are compared closely with their models in the development and recapitulation, a remarkable fact becomes apparent: the changes made to them are without exception calculated to reinforce the listener's sense of an impending end. The 'chain of fourths' motif (borrowed from the first subject via the development) has had its pointed rhythms smoothed out, thereby becoming broader; the loud statement of the opening motif heard soon afterwards appears a fourth lower than previously (in D major instead of A major); the first and second subjects, appearing one last time, are more tightly gripped than before by tonic and dominant pedal notes; the back-ground of repeated notes in triplets has become more insistent.

It is its single-minded focus on closure that distinguishes a coda (a final section) from a finale (a final movement). Borderline cases are hard to find. One might take as a test case Nielsen's Clarinet Concerto, which, exception-ally for the composer in his maturity, ends in the same key in which it begins, F major. Despite the complete absence of internal thin–thick barlines or any other indications of movement divisions, this is clearly a three-movement, continuously running work by virtue of the fact that each of its three components, taken separately, makes a rounded whole. Each starts with exposition, continues with development (or contrasting material), and finishes with restatement. Even though much of the concerto is through-composed (cadenzas for the soloist have a prominent role), there are just enough reprises and developments of identifiable material to sustain this conclusion. In contrast, the six tone-poems of Smetana's *Má vlast*, super-ficially constructed according to similar principles, are all composite one-movement works. In each of them the individual components, which form a chain of more or less discrete sections (including occasional reprises, mostly leitmotif-style), are functionally specialized according to their position and therefore fail to become rounded wholes. Even though the Lisztian tone poem may have aspired to be regarded as 'music of the future', it unwit-tingly looks back to the early seventeenth century for its constructional

principles. The technique of thematic metamorphosis, so progressive from
an organicist point of view, harbours, ironically, a retrogressive side in that
it encourages parataxis (the placing of different elements in a straight row)
instead of the hypotaxis (the hierarchical, interdependent ordering) that the
Classical style favoured. Unity of theme pursued as an end in itself may act
to the detriment of unity of form.

So far, we have not spoken on the other kind of single-movement design,
in which a single form (usually sonata-form or rondo) encompasses the
entire structure, but where the dimensions of the movement are so large
that they permit the formation of enclaves that take on the character of
different movements. The classic work answering to this description—and
one of the very first of its kind to be written—is Liszt's Piano Sonata in B
minor, S178 (1854), which takes up to half an hour to perform. As we saw
earlier, Newman speaks of it as having a 'double-function' form, in which
'its several components also serve as the (unseparated) movements of the
complete [multimovement] cycle'.[19] The terminology is unfortunate, since
the function of the components is unambiguously single (as first subject,
first theme of second subject, etc.). It is their character (as 'second movement', 'scherzo', etc.) that introduces the extra dimension. Once again, the
concept of mimicry can help us to arrive at an adequate description. We can
say, for instance, that whereas the first theme of the movement's vast second
subject group (the 'grandioso' melody in D major that begins in bar 106) has
an authentically 'first-movement' quality, as does the more *cantabile* second
theme in the same key (beginning in bar 154), the 'andante sostenuto' theme
that introduces the part of the second subject group based in F sharp major
belongs in spirit to a slow movement. Because a slow movement is customarily an interlude separating two faster ones, it is easy to produce an
analogous impression by fitting a slow enclave into a generally fast movement. To mimic a scherzo is equally unproblematic. Most commentators
identify the 'scherzo' episode of Liszt's sonata with the extended fugato
based on a subject adapted from the principal first subject theme, which is
shown as Ex. 9.2 (starting with the third entry of the subject).

But, it could be argued, is it not a finale that Liszt intends to mimic here?
Certainly, the tempo, the metre, the technical difficulty, and the uncompromising severity of the counterpoint seem more characteristic of such
movements as the finale of Beethoven's 'Hammerklavier' Sonata than of
ordinary scherzos in piano sonatas. However, this identification soon
proves stillborn. Finales cannot ever escape from their essential nature as
'edge' movements. A scherzo or an 'andante' can insinuate itself into the
centre of a movement by virtue of naturally being a middle movement, but a
finale derives its whole *raison d'être* from coming last. If one were to think of
plausibly mimicking a finale in a single-movement composition, the episode

---

[19] Newman, *The Sonata since Beethoven*, 134.

Ex. 9.2.   Liszt, Piano Sonata in B minor, bars 480–7

would have to come at or near the end of the movement. But this is precisely the point at which coda principles emphasizing closure begin to operate. The composer has the choice either of making the coda his 'finale' (a pointless task, since a coda already possesses so much of the same general character) or of expanding the coda into a fully rounded structure (which would result in the formation of a new movement with its own, separate coda).

We are therefore drawn back to the criteria that were proposed in Chapter 2 for differentiating sections and movements. Codas and finales may sometimes be remarkably similar in character, but in the last analysis they always remain apart and non-interchangeable on account of their different structural function vis-à-vis other units. In this instance, size is unimportant: what matters is relationship.

# 10

# *Final Thoughts*

ANY system of classification needs constantly to be interrogated. The fundamental questions are always primarily two. Why classify at all? Why use precisely these categories and not others?

The first question has to be answered pragmatically. If it is true, as nominalists would argue, that every manifestation is unique—that no two pieces of music are the same (for otherwise, we would not recognize them as separate pieces)—then no attempt to yoke them together under some heading will capture their real essence. This is undeniable. However, the historian's or the analyst's aims are more modest. The objective is not to reveal the complete truth or the full information but to expose a selected part of both. Calling the finales of Beethoven's Ninth Symphony and Bruckner's Eight Symphony 'summative' or those of Mozart's 'Haffner' Symphony and Schumann's 'Rhenish' Symphony 'relaxant' is a convenient way of drawing attention to one particular aspect of them that is of special interest because it relates to a tradition. For other, equally valid, purposes one might classify works or movements according to entirely different criteria. For example, one might speak of a class of 'D major' works related by a complex history of, first, modal transposition and, later, instrumentation and style.

The criterion for the broad classification of finales into 'relaxant', 'summative', and 'valedictory' is that of their effect in relation to the preceding part or parts of the multimovement work (and also, in fact, to the silence that follows the performance). What the labels for these categories should be, in English and in other languages, is naturally open to debate. More important at this stage, however, is to decide whether three categories is the right number.

My belief is that what I have called the 'relaxant' finale is the most natural kind—the kind that goes with, not against, the grain. A return (to the home key and to quick tempo) is inherently relaxing because it restores the known after the unknown. This argument can be tested by considering strict ABA arrangements of movements (for instance, the Classical minuet and trio). Is it not the case that, however many musical surprises the minuet contains on its first outing, these will lose something of their force on its repeat because of their familiarity? But even if it remains true that, as Tarasti argues, 'second times' are always experienced differently from 'first times' no matter how great their surface resemblance, the listener can also appreciate, and respond to, their similarity. A long, entirely serious movement such as the finale of Brahms's Fourth Symphony and a short, frothy one such as that of Bach's Third 'Brandenburg' Concerto have in common that from their very first note they represent a kind of homecoming. However different in all kinds of ways these finales may be from their respective first fast movements (which, of course, are not always the first movements *tout court*), there is an inescapable sense of their being 'second times'.

There are only a limited number of ways in which this pattern can be inflected. One is to defer the homecoming to a later stage in the movement. This is the strategy employed by a summative finale. By referring back extensively to earlier material, by juxtaposing new material that contrasts strikingly with it and sustains a sense of conflict, and by making free use of the devices of cumulation and regression, it turns itself from a matching bookend into a varied résumé.

In a valedictory finale the homecoming is pushed back still further— beyond the boundary of the work, in fact. Its mandatory slow tempo, ostensibly calming, is by a strange paradox profoundly tense, as Seidel recognized. Only a final silence, by relieving this pervasive tension, can deliver the true homecoming.

So the three types of finale are identified, in the last analysis, by three different points of psychological homecoming: at the beginning of the movement (relaxant); during the course of the movement (summative); after the movement (valedictory). Between them, these cover all possibilities and in that respect form a complete, self-contained system. This is not, of course, to deny the existence of borderline cases or ambiguities but to argue that any individual case can be assessed and described in relation to the triad relaxant/summative/valedictory without reference to extra factors.

Since we have already examined each of the three types in period-based and genre-based contexts, it will be appropriate to end this study by considering them in relation to a single composer. For this purpose I have chosen the fifteen string quartets of Dmitri Shostakovich (1906–75), which form a substantial corpus of music acknowledged to be highly representative of their composer and among the most important contributions to their genre made during the twentieth century. Shostakovich's works in general, and his quartets in particular, are saturated with 'extroversive' elements both overt and covert.[1] These refer to private life, public life, and the interactions between the two. Intertextual musical references are almost embarrassingly copious, especially in the later works. Besides the expected 'cyclic' links between the movements there are likely to be more or less literal quotations from other Shostakovich compositions and sometimes from music by other composers. In a certain sense, Shostakovich must have considered his whole oeuvre as a 'super-work' within which each

---

[1] 'Extroversive' and 'introversive' are terms coined by Kofi Agawu to distinguish between forms of reference to music (or anything else) standing outside the piece analysed and those that exist within the piece itself.

TABLE 10.1. *Shostakovich's string quartets*

| Opus | No. | Key | Completed | Première | Dedication |
|------|-----|-----|-----------|----------|------------|
| 49 | 1 | C | 1938, July | 1938, Oct. | none |
| 68 | 2 | A | 1944, Sept. | 1944, Nov. | V. Y. Shebalin (composer) |
| 73 | 3 | F | 1946, Aug. | 1946, Dec. | Beethoven Quartet |
| 83 | 4 | D | 1949, Dec. | 1953, Dec. | P. V. Williams (designer)* |
| 92 | 5 | B♭ | 1952, Nov. | 1953, Nov. | Beethoven Quartet |
| 101 | 6 | G | 1956, Aug. | 1956, Oct. | none |
| 108 | 7 | f♯ | 1960, Mar. | 1960, May | Nina Shostakovich (first wife)* |
| 110 | 8 | c | 1960, July | 1960, Oct. | the victims of fascism and war |
| 117 | 9 | E♭ | 1964, May | 1964, Nov. | Irina Shostakovich (third wife) |
| 118 | 10 | A♭ | 1964, July | 1964, Nov. | Moisei Vainberg (composer) |
| 122 | 11 | f | 1966, Jan. | 1966, Mar. | Vasili Shirinsky (second violinist in the Beethoven Quartet)* |
| 133 | 12 | D♭ | 1968, Mar. | 1968, June | Dmitri Tsyganov (leader of the Beethoven Quartet) |
| 138 | 13 | b♭ | 1970, Aug. | 1970, Dec. | Vadim Borisovsky (original violist of the Beethoven Quartet) |
| 142 | 14 | F♯ | 1973, Apr. | 1973, Oct. | Sergei Shirinsky (cellist in the Beethoven Quartet) |
| 144 | 15 | e♭ | 1974, May | 1974, Oct. | none |

* In memoriam

individual composition occupied its allotted niche (rather as a movement does within a larger work). This intricate network of allusion invests Shostakovich's finales with a 'poetic' meaning that validates, reinforces, and sometimes inflects the conclusions than can be reached via simple musical analysis. Table 10.1 offers a simple overview of the quartets.

It will be useful to start by considering some points that arise directly from this table. As its first and fourth columns show, Shostakovich began to write quartets only in the second third of his active career, by which time he had completed five symphonies. Because of external pressures (to be explained in the discussion of 'socialist realism' that follows shortly), and perhaps also on account of the natural process of maturity, the Shostakovich quartets exhibit no 'modernist' or experimental period as represented by the composer's second and third symphonies. On the other hand, the composer continued to produce quartets with some regularity almost up to his death (the Viola Sonata, Op. 147, is the only completed instrumental work to postdate the Fifteenth Quartet), and the last four—or perhaps five—quartets are self-consciously 'late-period' in manner.

The third column reveals that no keys are duplicated, allowing for the distinction between major and minor (the fact that Shostakovich recognized a distinction is naturally significant). The absence of duplication conforms to Shostakovich's reported statement that he was working towards a cycle of twenty-four quartets, one in each key.[2] The first six quartets, all in major keys, descend alternately by minor and major thirds. Descent or ascent by thirds of alternate type is a common enough method of progressing through the keys (we see it applied, for instance, to the first eight works in Purcell's *Sonatas of Three Parts* of 1683), but it is usually combined with alternation of the two modes. This is the pattern employed in Chopin's set of twenty-four preludes (and also those of Skryabin's Op. 11); Shostakovich uses it himself for his Op. 34 preludes and the prelude–fugue pairs of his Op. 87. What is unusual about the key sequence of the first six quartets is that all the keys are major. Had the pattern continued unaltered, C major would have returned in Quartet No. 8. This may be the reason why the original scheme was abandoned after six works. Quartet No. 7, in F sharp minor, is an apparent singleton, and from Quartet No. 8 onwards the alternation of major and minor modes complements the pattern of descending major and minor thirds so that the keys travel backwards through the circle of fifths in the traditional manner.[3]

It can be seen from the fourth and fifth columns that the première of each work followed closely on its completion. The two notable exceptions are Nos. 4 and 5, which had to wait for the death of Stalin, on 5 March 1953, before the composer deemed it safe to release them. From No. 2 onwards Shostakovich entrusted their first public outing to the Beethoven Quartet (consisting originally of Dmitri Tsyganov, Vasili Shirinsky, Vadim Borisovsky, and Sergei Shirinsky).[4] Two quartets (Nos. 3 and 5) were dedicated to the Beethoven Quartet collectively; each of its individual members much later received, in quick succession, the dedication of a quartet (Vasili Shirinsky posthumously). In the four works concerned (Nos. 11–14) Shostakovich makes clear allusions to the personalities and technical accomplishments of the dedicatees.[5]

[2] See Elizabeth Wilson, *Shostakovich: A Life Remembered* (London, 1994), 389. The statement, dating from 1960, was recalled by Dmitri Tsyganov, leader of the Beethoven Quartet. Shostakovich's fifteen symphonies also begin by avoiding key duplication, but No. 8, which returns to the key of No. 4 (C minor), breaks the pattern, as do Nos. 9 and 12 later.

[3] The key plan of the quartets is discussed in Iain Strachan, 'Shostakovich's "DSCH" Signature in the String Quartets', *DSCH Journal*, 10 (Winter 1998), 48–9. Strachan observes that the quartets in the major keys whose key notes belong to the composer's monogram (D, E♭, and C) all bear numbers that are perfect squares (4, 9, and 1, respectively)—and so, too, would a hypothetical sixteenth quartet in B (H) major. (For an explanation of the monogram, see p. 203.) The necessity of placing the E flat quartet in ninth position could explain why it follows, instead of preceding as elsewhere within the 'second' scheme, the quartet in its relative minor key (No. 8). More generally, the wish to build the monogram into the key scheme could be the reason why no unified plan (in a conventional sense) was implemented.

[4] Because of Sergei Shirinsky's death, which occurred during the rehearsal of No. 15, its première was given by the Taneyev Quartet, although the Beethoven Quartet, joined as cellist by Yevgeni Altman, repeated it soon afterwards.

[5] This 'personalization' echoes, probably unwittingly, Nielsen's commemoration of the members of the Copenhagen Wind Quintet in a set of concertos, only two of which came to fruition.

During the entire period spanned by these quartets, and with greatest rigour during Stalin's years, Soviet music was expected to adhere to the norms of 'socialist realism', offspring of the 'social realism' practised and advocated by the veteran writer Maxim Gorky, whose personal rapport with Stalin was certainly one of the factors that contributed to the elevation of the doctrine to state policy. The very description 'socialist realism' has sometimes been seen as a bizarre oxymoron. This is unfair, since in the literary sphere, and even in the visual arts, the phrase can meaningfully be applied to a realistic representation chosen or viewed in a socialist spirit. Naturally, music, the quintessentially self-referential art, can be fitted into such a scheme only by analogy and always to some extent arbitrarily. For that reason, 'socialist realism' was in practice applied to music as a cover word for agendas that had little to do with socialism and less with realism.

Richard Taruskin has equated socialist realism with a style and approach that he terms 'heroic classicism'.[6] This definition accounts for a high proportion of the Soviet music that met with official approval in its time, but neither word is quite flexible enough to accommodate all the possibilities that existed. Heroism was undoubtedly appropriate for music designed to illustrate the building of, or struggle for, socialism, but a necessary place was likewise reserved for music depicting the pleasures of life under the socialism already achieved. Moreover, the Stalinist doctrine of 'socialism in one country' (as opposed to world revolution) favoured the co-option of folkloristic elements, exactly as in the Tsarist past, and these were always more likely to be more lyrical than heroic. In short, any manner was acceptable, provided that it could be read by a lay audience as 'optimistic'.[7] Since optimism relates to the future, it was a work's ending—the finale and perhaps also its coda—that was most carefully perused.

'Classicism', for its part, has to be interpreted in a broad, specifically Russian, context. The concept certainly includes the Viennese Classical style from Haydn to Schubert—a parody such as Prokofiev's 'Classical' Symphony might even have elicited approval if composed in the 1930s or 1940s. But it includes also the classicizing, though outwardly 'Romantic' or 'Russian-national', style inculcated in the conservatories of Moscow and St Petersburg from their foundation in the 1860s until fairly recent times. A common feature of the entire twentieth-century Russian 'school'—whether at home (Shostakovich, Prokofiev) or in emigration (Rakhmaninov,

---

[6] Richard Taruskin, 'Public Lies and Unspeakable Truth: Interpreting Shostakovich's Fifth Symphony', in David Fanning (ed.), *Shostakovich Studies* (Cambridge, 1995), 17–56 at 55.

[7] The official disappointment at Shostakovich's Ninth Symphony (1945), a *sinfonia buffa* if there ever was one, had nothing to do with style as such: it resulted from Stalin's expectation that a work bearing this hallowed number and completed at war's end would glorify him, the *Generalissimo*, in music of appropriate grandeur. Ironically, the work was used in 1985 for a ballet in Leningrad marking the fortieth anniversary of the victory over fascism, its levity serving the purpose of belittling the *Führer*, not glorifying the *Vozhd*.

Stravinsky), whether radical (Skryabin, Roslavets) or conservative (Myaskovsky, Medtner)—has been its loyalty to inherited genres and their associated musical forms.[8] As in Tsarist times, the idea of 'classicism' also extended backwards to embrace Bach (to whom even the iconoclast Musorgsky had paid affectionate homage in his *Intermezzo in modo classico*) and the forms (prelude, fugue, passacaglia, suite, etc.) of his period. Unsurprisingly for a society constantly exhorted to combat first 'leftism' (anarchism, Trotskyism), then 'rightism' (social democracy, Bukharinism), then both in alliance with each other and (objectively) with fascism, Soviet 'socialist realism' was above all a recipe for caution and the golden mean: music poised between the past and the present, between diatonicism and chromaticism, between simple and extended tonality, between particularism and universalism, between anonymity and individualism. The parallel with France during the *Grand Siècle* is remarkable. There, too, a conformist spirit reinforced from above coupled with a thorough and uniform system of musical education produced a distinctive national musical style, within which a few composers of exceptional talent stood out from the crowd.

We will not enter here into the continuing debate over whether Shostakovich was an open dissident, a closet dissident, a reluctant collaborator with the régime, or even a compliant collaborator (though this last possibility seems very remote). Two things, however, are indisputable: he was an individualist to the core, and he had a strong consciousness of belonging to an international community of composers (and of creative artists in general) handing on the torch from generation to generation. This desire to locate himself in history on a world stage already proclaims his lack of genuine interest in any supposedly specific qualities of 'Soviet man'.

As for the individualism, this is apparent even if one holds a miniature score of one of the quartets a metre away from one's eyes. As Paul Griffiths has observed, this music exhibits 'an astonishing thinness of texture... Shostakovich throughout his cycle takes the quartet into regions of bareness only otherwise approached, rather differently, by Cage'.[9] Unaccompanied solos for one or other of the instruments, or passages for just a pair of them, occupy system after system.[10] Already, this insistence on unaccompanied utterance challenges the priorities of a collectivist society by implying that consciousness is ultimately rooted in the individual alone.

---

[8] During the mid-1920s this dominance seemed to waver in the Soviet Union, but the social conservatism accompanying the rise of the *nomenklatura* during the next decade led inevitably to the re-*embourgeoisement* of Soviet cultural life.

[9] Paul Griffiths, *The String Quartet* (London, 1983), 213. The bareness only increases in the late works.

[10] This is in fact a feature of Shostakovich's style in general (consider, for example, the monophonic enunciation of the long theme in the variation finale of his Second Piano Sonata, Op. 61).

Equally astonishing is the paucity of dynamic marks or marks of phrasing and articulation—of which there are fewer than in the average late Haydn quartet. Special effects are severely rationed and notably infrequent by comparison with, say, Bartók or Berg.[11] The type of supplementary marking of which one is most aware is a pair of crotchets or minims separated by an 'equals' sign, by which Shostakovich instructs the players to keep the beat note constant in value during the relatively frequent metrical shifts. He is happy to grant players a wide degree of latitude in their interpretation of these quartets, which can taken both as a token of confidence in their ability to understand and execute his music and as a statement of belief in its elemental, transcendent qualities.

Although much of Shostakovich's musical language is tonal according to the major–minor system, there is also a strong admixture of octatonic elements based on an eight-note scale of regularly alternating tones and semitones.[12] Whereas the heptatonic scale is formed from two tetrachords overlapping at one end (e.g., G–C, C–F), its octatonic counterpart is based on a continuous chain of four overlapping trichords (e.g. G–B♭, B♭–D♭, C♯–E, E–G). The separation of trichords belonging to the same octatonal scale by minor thirds (or diminished fourths) explains some of the apparently remote, but in reality proximate, key relationships that occur in the quartets and elsewhere in Shostakovich's music. For example, the C minor and G sharp minor juxtapositions in Quartet No. 8 and the A flat major and E minor juxtapositions in Quartet No. 10 are of this type.

The bitter-sweet ambiguity between major third and diminished fourth inherent in octatonal writing pervades this music (there is a similarity here to Mahler, one of Shostakovich's idols, who also likes to exploit the uncertainties generated by oscillations between notes a semitone apart that can be interpreted either as minor and major third or as minor third and diminished fourth). Further, the octatonic scale encompasses, at three different levels simultaneously, the interval structure of Shostakovich's celebrated musical monogram formed from the letters D–S–C–H (for D. SCHostakowitsch (in German spelling), resulting in the notes D–E♭–C–B). Because this motto, including its multitude of anagrammatic forms and transpositions, fits so neatly into the octatonic system, it can be said to belong more to *langue* than to *parole*, maintaining as obtrusive or unobtrusive a presence as the composer desires.[13]

---

[11] David Fanning has pointed out to me, however, that muting, which qualifies as a 'special effect' (albeit of a very familiar and technically undemanding kind), is employed exceptionally copiously by Shostakovich.

[12] The octatonic scale is naturally subject to exactly the same kind of chromatic inflection and modulation (through transposition to another level) as the heptatonic scale. Many of the variant scales and modes that theorists have identified in Shostakovich's music can be explained more simply by reference to these two processes.

[13] The first prominent untransposed and unanagrammatized statement of the Shostakovich monogram is stated in the literature to occur in the third movement of the Tenth Symphony,

Another coincidence (or not): the trichord spanning a diminished fourth is a prominent and characteristic feature of the so-called Phrygian (*freigish*) mode in Jewish folk music from Eastern Europe (as performed by Klezmer bands), where the second degree of the scale is flattened and the third raised.[14] A *freigish* scale beginning on G includes the notes of Shostakovich's monogram between degrees 3 and 6. Shostakovich's infatuation with the melody, rhythm, and texture of Jewish folk music (which, in view of the marginalized, threatened position of Jews in Soviet Russia, especially under Stalin, was in itself tantamount to an act of solidarity with actual and potential enemies of the state) seems to date from his completion in early 1944, as a labour of love, of the opera *Rothschild's Violin* by his lately deceased Jewish pupil Veniamin Fleishman (1913–41).[15] The incidence of identifiably Jewish elements in Shostakovich's music written from 1944 onwards is extraordinarily high—certainly higher than most commentators have ventured to claim. Once again, they are so thoroughly assimilated as to have become part of his everyday *langue*.

Shostakovich betrays the characteristically twentieth-century preoccupation with 'organic' unity by favouring inter-movement links, or at least *attacca* connections (a subsidiary reason for the links may be—exactly as in Mendelssohn's concertos—a desire to foster concentration on the part of his listeners). No fewer than six of the quartets (Nos. 5, 7, 8, 9, 11, and 15) have all their movements linked, and a further six (Nos. 2, 3, 4, 6, 10, and 14) have links between their two last movements only.[16] The privileging of the last pair of movements in respect of linkage is interesting and important; it certainly contributes to the sense of end-weighting (allied, in certain cases, to summativity) that most of the quartets display. It is interesting that these connections exist irrespective of whether the penultimate movement has 'scherzo' or 'slow movement' character. Noteworthy, too, is the high incidence of movements marked either 'allegretto' or 'moderato'; only quartets Nos. 13 and 15 fail to use at least one of these directions (Nos. 3 and 4 each have three such movements). The composer's fondness for 'middling' tempi is perhaps not unconnected with his difficulty, to which he himself

Op. 93 (1953). It remains to establish whether the motto drew Shostakovich to the octatonic scale or the reverse.

[14] The presence of Jewish motifs and musical elements in Shostakovich's music is discussed in Joachim Braun, 'The Double Meaning of Jewish Elements in Dmitri Shostakovich's Music', *Musical Quarterly*, 71 (1985), 68–80. Braun recognizes Jewish elements in Opp. 67, 77, 79, 87, 91, 107, 110, and 113.

[15] *Testimony*, claimed to be the memoirs of Shostakovich as dictated to and edited by Solomon Volkov (London, 1979), is today generally agreed to represent the composer's views fairly accurately, although the extent of Volkov's intervention remains unclear. The book contains (on pp. 118–20) a lengthy excursus on the composer's fondness for Jewish music, his use of elements drawn from it in his own compositions, and on his, and his family's, opposition to Russian and Soviet anti-Semitism.

[16] In No. 2 the *attacca* link is unstated; it is strongly suggested, however, by the off-tonic beginning of the finale with the very note (E♭) on which the preceding 'Valse' closed.

admitted, with writing opening sonata allegros; he thinks naturally in spacious paragraphs that need time for their unfolding but, on the other hand, are too urgent to linger over. A relatively narrow ambit of basic 'pulses' employed during a work can also aid Shostakovich in his drive to establish inter-movement (as well as intra-movement) relationships.

The shadow of Beethoven hangs over all of Shostakovich's quartets. Not for nothing did he pointedly inscribe 'In memory of the great Beethoven' over the last movement of his last work (the Viola Sonata), which relays echoes of the 'Moonlight' Sonata. Noting this influence, Griffiths points to their 'symphonic spaciousness', the prominence within them of solo recitative and song, the frequency of structures that deviate (in either the character or the number of the movements) from the conventional, and the composer's use of the quartet genre as the vehicle for a 'consciously articulated late style'.[17] To these influences one could add a fondness for intensive development (like Beethoven, Shostakovich is a master of development sections organized in several discrete phases, one such phase acting identifiably as the section's—and the movement's—climax), as well as for long-drawn-out codas. Beyond these technical matters, one often catches a 'tone' (heroic, elegant, elegiac, *faux-naïf*, or whatever) that takes one straight back to Beethoven. Admittedly, a similar 'tone' (usually less expertly captured) informs much Russian and Soviet music from Borodin onwards; Beethoven's triumph over personal adversity and his concern for the broader human condition provided an inspiring role model equally for reform-minded intellectuals under Tsarism and for the later fulfillers of Five-Year Plans.

To Beethoven's influence Shostakovich adds (often within the same composition) that of Bach. The Bachian legacy is most evident in Shostakovich's bass lines, which have the same sculpted melodic shape and importance for the thematic discourse. Indeed, one could well argue that Bach and Shostakovich are the two composers since 1600 who have invested the most musical weight and meaning in their bass lines. Baroque-style counterpoint is also much in evidence, manifesting itself in ostinatos, canons, fugatos, and many other artifices.

The scene is now set to discuss the quartets, and in particular their finales, individually.

*Quartet No. 1 in C major, Op. 49.*   Shostakovich suppressed the title *Springtime* that he originally gave this quartet. It was written in a year, 1938, when the Great Terror was starting to recede (for want of more victims, one might say) and the material benefits of the Second Five-Year Plan, in terms of consumer goods, were just beginning to come on stream. Even if the composer privately regarded the title of the quartet as a reference to an aspiration rather than an actual achievement, there can be no doubt about the bubbling

---

[17] Griffiths, *The String Quartet*, 215. In *Testimony* (p. xxxiii) Volkov aptly describes Shostakovich's late works as being, for the first time, 'about himself *for* himself [original emphasis]'.

mood of the work. It outdoes in neo-Classicism Prokofiev's First Quartet, a work that may have influenced it, although traces of Tchaikovsky's quartets are also evident. Lasting about fourteen minutes, it is shorter than any of the other quartets except No. 7 (which is a mere twelve minutes long).[18]

Its four-movement plan is ultra-conventional. An opening sonata-form movement is succeeded by a short set of variations on a theme of markedly Russian character (initially presented monophonically), a fast scherzo resembling a waltz that has spun out of control, and a sonata-form 'allegro' to conclude. Even though the inner movements are set in minor keys (A minor and C sharp minor respectively), they each preserve the 'prettiness' of the opening 'moderato' (a comparison with Haydn's instrumental works of the late 1770s would not be inapt). Although shorter in duration than the first movement, the finale is by far the more complex movement. Whereas the first movement has only a residual development section (a feature that also has Viennese Classical roots), the finale has a well-developed, even slightly strenuous one, followed by a recapitulation and coda that exhibit the same cunning juggling and intercutting of material that we admire in Haydn. This movement abounds in such subtleties as the augmentation and diminution of themes, playful metrical shifts (the passages in 3/4 metre seem a deliberate back-reference to the third movement), and the canonic presentation of material (near the start of the recapitulation, at figure 66). All these devices recur constantly in the later quartets. The result is a work that is unambiguously end-weighted, even if the finale cannot be considered other than relaxant. From a thematic point of view, the quartet is uncommonly well unified, its germinal melodic idea being a series of three (or more) superposed fourths.

The markedly unproblematic nature of this quartet has been its problem, as viewed by commentators. The suggestions have sometimes been advanced that Shostakovich chose to be ultra-cautious in the aftermath of his official rehabilitation (after the *Lady Macbeth* scandal) via the Fifth Symphony, Op. 47 (1937), or that the string quartet genre itself was a 'bourgeois' genre under threat that needed especially careful handling. Neither possibility can be discounted altogether, although we should not deem the composer incapable of sometimes taking a holiday from problematizing and instead simply 'making music', as Richard Strauss called it. It is probably no coincidence that Shostakovich's 'Simple Quartet' is his first piece in the genre and also has C major as its key. To judge from Shostakovich's other C major pieces opening a series or collection (the 24 *Preludes*, Op. 34, and the 24 *Preludes and Fugues*, Op. 87, are the cases in point), he appears to have regarded a short, heavily stylized composition as the appropriate beginning for a long cycle (as if to symbolize the idea that from simple

---

[18] Timings are based on the figures given in Derek C. Hulme, *Dmitri Shostakovich: A Catalogue, Bibliography, and Discography* (Oxford, 1991[2]), a work on which I have relied for much of the simple factual information concerning Shostakovich's quartets.

origins more complex things later emerge) and to have taken on board the traditional 'ethos' of C major, whose notation, unencumbered by a key signature, hints at a similarly transparent quality in the music itself.[19]

As the only Shostakovich quartet that predates the Second World War (which for the Soviet Union began in 1941), the First Quartet stands a little apart from the rest. Its true and immediate successor is not the Second Quartet but the Piano Quintet, Op. 57 (1940), whose only slightly more expansive neo-Classicism garnered a Stalin Prize.

*Quartet No. 2 in A major, Op. 68.* This is the most 'patriotic' of Shostakovich's quartets. Its Russian character shines through each of its movements—and yet, as we shall see, there is a twist. Its folkloristic tinge seems to be a riposte to that of Prokofiev's Second Quartet, on Caucasian (Kabardinian) themes, composed in 1941. The affinity of their opening movements, both of which begin *con slancio* with heavy accompanying chords, is undeniable. In the autumn of 1944 the Soviet army had all but liberated its native territory and victory appeared a mere matter of time. However, the recovery of occupied land brought only more tales of atrocity and death. In his Second Piano Trio, Op. 67, completed only shortly before, Shostakovich addressed for the first time the specific dimension of Jewish suffering. Its third movement, although described as a passacaglia by the composer and most commentators, is in reality modelled on a popular type of *doina* cultivated by Klezmer musicians in which a pair of melody instruments weave dialoguing arabesques over a repeated background of evenly spaced chords.[20] The finale, a kind of eerie *Totentanz*, relates even more closely to Jewish folk idiom.

The first intrusion of this new element occurs soon after the opening movement's second subject group gets under way (three bars before figure 6). It takes the form of a 'sighing' form of delivery (a chain of *Seufzer*, as German Baroque theory would have described it) that is especially characteristic of Jewish music both inside and outside the synagogue.[21] From then on, this figure (which much of the time applies itself to oriental-sounding semitonal rotations around a central note) partners the 'Russian' material in counterpoint or dialogue. Under the influence of its *melos* the recapitulation of the entire exposition material (at figure 22) is chromatically, and thus also modally, transformed.[22] Shostakovich introduces a

---

[19] David Fanning has explored Shostakovich's relationship to the key of C major in a paper, 'Shostakovich in C', read in Oct. 1998 to a conference on 'Nation, Myth, and Reality' at the University of London.

[20] In a conventional passacaglia, as it exists within Western art music, the ostinato principle is applied to a single line, variously harmonized, rather than to an entire chordal texture. The *doina*, distinguishable by its improvised character, originates from Romania.

[21] In Braun's terminology this is the 'iambic prime': each note in a series is introduced by its unaccented anticipation, usually slurred to the previous note.

[22] The change to the character of the first and second subjects is so radical that the recapitulation was mistaken for part of the development by one commentator, who therefore had to locate it in the coda (and comment how severely abridged it was). See Niall O'Loughlin, 'Shostakovich's String Quartets', *Tempo*, 87 (1968–9), 9–16 at 11.

lightly anagrammatized version of his untransposed monogram at figure 22, the climactic point of the strenuous development section, as if to express a personal solidarity.

For our present purposes, we may pass quickly over the inner movements, a 'Recitative and Romance' in B flat major, in which the 'repeated sighs' figure features even more prominently, and a ghostly 'Valse' in E flat minor whose second theme is similarly characterized.[23]

In planning his finale, Shostakovich was faced with the same problem as Beethoven after three movements of the 'Eroica' Symphony: how to achieve a movement of equal weight to the first, but of sufficiently different form and character. Once again, the solution was variation form—but on a scale, and with a degree of internal complexity, appropriate to its position. Another point of difference is that the finale is emphatically in the minor mode (the repeated close-position tonic triads with which it closes, strikingly similar to, and perhaps influenced by, those ending Sibelius's Fourth Symphony, seem to express grim determination), joining the very select group of consistently minor-key finales ending major-key works on which comment was made in Chapter 4.

The complexity arises mainly from the fact that the long main theme, which enters at figure 92, has a prefatory theme (also monophonic, and shaped as a dialogue between a repeating, *tutti*-like bass motif and recitative-like responses on the first violin) from which it draws the material of its last bars. This prefatory theme returns, with variation, three times in the closing stages of the movement, as if to claim parity with the main theme, and finally merges into it in the coda. So this is a 'double' variation form, albeit of an unconventional kind. The shape of the movement is summarized in Table 10.2.

The first four statements of theme 1, which assign the melody to the four instruments in turn (as at the start of the slow movement of Haydn's Op. 76 No. 3, the 'Emperor' Quartet), are the kind of 'limbering up' that one recognizes from Classical usage (the 'Eroica' finale is a case in point). In variations 5 and 6 the theme is taken to new tonal areas and subjected to contrapuntal processes. Variations 8–10 are 'character' variations, in which the acceleration of the theme (via changes in tempo and/or note values) is taken to its furthest point.[24] The *maggiore* variation begins a process of deceleration, which continues to the end of the movement.[25] The variations

---

[23] Surprisingly, Griffiths (*The String Quartet*, 213) refers to 'the cheapening subtitles for the middle movements [which] imply, as the music itself implies, a mistrust of the confident, archetypical structures that are being re-embodied'. And what of the 'Cavatina' in Beethoven's Op. 130?

[24] The repeated pedal note in variation 10 recalls, and may be a conscious reference to, the bass in the sixth variation, 'un poco più vivace', of the finale of Beethoven's 'Harp' Quartet, Op. 74.

[25] A good comparison could be made with the fourth variation in the second movement of Schubert's 'Death and the Maiden' Quartet (D. 810). In both cases, the major-key sweetness appears saccharine (for legitimate effect) and forced.

TABLE 10.2.   *Plan of the finale of Shostakovich, Quartet No. 2 in A major, Op. 68*

| Figure | Theme | Time | Key | Comment |
|--------|-------|------|-----|---------|
| 90 | 1 | 1 | E♭ → e | treble/bass dialogue |
| 92 | 2 | 1 | a | theme in viola, unaccompanied |
| 93 | 2 | 2 | a | theme in violin 2 |
| 95 | 2 | 3 | a | theme in violin 1 |
| 97 | 2 | 4 | a | theme in cello |
| 99 | 2 | 5 | f♯ | triplets in violin 1, decorative |
| 101 | 2 | 6 | f | fragmented, with canonic imitation |
| 105 | 2 | 7 | a | even more fragmented, using hocket |
| 107 | 2 | 8 | a | moto perpetuo semiquavers on violin 1 |
| 110 | 2 | 9 | b♭ | energetic on all instruments, quasi-orchestral |
| 112 | 2 | 10 | A♭ | over an E♭ pedal in repeated triplet quavers |
| 115 | 1 | 2 | E♭ → B | theme 1 (*tutti* motif) in bass |
| 116 | 2 | 11 | B → d | parody of Classical *maggiore* variation |
| 120 | 1 | 3 | d → a | over a drone bass (alternating *D* and *A*) |
| 123 | 2 | 12 | a | with the *tutti* motif of theme 1 as descant |
| 128 | 1 | 4 | a | chordally reinforced reprise of the first statement |
| 129 | 1 | 13 | a | massively chordally reinforced, quasi-orchestral |

at figures 120 and 123 act as a recapitulation of the opening, and the last two as a coda. The movement is notable for the richness of variation processes it employs and their transparency. In *Testimony* Shostakovich (reportedly) criticizes Glazunov for not creating enough energy and tension;[26] this is decidedly not a fault he shares.

The Russian character of the main theme is emphasized by its similarity in its opening two bars, and again in its twelfth bar, to the opening theme of Musorgsky's *Boris Godunov*, for which Shostakovich had provided a new orchestration in 1939–40—see Ex. 10.1, which shows its second appearance. By compressing Musorsky's sequence of notes A–G♯–F♯–E–G♯ into a diminished fourth, F♭–E♭–D♭–C–E♭, and prefixing an upbeat E♭, Shostakovich even manages to smuggle in the notes of his monogram. Already in this first variation a complementary Jewish presence makes itself felt in the shape of the loping, 'clip-clop' rhythm of the bass, a style much favoured by Klezmer musicians.[27] In its sixth statement, after figure 103, the intervals

[26] Volkov, *Testimony*, 124.
[27] This style of accompaniment occurs often in Shostakovich's song-cycle *From Jewish Folk Poetry*, Op. 79 (1948, first performed in 1955), which, because of its subject, can function as a useful 'control' by which to determine what features are, or are not, intended as 'Jewish' by the composer. It also figures prominently in Prokofiev's *Overture on Hebrew Themes*, Op. 34.

Ex. 10.1.    Shostakovich, String Quartet No. 2 in A major, Op. 68, last movement, bars 31–45

of the theme's twelfth and thirteenth bars become compressed into the interval of a diminished third (i.e. the semitonal rotation around a central note mentioned in connection with the first movement), a recognizably Jewish feature seen also in the opening theme of the finale of the Second Piano Trio. In its subtle bi-nationalism the finale seems to plead for unity and inclusiveness amid tragic events.

*Quartet No. 3 in F major, Op. 73.*   Like Mahler, in his First Symphony, Shostakovich originally provided informal programmatic descriptions, not intended for publication, for each of the movements in this quartet. The titles are revealing and help to explain the otherwise puzzling contrast of mood between the first movement and the four movements that follow it. They are, respectively: 'Calm unawareness of the future cataclysm'; 'Rumblings of unrest and anticipation'; 'The forces of war unleashed'; 'Homage to the dead'; and 'The eternal question—Why? And for what?'[28]

Written a year after the end of the 'Great Patriotic War', the quartet reviews the experience of this event in the context of the weary picking up of pieces afterwards (and the disappointment of widespread hopes that Stalin would not reimpose his dictatorship in its pre-war severity). It runs parallel to the slightly earlier Eighth Symphony in some aspects of structure. In both cases, the central group of movements follows the sequence of (a) menacing scherzo, (b) ferocious scherzo, and (c) funeral march styled as a passacaglia leading into, and later reintroducing itself as an episode in, the finale. The last movement of both works is a languid rondo, wistful rather than cheerful. Their first movements could not, however, be more different. That of the Eighth Symphony is brooding and laboured, while the Third Quartet's opening 'allegretto' is sparkling in the manner of the finale of the First Quartet—only a highly dissonant development section (based, un-usually, exclusively on the opening theme) hints at darker things to come.

This quartet's finale, like those of the first two quartets, falls into the 'relaxant' category. Yet its tender, elegiac tone is highly unusual for the context. One could describe the movement as a relaxant finale wearing valedictory clothing. A valedictory finale *tout court* it is not, since it repre-sents the extinction not of life, but (perhaps only temporarily) of hope. Behind the lamentation there is staying power. The finale's and the quartet's message is encapsulated in the last statement of its refrain, transformed into a coda by its inability to proceed beyond its first phrase, which soars upwards into celestial transfiguration over an inert F major chord. Final redemption through escape to a (literally) higher sphere is a motif Shosta-kovich will employ again in quartets 4, 5, 10, 11, and 13.

*Quartet No. 4 in D major, Op. 83.* This is commonly regarded as 'the' Jewish quartet of Shostakovich, although in that respect it merely emphasizes more strongly what was already apparent in the Second Quartet and will recur in at least one later quartet. In general terms, the Fourth Quartet could be said to retreat from the heroic temper of the two intervening works, which are comparable with Beethoven's Op. 59, to recapture the chamber-music intim-acy of the First Quartet. Once again, the first movement presents, in simpli-fied guise, the sonata-form structure to be deployed on an ampler scale in the finale, while the two central movements are cameos of strongly 'generic' character.

The first movement is pseudo-idyllic in a manner familiar from the closing songs in *From Jewish Folk Poetry*, composed only a short time before. It is dominated by its bucolic pedal-points and nagging, sinuous melodic lines, in which occasional progressions of parallel perfect fourths suggest folk polyphony. One interesting novelty, which recalls the modal

---

[28] The translations are as given in Hulme's catalogue.

transformations in the finale of the Second Quartet, is that the first subject (there is no development section) is recapitulated over an E, instead of a D, pedal. The discursive 'andante' in F minor is at first sight styled as a straightforwardly 'Russian' romance (its elegant coolness could be compared with that of the F minor prelude in Op. 87); it stands a little apart from the other movements in style and temper and for that reason is arguably a weak part of the quartet. Nevertheless, a vestige of the 'Jewish' character remains (consider, for example, the first violin line at figure 23). In the 'trio' section of the beautifully crafted 'allegretto' scherzo, in C minor, Shostakovich employs Jewish elements—notably the 'semitonal rotation' figure—more conspicuously. In its coda, which is continued to become an introduction to the finale, also 'allegretto', he gives the viola declamatory phrases composed almost entirely of 'repeated sighs' in implied *tempo rubato*, which are punctuated by pizzicato chords evocative of the *tsimbl*, or cimbalom. This heralds the beginning of a movement whose main theme (at figure 58), wrenched up a tone to D (Dorian minor), has a strong flavour of a Hasidic dance, complete with 'clip-clop' bass. The long and brutally intense development section (between figures 69 and 84) places this theme on the rack. At its *fortissimo* climax (figure 78, repeating at figure 81), Shostakovich uses the same variant of his monogram (its second and third notes connected by a passing note) that had appeared in the finale of the Second Quartet to add his voice to the cry.

The recapitulation is signalled by the irruption of the C minor introduction, amplified in quasi-orchestral style (the 'tsimbl' now hammers *tremolando* chords). It soon subsides, however, into the muted, melancholic amble (almost shamble) of the exposition. The movement peters out tenderly with dirge-like fragments suggesting solemn choral intonation and shreds of yearningly arching melody. Were one to invent a simple narrative for this movement, one could visualize it as the course of Soviet Jewish life before (exposition), during (development), and after (recapitulation) the War.

This is unquestionably a summative finale. The point is not that it is more complex or longer than the first and middle movements (which it is) but that it is far richer in content and, as it were, distils and concentrates the work's essential hermeneutic meaning. This effect is achieved not by direct thematic requotation but by recasting what was diluted and fragmented in earlier movements into a definitive, more uncompromising shape. In other words, it is the finale (and only the finale) that 'stands for' the meaning of this work.

*Quartet No. 5 in B flat major, Op. 92.*   The Fifth Quartet almost matches the Second and Third for length—a remarkable fact when one considers that it is one of three quartets in the series to have only three movements, here configured F–S–F. All are in sonata form (the slow movement lacks a development section).

In general, composers take care, when the plan is as symmetrical as this, either to differentiate the outer movements clearly or to turn the finale into a reprise (normally varied) of the first movement. Shostakovich lives dangerously by doing neither one thing nor the other. The movements are similar in length (about ten minutes), and the only really conspicuous difference in their form is that the first movement has a repeated exposition (as in Quartet No. 2) and the finale is framed by two versions of a ruminative section that in a quicker tempo ('moderato') connects it with the slow movement and in a slower tempo ('andante') winds it down in conclusion.[29] Both open insouciantly, become darker-hued during the transition and the second subject group, enter a world of harrowing drama in a long development section, and revert to their former existence clearly marked by the experience. The differences of tempo, metre, and style of movement are relatively slight (each contains episodes of waltz character). In both the diminished fourth dominates as never before; it encloses the composer's monogram in various permutations (starting with the viola's phrase in bar 2 of the opening movement), as well as countless more or less inter-related dispositions of diatonic and chromatic notes.

Extroversive reference also occurs. The motif on the violins presented in the first movement at figure 3 is 'distorted' (compressed into a diminished fourth) at figure 25, a climactic point in the development; in this form, as Ex. 10.2 shows, it is identical with the 'altered' monograms appearing at the climaxes of the finales of the second and fourth quartets. This time, however, it is less apparent to what the composer is bearing witness. Four bars

Ex. 10.2.   Shostakovich, String Quartet No. 5 in B flat major, Op. 92, last movement, bars 233–6

[29] The development section of the finale opens with a statement of the first subject in the tonic, as if it intends to follow the routine of the first movement—but this is only a feint, similar to that in the first movement of Beethoven's Op. 59 No. 1.

Ex. 10.3.   Shostakovich, String Quartet No. 5 in B flat major, Op. 92, last movement, bars 341–9

after figure 117 in the finale, the pizzicato strings present, in full chords, Shostakovich's characteristic 'rat-tat-tat' (or 'anapaestic') rhythm—the one that develops into a quotation from Rossini's overture to *Guillaume Tell* in the Fifteenth Symphony; between its statements is inserted an enigmatic scrap of diatonic melody that appears to have immigrated from Rimsky-Korsakov's *Sheherazade*.[30] The passage is given as Ex. 10.3. This deliberately incongruous insertion, whether intended a quotation or not, has an effect similar to the 'barrel organ tune' in the last movement of Bartók's Fifth Quartet. It shows how the process of regression (in this case, the diatonicization of what was previously chromatic) can be used, in twentieth-century

---

[30] It is a simplification of the melody first heard at bar 141 in the fourth movement of the suite, which in its turn derives from the main theme of the third movement.

music, for humorous or ironic ends: the simpler the material becomes, the more connections it is able to forge with music of the past.

As Colin Mason has pointed out, a significant theme introduced in the development section of the first movement—initially at figure 29—recurs in that of the third, initially at figure 109.[31] David Fanning has recently identified the provenance of this theme: a Trio for Clarinet, Violin, and Piano (1949) by Shostakovich's composition pupil Galina Ustvolskaya.[32] On both occasions, the quotations occur in a high register for the respective instrument (violin in movement 1, cello in movement 3), as if to express both the composer's erotic passion and the beloved's unattainability—Fanning relates that he proposed marriage to her twice and was rebuffed both times.

Immediately before this undoubtedly significant 'extroversive' reference, at figure 108, the finale reaches back to the quartet's own slow movement for another theme. It has to be said, however, that the two borrowings, important though they are for the micro-structure of the finale (as well as the quartet's hermeneutic import), make no deep impact on its macro-structure. In the last analysis, it remains relaxant in type, even if the 'relaxation', in a literal sense, is fitful.

*Quartet No. 6 in G major, Op. 101.*  This quartet provides convalescence after the rigours of Quartet No. 5. It is by far the most melodious (in the traditional *cantabile* sense) and the most conventionally tonal in overall effect of any of the series. Shostakovich's melodic spans are here huge, approaching the scale of those favoured by Prokofiev although not abandoning his characteristically piecemeal, 'modular' system of construction. The basic material is that already presented in the *Sheherazade*-like reference in Ex. 10.3: three-note linear progressions between the notes of the major triad. Emphatic, rising V–I progressions are also a recurrent idea.

The first movement, largely in common time, is in ordinary sonata form. Especially noteworthy is its undisguised borrowing of material, in the second subject group, from the corresponding section of the first movement of the Third Quartet. Its 40-bar coda, in which the tonic triad is playfully elaborated, Beethoven-style, with dissonant chromatic notes (C♯, A♭), is achingly beautiful. As his parting gesture, Shostakovich plucks a bass motif from bars 11–13 and reuses it, in a more solemn guise, as a motto phrase; the same phrase, similarly harmonized, is then brought back to conclude each of the movements (appropriately transposed in the case of the second movement, a lilting waltz in E flat major). The third movement, in G flat major, is a genuine passacaglia (not a *doina*, this time) with seven statements of the bass theme; between the fifth and sixth statements the composer has an interlude, during which he introduces a haunting theme

---

[31] Colin Mason, 'Form in Shostakovich's Quartets', *Musical Times*, 103 (1962), 531–3 at 532.

[32] See David Fanning's commentary to catalogue entries 115 and 116 in Felix Meyer (ed.), *Settling New Scores: Music Manuscripts from the Paul Sacher Foundation* (Basle, 1998), 235–8.

whose opening is strikingly similar to the first theme of the slow movement of Prokofiev's Second Quartet.

The finale, like that of the preceding quartet, recasts, but does not radically depart from, the form, mood, and material of the first movement. Once again, triple metre dominates (though the second subject's main theme is an eerie 'fairy' march in cut time). Unusually for him, Shostakovich opts for a 'mirror' recapitulation: the first subject returns after the second, and the coda is merely its extension.

This ending, like the quartet as a whole, is certainly light (in the manner of the First Quartet, in fact), but not flippant or facile.[33] It radiates an undramatic, simple beauty that is beyond profundity or, better, is profound by virtue of its mysterious grace and ease.

*Quartet No. 7 in F sharp minor, Op. 108.*   This highly compact work is a favourite among commentators. Its laconic manner, enigmatic expression, and inventive, well-integrated structure have justly earned it admiration. Once again, a three-movement plan, F–S–F, is adopted. In this quartet we catch the first glimpses of the economy and audacious simplification of style that characterize the late period.

Its first movement is dominated by the 'rat-tat-tat' figure commented on earlier, which serves as the pendant to a striking opening motif, utilizing the same three-note cells as in Quartet No. 6, only now 'deformed' chromatically (diminished thirds and fourths are on the march again). The second subject, profiled in short, breathless phrases against a background of 'scrubbing' semiquavers, has almost a *buffo* character. The movement is otherwise in normal sonata form, except for the Bartók-like metamorphosis (from 2/4 to 3/8 metre) of the recapitulated first subject.

The 'lento' is in cantilena style. At figure 20 the viola and cello playing in octaves introduce reminiscences of the First Cello Concerto, Op. 107, which had been composed in the previous year, 1959. The unaccompanied viola ends the movement with the motto phrase B♭♭–A♭–G♭–F (or enharmonically, A–G♯–F♯–E♯), which, previously concealed under layers of elaboration, comes to the fore in the finale.

This is, technically, a 'divided' finale, as the term was defined in Chapter 7. Its structure is shown in Table 10.3. It begins as a fugue and ends as a waltz, the point of division occurring between figures 37 and 41. Despite the small scale of the work, the movement qualifies fully for the label 'summative', since it takes into itself and distils the essence of the two preceding movements, which are retrospectively recognized to be 'incomplete' statements of the central idea. From an aesthetic point of view, the ending is remarkable for its quiet intensity (the oxymoron is deliberate) and quizzical manner.

---

[33] Griffiths' reference to the 'strolling inconsequentiality' of the first movement (*The String Quartet*, 217) is surely over-harsh. May great music never stroll?

TABLE 10.3. *Plan of the finale of Shostakovich, Quartet No. 7 in F sharp minor, Op. 108*

| Figure | Description | Comment |
|---|---|---|
| 23 | Introduction | Based on an inversion of the theme opening movement 1. In bars 4–7 the unaccompanied viola repeats, in semibreves, the motto phrase (which resembles one of Schumann's 'Sphinxes' in *Carnaval*—except that it is actually played) |
| 24 | Fugato | The subject has two components: the first derived from the introduction, the second from dotted figures in the second movement. The fugal treatment is regular and includes a *stretto* at fig. 34 |
| 37 | Transition (i) | Return of the main theme of the second movement, once more in D minor |
| 38 | Transition (ii) | Return of the first-movement opening theme in B flat minor, in dissonant parallel chords. Continued with the 'rat-tat-tat' figure, developed freely |
| 41 | Waltz | The fugue subject returns, metamorphosed into an insubstantial 'valse oubliée', with all instruments muted |
| 46 | First-movement opening theme | *Détaché*, muted, and in the 3/4 metre of the waltz |
| 48 | Waltz | Reprise of the earlier section, now in C minor |
| 49 | First-movement opening theme | Pizzicato, otherwise similar to before (at fig. 46) |
| 52 | Coda | The head of the waltz and the tail of the opening theme combined. |

*Quartet No. 8 in C minor, Op. 110.* The Eighth Quartet is popular with audiences but controversial among commentators, who have sometimes found it obvious or over-repetitive (and perhaps shrink in any case from its no-holds-barred emotionalism). In short, it shares the fate of the overtly programmatic symphonies (in particular, Nos. 7, 11, and 12).

Confusingly, though also intriguingly, the quartet has two parallel programmes. The more politically 'respectable' one connects it with Germany, where Shostakovich composed it (in Görlitz, Saxony) in 1960. Its dedication 'to the victims of fascism and war' refers specifically to the Anglo-American bombing of Dresden in 1945, and the heavy repeated chords in 'rat-tat-tat' rhythm heard throughout the fourth movement represent the splutter of anti-aircraft fire. The fugal passages using the DSCH motto as their subject pay an obvious homage to J. S. Bach, the great Saxon composer of fugues on his own name (whom Shostakovich had already emulated in his Op. 87). Hence the nickname 'Dresden Quartet'.

The more subversive programme makes the work a memoir of Shostakovich's life and career—and also an intended suicide note.[34] According to this scenario, the monogram (treated variously as fugue subject and ostinato phrase) functions rather like the 'Promenade' in Musorgsky's *Pictures at an Exhibition*, linking one episode to the next and symbolizing the composer's constant presence. These episodes present a kaleidoscopic succession of images. In the first movement ('lento') we hear the opening of the First Symphony and a snippet from the Tenth Symphony; the fierce 'allegro molto' in G sharp minor that follows evokes the whirlwind-like second scherzo from the Eighth Symphony and uses the second theme, in C minor, of the finale of the Second Piano Trio for contrast (but hardly relief); the third movement, a malicious waltz, introduces the main theme of the opening movement of the First Cello Concerto and also very fleetingly (just before figure 45) that of the finale of the Third Quartet. The same theme from the Cello Concerto, prolonged to produce the gunnery, carries over into the fourth movement, another 'largo'; it is succeeded by references to the third movement of the Eleventh Symphony, to the second subject of the first movement of Tchaikovsky's Sixth Symphony, and to two vocal items: the popular song *Zamuchon tyazholoy nevolej* (*Tormented by Grievous Bondage*) and lastly a theme from Act IV of *Lady Macbeth of the Mtsensk District*.[35] The final movement, based on the material of the first movement (shorn of its quotations from symphonies), introduces a motif from the same opera as a regular counter-subject to the monogram. Doubtless, there are other significant quotations that have so far escaped identification (Shostakovich himself referred to one from the Funeral March for Siegfried in Wagner's *Götterdämmerung* that has eluded me).

Despite this superabundance of intertextual reference and the *attacca* connections, each movement has an adequately cogent structure. For the first, Shostakovich chooses an arch form; for the second, a scherzo and trio form (the trio returns as coda-cum-link); for the third, a similar ABA form; for the fourth, rondo form; and for the fifth, a through-composed form that at last allows the monogram fugue subject to be treated at length without interruption—in effect, we hear a purified version of the opening movement, in which the new counter-subject, frequently forming false relations with the subject, revitalizes the counterpoint and lends the expression a painful intimacy. These three final pages lay the work to rest not in a lachrymose but in a quietly dignified fashion, setting aside all the roughness of the middle movements (Ex. 10.4 shows the first entries). This is

---

[34] The suggestion that Shostakovich, depressed at having been coerced into membership of the Communist Party, seriously contemplated suicide, as reported much later by his friend Lev Lebedinsky (see Wilson, *Shostakovich*, 340–1), is certainly not to be rejected out of hand, though one should remain very cautious. The 'rat-tat-tat' figure, according to this scenario, can be interpreted as the knock on the door at midnight by the security police.

[35] The theme is the one with which Katerina declares to Sergei (in vain) her continuing love.

Ex. 10.4.  Shostakovich, String Quartet No. 8 in C minor, Op. 110, last movement, bars 7–18

Shostakovich's first valedictory finale in the quartets, and one to treasure. The composer himself wrote to his friend Isaak Glikman of the quartet's 'marvellous unity of form';[36] the way in which—almost in the manner of early seventeenth-century sonatas such as those by Dario Castello discussed in Chapter 2—the finale returns to the opening material but subtly transforms it contributes greatly to this effect.

*Quartet No. 9 in E flat major, Op. 117.*   This quartet takes the 'cyclic integration' aspect of Quartet No. 7 a stage further. Each of the four movements following the first is meticulously prepared at the end of its predecessor so that the flow of thought as well as of motion is uninterrupted. The opening bars of the first movement, shown as Ex. 10.5, contain *in nuce* the primitive thematic elements that the rest of the work will 'compose out' and combine. The first thing to note is the opposition between tonic and dominant, first expressed between the outer voices in bar 4. The second is the undulating line on violin 2. Figures of this type appearing in Shostakovich's works are

[36] Quoted in Wilson, *Shostakovich*, 340.

Ex. 10.5. Shostakovich, String Quartet No. 9 in E flat major, Op. 117, last movement, opening

commonly related to the leitmotif for Pimen's Narrative in *Boris Godunov* or to the new motif, elaborated contrapuntally, that appears in the development section of the opening movement of Beethoven's First 'Rasumovsky' Quartet. In fact, this is a topos that has been used for centuries to represent the minute up-and-down motions of handwriting (one meets it, for instance, in the motif for the central syllable of the word 'beschreibet'—'de-scribe-s'— in the Introit of Schütz's *St Matthew Passion*). The three-pitch motif on violin 1 is bounded by a perfect fourth; this will compete during the rest of the quartet with the diminished fourth, already in evidence (in the descent from G♭ to D) in bar 5. In the same bar, the second violin also presents the 'hump' shape 1–2–3–2–1 (with a minor third) that underlies several later themes. Versions of all these motifs will recur in many of Shostakovich's later quartets; like the notes of the upper tetrachord of the harmonic minor scale in Beethoven's late quartets, they act as elementary building blocks— 'pre-motifs' one might call them.

The opening movement, 'moderato con moto', is in the same kind of sonata form without a development section that we have encountered many times earlier. It is followed by a very brief 'adagio' in F sharp minor (a theme with episodes) and an equally brief, hectic scherzo in the same key that recalls, almost, that of the First Symphony. The triad of short cameo movements (in the spirit of Mahler) is rounded off by a lugubrious 'adagio' in E flat minor that takes the form of a quasi-vocal chant whose phrases are interspersed with recitative-like episodes.

It has been noted that the finale, in a very long and elaborate sonata form, begins almost as a second scherzo.[37] There is no disguising its playful mood, but its infallible pacing, combinatorial inventiveness, and ability to coax the

[37] G. W. Hopkins, 'Shostakovich's Ninth String Quartet', *Tempo*, 75 (1965–6), 23–5 at 24.

material into ever-new patterns (it provides another example of the metrically altered recapitulation) reveal an utter seriousness of compositional intention. The 'Guillaume Tell' fanfare motif (most regressive of all the manifestations of the perfect fourth), which was introduced already in the third movement, stamps its presence on the movement with telling effect. At figure 101, close to the start of the coda, Shostakovich veers abruptly into D major as if to signal the arrival of the Seventh Cavalry; this is a classic example of 'codal disruption'—the equivalent of the F sharp minor episode in the finale of Beethoven's Eighth Symphony.[38]

In a technical sense, this finale could be called summative: it collects the most important material of the earlier movements and delivers it in an integrated package. In a hermeneutic sense, however, it is not summative, since it adds or reveals no new meaning—and this is where it differs significantly from the finales of the seventh and fourteenth quartets.

*Quartet No. 10 in A flat major, Op. 118.* Although it was completed immediately after the Ninth Quartet and given its première at the same concert in 1964, the Tenth Quartet is some respects a throwback to the quartets of the immediate post-war period, even turning its back on the technical 'tricks' that figure so strongly (for Shostakovich) in its predecessor. It was dedicated to the talented composer Moisei Vainberg, a Polish Jew who had emigrated to the Soviet Union at the start of the War. In 1953 Shostakovich had even risked severe official displeasure by interceding with the feared minister of the interior, Beria, to have Vainberg released from prison, into which he had been thrown at the time of the campaign against 'rootless cosmopolitans' in its last, most vicious phase.

Unsurprisingly, this is another 'Jewish' work. The *freigish* flattened second is prominent from the start and develops in the second movement, yet another demonic scherzo, into a 'semitonal rotation' figure. The third movement starts as another *doina* (with an ostinato melody for the accompaniment), although it evolves to become a 'true' passacaglia at figure 45, when the ostinato melody migrates to the bass. The 'allegretto' finale rounds off this parade of Jewish features by introducing the 'clip-clop' bass at figure 54 (this reappears in augmentation at figure 59).

However, the most individual among the germinal ideas in this quartet is the plagal cadence (of which the accompanimental pattern in the 'adagio' presents no fewer than four in a row). First arriving at bars 18–19 in the first movement, it imparts a restful, on occasion mournful, feeling to the music.

The finale is the first in the quartets that could be confidently described as being in rondo rather than sonata form. Its outline is given in Table 10.4. Almost throughout, the 'tone' of this movement is popular. It invokes not only Klezmer music but also a broader, more *gemütlich* Central European idiom described in earlier pages as 'café-Hungarian'.

[38] There are two further disruptions (in D and A major respectively) before the end.

TABLE 10.4.  *Plan of the finale of Shostakovich, Quartet No. 10 in A flat major, Op. 118*

| Fig. | Description | Key | Comment |
|------|-------------|-----|---------|
| 52 | A | A♭ | refrain |
| 56 | B | d | first couplet (with 'Dorian' inflection) |
| 59 | A | A♭ | refrain, with varied accompaniment |
| 61 | C | f♯ | second couplet (with 'Phrygian' inflection) |
| 64 | development | → | uses all themes; the *doina* theme from movement 3 is introduced at fig. 74, preceded by hints of the second movement |
| 77 | B | d | reprise, with key unchanged from the original statement |
| 80 | A | A♭ | refrain: opening only, continued into... |
| 81 | Coda | A♭ | combines refrain material with a reprise of elements from movement 1 |

*Quartet No. 11 in F minor, Op. 122.*   This quartet has been described variously as a suite and as 'an insolent gloss...on Beethoven's C sharp minor quartet'.[39] Both characterizations have a point (forgetting the insolence). To offset the extreme economy and integration of the quartet's thematic substance, the composer finds it necessary to diversify the 'surface' of the composition by casting each movement (none too rigorously, it has to be said) as a genre piece. What is ostensibly 'light' (a chain of seven short, titled movements) is, in reality, only a mask for something distinctly 'heavy'.

An 'Introduction' presents the basic material: (i) a swirling melodic arc (spanning over two octaves) centred on the tonic (F); (ii) a pithy phrase (at figure 1) comprising the sequence of notes F♯–G–F♯–E–A–G–F♯; (iii) a funereal phrase, accompanied in pseudo-choral style, on the notes D–E♭–D–C–B (shortly after figure 2). These ideas will suffice for the whole quartet.

There follow a 'Scherzo' full of whimsical chatter, a harshly dissonant 'Recitative' whose 'melodic' line consists of laconic double-stopped phrases, *fortissimo*, on first violin, an 'étude' in which moto perpetuo semiquavers on violin 1 pass eventually to the cello, a 'Humoresque' in which violin 2 inanely repeats alternating quavers on *g″* and *e″*, and an 'Elegy' in the familiar funeral march style going back to the 'Eroica' Symphony.

The 'Finale', which remains at *pianissimo* level almost throughout, provides a soothing conclusion, bringing together in new combinations material from the first two movements. The rocking figure in quavers that appears in the second violin in the first part of the movement is borrowed from the finale of Quartet No. 6, where it conveys a similar calm. Although this is a *Moderato* movement, it can be classified as a valedictory finale according to the usual criteria.

[39]  Griffiths, *The String Quartet*, 215.

There is, of course, an external rationale for the sadness and softness of the music. It is dedicated to the memory of Vasili Shirinsky, the original second violinist of the Beethoven Quartet. Throughout the work, one is conscious of the 'empty seat'; the part for Shirinsky's replacement, Nikolai Zabavnikov, is kept tactfully discreet. The one movement that brings the second violin into prominence, the 'Humoresque', may harbour a private, posthumous joke.

*Quartet No. 12 in D flat major, Op. 133.* This is Shostakovich's famous 'twelve-note' quartet. Those who search for such things have identified twelve-note (or rather: almost-twelve-note) rows in the fourth movement of Quartet No. 3 and the opening movement of Quartet No. 8. But these are probably only the fortuitous outcome of highly chromatic writing, as the composer himself intimated, comparing them with a similar appearance in Mozart (probably the well-known passage in diminished sevenths near the beginning of the development section of the finale of Symphony No. 40).[40] In Quartet No. 12, by contrast, the twelve-note passages are demonstrably intentional, inserted into the music at intervals almost in the manner of a collage. Shostakovich treats the row thematically, like any other melodic material, not serially. In this respect the admiration of the late Hans Keller, who discerned in it a homage to Schoenberg's *First Chamber Symphony*, is as misleading as it is welcome and unexpected.[41] Shostakovich is on record as voicing his doubts about the utility of the Schoenbergian method (some will insist: 'methods') of composing with twelve notes. But he defended as a matter of principle the right of composers to use this or any other technique relevant to their artistic purposes. In that sense, the note row on unaccompanied cello occupying bar 1 and the first note of bar 2 (the tonic, D flat) is a deliberate political provocation, an opening of the forbidden gate by someone harder (by 1968) to thrust back than the many younger composers who had a genuine interest in serial composition. Every now and again, Shostakovich repeats (with permutations) his row theme, just in case the challenge was overlooked.

The quartet is dedicated to Dmitri Tsyganov, leader of the Beethoven Quartet. Appropriately, Shostakovich writes a showy first violin part, but he also pays homage to the composer whose name the quartet bears (and which Tsyganov founded) in the form of two quotations from the 'Rasumovsky' Quartets, with which, significantly, Beethoven is linked to Russia. The first is the 'writing' motif (movement 1, bars 2–3) appearing at the start of the development section in the first movement of Op. 59 No. 1; the other, possibly unrecognized until now, is another phrase in quavers (movement 1, bars 8–10), which comes straight from bars 80–1 of the first movement of Op. 59 No. 3. More generally, fragments of the *thème russe* of the fourth

---

[40] Wilson, *Shostakovich*, 409.
[41] Hans Keller, 'Shostakovich's Twelfth Quartet', *Tempo*, 94 (1970), 6–15.

movement of Op. 59 No. 1 crop up all over the quartet, lending it a Beethovenian sheen.

Most two-movement works written after Beethoven's Op. 111 have summative or valedictory finales, and the reason is not hard to find. It is that compensation for the 'lack' of a movement (or two) is seen as necessary, and this compensation has to take the form of bolstering the second movement in some way. In the post-Beethoven age a relaxant finale for a two-movement work, such as the master himself earlier provided in the two cello sonatas of his Op. 5, is no longer good enough.

Shostakovich takes this lesson to heart. The first movement is a mere prelude: three short sections based on the Beethoven material (and garnished with 'serial' accretions) alternating twice with a fairly unmemorable contrasting section. In comparison, the second movement is massive. Its opening section, recapitulated in varied form as the coda, is a mercurial scherzo (complete with trio section) that recovers some of the swagger of the second movement of the early *Prelude and Scherzo*, Op. 11, for string octet (1925). The scherzo encloses an 'adagio', which in turn encloses a development section devoted to all the main themes of both movements. There is a separate reference to the first movement just before the coda based on the material of the scherzo.

The finale is therefore classically summative: it both adds and incorporates, containing within itself a scherzo, a slow movement, and a development of the material given out (but barely developed) in the first movement.

*Quartet No. 13 in E flat minor, Op. 138.* Since this sombre work, uniquely for Shostakovich's quartets, is in a single movement, discussion can be brief. Dedicated to Vadim Borisovsky, the retired violist of the Beethoven Quartet, it gives the viola pride of place, celebrating the ability of Borisovsky's pupil and replacement in the Quartet, Felix Druzhinin, to play ultra-high notes.[42] Its form is ternary, with a slow outer section and a 'doppio movimento' central section, flanked by a transition and a retransition, in which Shostakovich, who was gravely ill at the time, gives us the most sinister of his *Totentänze*, complete with intermittent raps from the players with the wood of the bows on the belly of their instruments. The opening twelve-note theme, for solo viola, recalls the 'Faust' motif from the homonymous symphony by Liszt in its brooding, questioning manner. Unlike in the preceding quartet, this theme and its derivatives are fully integrated into the form and thematic treatment. In fact, Quartet No. 13 represents the furthest *rapprochement* Shostakovich made in his quartets with the main current of modernism—a few passages have almost the textural and timbral complexity of Bartók.

---

[42] The viola, joined at the same pitch by the violins, ends the work in the treble clef with a B♭ *in altissimo.*

*Quartet No. 14 in F sharp major, Op. 142.* Shostakovich's dedication of this quartet to Sergei Shirinsky, cellist of the Beethoven Quartet, is reflected in the prominence of the cello part throughout.[43] The quartet also has in places a very Bachian feel; in the opening theme, and many times subsequently one has the sensation of eavesdropping on private practice of the Bach suites for unaccompanied cello; this impression is heightened by the prevalence of quadratic phrase structure, which Shostakovich does not usually favour.

The opening movement is cast in a sonata form that proceeds straightfor-wardly, except for the off-tonic beginning of the recapitulation. The 'adagio' begins as a 'strophic variations' movement (a form associated with the early Baroque in which a melodic strand, usually in the bass, is repeated with changes each time to its metrical and/or rhythmic structure). However, after the cello has reproduced, with rhythmic variation, the unusually long, discursive melody initially stated by the first violin, this idea gives way to a new lyrical theme, also for cello, which has a much more emphat-ically 'major' colouring than one is accustomed to find in late Shostakovich. The variation theme then returns once, but is this time truncated and shared out among the instruments.

The finale is in a complex form, the most 'regular' component of which is a series of variations on a repetitive melodic pattern (a childlike, regressive version of the first movement's opening theme) given out at the start by the unaccompanied first violin. Between the variations, however, there occurs a succession of memorable episodes and digressions. These acquire more prominence than the variations themselves, whose main function is to provide continuity—their use is in this respect comparable with that of the composer's monogram in the Eighth Quartet. From figures 62 to 64 the first violin has a new melody in the home key, F sharp major. The cello responds with its own melody (this time, a close paraphrase of the first movement's opening theme) in the same key at figure 64. Between figures 67 and 74 Shostakovich introduces a skittish new cello melody (very much in the style of second subjects in the early quartets) and then subjects it to a series of three fantastic quasi-variations: 'quasi', because although the hocketed fig-uration of each variation is entirely regular (the four instruments toss around tiny thematic particles initially of quavers, then of triplet quavers, and finally of semiquavers), there is no regularity in the melodic and harmonic shape of the particles themselves—no apparent theme, in fact. At figure 75 the cello intones the same melody from *Lady Macbeth* used in Quartet No. 8—but here with a special punning intention, since Katerina's lover, whom she is passionately addressing, bears the same given name, Sergei (the opera's text uses the diminutive form, Seryozha), as the dedica-tee. At figure 76 there is another miniature set of variations, on a new

---

[43] The first violin, too, has remarkable salience; it constantly dialogues or 'duets' with the cello. If one knew more about the interpersonal dynamics of the members of the Beethoven Quartet, one might attempt to account for this.

metamorphosis of the first movement's opening theme. The first episodic theme, nudged up a semitone to G major and transferred to the cello, returns at figure 83. At figures 86 and 89, respectively, the two themes of the slow movement return to close the movement in an unexpectedly lyrical vein.

It is conventional among commentators to describe the last three Shostakovich quartets as haunted by thoughts of death. This seems totally inappropriate for No. 14, which begins with good-humoured drollery and ends in radiant consolation. The form of its finale, so episodic on the surface, is in fact more complex, and thematically richer, than any other in the quartets. It interweaves several ideas of its own into ones taken from the previous two movements and combines introversive and extroversive reference in a fascinating tapestry. Like the finale of No. 7, but in a much more lyrical spirit, it shows that summativity need not be coupled with monumentality.

*Quartet No. 15 in E flat minor, Op. 144.*   Shostakovich must have resigned himself to the probability that Quartet No. 15 would be his last. This is a valedictory quartet with a valedictory finale. Superficially, the quartet, with its six movements, resembles the suite-like No. 11. But there are two important differences: the first is that all the movements have the same tonic, E flat minor (this unexpected homotonality provides a link with the Baroque suite); the second is that all the movements are, in differing degrees, slow—this fact calls to mind such cycles as Haydn's *Seven Last Words from the Cross.*

The language of the quartet is late-period Shostakovich at its most etiolated and enigmatic. Its movements subsist on tiny musical particles, which are centonized into larger units that always sound fragile and provisional, ready to transmute at the first opportunity. Here and there, one catches a fleeting allusion to another work, but nothing remains long enough to be consolidated. Shostakovich starts with an 'Elegy', the most extended and also the most regularly formed movement; its sonata-form structure has a kind of fugato and a 'consolation' theme as its two subjects. There follow a shadowy 'Serenade' with grotesque interludes; an 'Intermezzo', in which a motif from the Fifth Symphony is introduced;[44] a 'Nocturne' in which a sinuous melody stealthily glides through enveloping broken chords; and a 'Funeral March', in which the characteristic Beethovenian (and Chopinesque) dotted rhythms appear. Last comes the 'Epilogue', which until the very end is merely recollective, recalling (though always with modifications) ideas from each of the previous movements. But then Shostakovich springs a surprise: nervous tremors on the three upper strings (see Ex. 10.6) evoke the first stirrings of the fire music with which, at the end of Wagner's *Die Walküre*, Loge surrounds the sleeping Brünnhilde as Wotan finally leaves her. Is this the composer's way of saying that death is only a sleep, from which a future awakening is possible?

---

[44]  At figure 43 we hear the motif that appears at the same figure, 43, in the first movement of the symphony.

Ex. 10.6.   Shostakovich, String Quartet No. 15 in E flat minor, Op. 144, last movement, bars 74–85

In this quartet, and in all the others, Shostakovich treats the finale as an opportunity rather than as a problem. He is a composer blessed with the ability to handle successfully both long-range thematic or tonal relationships (e.g. how the finale stands in relation to the first movement) and short-range ones (e.g. how the end of the preceding movement connects with the start of the finale). He understands how to make a finale 'belong' without taking anything away from its individuality. Above all, he never loses sight of the finale's role as the last part of a narrative that has to be concluded satisfyingly, whether in a conventional manner or otherwise.

And so we reach the end of the investigation. One further question, however, remains to be asked. If there is such a thing as 'finale studies', could one not also have 'slow movement studies', 'extra movement (minuet, scherzo, etc.) studies', and 'first movement studies'?

I believe that all of these are possibilities which, if tackled in the right way, would prove interesting and enlightening. In relation to the first of them, we would have to distinguish between an external slow movement (our 'valedictory' finale is in fact one of these) and an internal one; we could profitably trace the development of the lyrical middle movement from its origins in concertos by Albinoni and Vivaldi (and perhaps other composers active around 1700) up to its modern apotheosis as 'mood music'. For the minuet and its later or substitute forms we could establish a complex typology and work out in more detail the rationale for placing it either before or after the slow movement. Of first-movement studies (even if not usually termed such) there is already no lack, although most of these treat an opening movement as a paradigm for the entire cyclic work rather than as a movement with a unique position and function. It would repay the effort to study first movements specifically as 'breakers of the silence' and also to examine the ways in which they sometimes withhold their own completion for the sake of the movements that follow—the finale, in particular. There is also much more to say about tempo and pulse relationships between the several movements.

But finales will always retain a special place by virtue of a simple fact. Every other movement can leave unfinished business behind it, but a finale cannot. It sweeps up, dusts down, disposes of the litter, rearranges the furniture, and switches out the lights. But it does not have to leave the room in exactly its original state, and it is this margin for change that constitutes one of its most fascinating aspects and an important theme of this book.

# BIBLIOGRAPHY

[Accademia della Crusca], *Vocabolario degli Accademici della Crusca*, 6 vols. (Florence, 1729–38).

AGAWU, V. KOFI, *Playing with Signs: A Semiotic Interpretation of Classic Music* (Princeton, 1991).

APEL, WILLI, *Die italienische Violinmusik im 17. Jahrhundert* (Wiesbaden, 1983).

BEKKER, PAUL, *Gustav Mahlers Sinfonien* (Berlin, 1921).

BERLIOZ, HECTOR, *The Art of Music and Other Essays (À travers chants)*, trans. and ed. Elizabeth Csicsery-Rónay (Bloomington and Indianapolis, Ind., 1994).

BONDS, MARK EVAN, *Wordless Rhetoric: Musical Form and the Metaphor of the Oration* (Cambridge, Mass., 1991).

BRAUN, JOACHIM, 'The Double Meaning of Jewish Elements in Dmitri Shostakovich's Music', *Musical Quarterly*, 71 (1985), 68–80.

BROSSARD, SÉBASTIEN DE, *Dictionnaire de musique* (Paris, 1703).

BROYLES, MICHAEL, 'Organic Form and the Binary Repeat', *Musical Quarterly*, 66 (1980), 339–60.

BUHLER, JAMES, '"Breakthrough" as Critique of Form: The Finale of Mahler's First Symphony', *19th Century Music*, 20 (1996–7), 125–43.

BURROWS, DAVID, 'Style in Culture: Vivaldi, Zeno and Ricci', *Journal of Interdisciplinary History*, 4 (1973–4), 1–23.

CAHN, PETER, 'Aspekte der Schlussgestaltung in Beethovens Instrumentalwerken', *Archiv für Musikwissenschaft*, 39 (1982), 19–31.

CARNER, MOSCO, 'The Orchestral Music', in Gerald Abraham (ed.), *Schumann: A Symposium* (London, 1952), 176–244.

CHAMBERS, EPHRAIM, *Cyclopaedia: Or, an Universal Dictionary of Arts and Sciences*, 2 vols. (London, 1728) (with subsequent editions in 1738, 1751–3, and 1779–83).

COLE, MALCOLM S., 'The Vogue of the Instrumental Rondo in the Late Eighteenth Century', *Journal of the American Musicological Society*, 22 (1969), 425–55.

—— 'Czerny's Illustrated Description of the Rondo or Finale', *Music Review*, 36 (1975), 5–16.

—— 'Haydn's Symphonic Rondo-Finales: Their Structural and Stylistic Evolution', *Haydn Yearbook*, 13 (1982), 113–42.

CONE, EDWARD T., *Musical Form and Musical Performance* (New York, 1968).

—— 'Schubert's Beethoven', *Musical Quarterly*, 56 (1970), 779–93.

—— *The Composer's Voice* (Berkeley and Los Angeles, 1974).

—— 'Schubert's Unfinished Business', *19th Century Music*, 7 (1983–4), 222–32.

CZERNY, CARL, *School of Practical Composition or Complete Treatise on the Composition of All Kinds of Music both Vocal and Instrumental from the most simple Theme to the Grand Sonata and Symphony and from the shortest Song to the Opera, the Mass, and the Oratorio: together with a Treatise on Instrumentation*, trans. John Bishop, vol. i (London, c.1848).

DAHLHAUS, CARL, 'Studien zu romantischen Symphonien', *Jahrbuch des Staatlichen Instituts für Musikforschung Preussischer Kulturbesitz* (Berlin, 1972), 104–19.

DAHLHAUS, CARL, *Esthetics of Music*, trans. William W. Austin (Cambridge, 1982).

DAHLHAUS, CARL, *Nineteenth-Century Music*, trans. J. Bradford Robinson (Berkeley and Los Angeles, 1989).

DAVERIO, JOHN, 'Formal Design and Terminology in the Pre-Corellian "Sonata" and Related Instrumental Forms in the Printed Sources' (Ph.D. diss., Boston University, 1983).

——*Robert Schumann: Herald of a 'New Poetic Age'* (New York and Oxford, 1997).

DELL'ANTONIO, ANDREA, *Syntax, Form and Genre in Sonatas and Canzonas, 1621–1635* (Lucca, 1997).

DENNY, THOMAS A., 'Articulation, Elision, and Ambiguity in Schubert's Mature Sonata Forms: The Op. 99 Trio Finale in its Context', *Journal of Musicology*, 6 (1988), 340–66.

DEVOTO, MARK, 'The Russian Submediant in the Nineteenth Century', *Current Musicology*, 59 (1995), 48–76.

DOWNS, PHILIP, 'Beethoven's "New Way" and the *Eroica*', *Musical Quarterly*, 56 (1970), 585–604.

DUNSBY, JONATHAN, 'The Multi-Piece in Brahms: *Fantasien* Op. 116', in Robert Pascall (ed.), *Brahms: Biographical, Documentary and Analytical Studies* (Cambridge, 1983), 167–89.

EIGELDINGER, JEAN-JACQUES, 'Placing Chopin: Reflections on a Compositional Aesthetics', in John Rink and Jim Samson (eds.), *Chopin Studies 2* (Cambridge, 1994), 102–39.

EVERETT, PAUL, *Vivaldi, The Four Seasons and Other Concertos*, Op. 8 (Cambridge, 1996).

FANNING, DAVID, commentary to catalogue entries 115 and 116 in Felix Meyer (ed.), *Setting New Scores: Music Manuscripts from the Paul Sacher Foundation* (Basle, 1998), 235–8.

FISCHER, WILHELM, 'Zur Entwicklungsgeschichte des Wiener klassischen Stils', *Studien zur Musikwissenschaft*, 3 (1915), 24–84.

FULLER, DAVID, 'Suite', in *The New Grove Dictionary of Music and Musicians*, ed. Stanley Sadie (London, 1980), xviii. 333–50.

GALAND, JOEL, 'Rondo-Form Problems in Eighteenth- and Nineteenth-Century Instrumental Music, with Reference to the Application of Schenker's Form Theory to Historical Criticism' (Ph.D. diss., Yale University, 1990).

GENETTE, GÉRARD, *Paratexts*, trans. Jane E. Lewin (Cambridge, 1997).

GIRDLESTONE, CUTHBERT M., *Mozart's Piano Concertos* (London, 1958²).

GOEHR, LYDIA, *The Imaginary Museum of Musical Works: An Essay in the Philosophy of Music* (Oxford, 1992).

GOMBRICH, ERNST, *The Sense of Order: A Study in the Psychology of Decorative Art* (Oxford, 1984²).

GRAYSON, DAVID A., *Mozart: Piano Concertos No. 20 in D minor, K. 466, and No. 21 in C major, K. 467* (Cambridge, 1998).

GRIFFITHS, PAUL, *The String Quartet* (London, 1983).

GROVE, SIR GEORGE, *Beethoven and his Nine Symphonies* (London, 1896²).

HAIMO, ETHAN, *Haydn's Symphonic Forms* (Oxford, 1995).

HOPKINS, G. W., 'Shostakovich's Ninth String Quartet', *Tempo*, 75 (1965–6), 23–5.

HOPKINS, ROBERT G., 'When a Coda is More than a Coda: Reflections on Beethoven', in Eugene Narmour and Ruth A. Solie (eds.), *Explorations in Music, the Arts and Ideas: Essays in Honor of Leonard B. Meyer* (Stuyvesant, NY, 1988), 393–410.

HULME, DEREK C., *Dmitri Shostakovich: A Catalogue, Bibliography, and Discography* (Oxford, 1991²).

KALLBERG, JEFFREY, 'The Rhetoric of Genre: Chopin's Nocturne in G Minor', *19th Century Music*, 11 (1987–8), 238–61.

KELLER, HANS, 'Shostakovich's Twelfth Quartet', *Tempo*, 94 (1970), 6–15.

—— *The Great Haydn Quartets: Their Interpretation* (London, 1993²).

KERMAN, JOSEPH, 'Notes on Beethoven's Codas', *Beethoven Studies*, 3 (1982), 141–60.

KERMODE, FRANK, *The Sense of an Ending* (New York, 1967).

KEYS, IVOR, *Brahms Chamber Music* (London, 1974).

KING, A. H., 'Mountains, Music and Musicians', *Musical Quarterly*, 31 (1945), 395–419.

KIRKENDALE, WARREN, *Fugue and Fugato in Rococo and Classical Chamber Music*, trans. Margaret Bent and the Author (Durham, NC, 1979).

KLENZ, WILLIAM C., *Giovanni Battista Bononcini of Modena* (Durham, NC, 1962).

KOCH, HEINRICH CHRISTOPH, *Versuch einer Anleitung zur Composition*, 3 vols. (Leipzig Rudolstadt, 1782–93).

—— *Musikalisches Lexikon* (Frankfurt am Main, 1802).

LANGER, SUSANNE K., *Philosophy in a New Key* (Cambridge, Mass., 1951).

LEICHTENTRITT, HUGO, *Musikalische Formenlehre* (Leipzig, 1952⁵ [repr. in facsimile from the 3rd edn. of 1907]).

LEVY, DAVID B., *Beethoven: The Ninth Symphony* (New York, c.1995).

LEVY, JANET M., 'Covert and Casual Values in Recent Writings about Music', *Journal of Musicology*, 5 (1987), 3–27.

LIVINGSTONE, ERNEST F., 'Das Formproblem des 4. Satzes in Beethovens 9. Symphonie', in *Bericht über den Internationalen Musikwissenschaftlichen Kongress Bonn 1970*, ed. Carl Dahlhaus *et al.* (Kassel, 1971), 494–7.

MARSTON, NICHOLAS, *Schumann: Fantasie, Op. 17* (Cambridge, 1992).

MASON, COLIN, 'Form in Shostakovich's Quartets', *Musical Times*, 103 (1962), 531–3.

MATTHESON, JOHANN, *Das neu-eröffnete Orchestre* (Hamburg, 1713).

—— *Der vollkommene Capellmeister* (Hamburg, 1739).

MERCER-TAYLOR, PETER, 'Mendelssohn's "Scottish" Symphony and the Music of German Memory', *19th Century Music*, 19 (1995–6), 68–82.

MEYER, LEONARD B., *Music, the Arts and Ideas: Patterns and Predictions in Twentieth-Century Culture* (Chicago, 1967).

MICZNIK, VERA, 'The Farewell Story of Mahler's Ninth Symphony', *19th Century Music*, 20 (1996–7), 144–66.

NATTIEZ, JEAN-JACQUES, 'Can One Speak of Narrativity in Music?', trans. Katharine Ellis, *Journal of the Royal Musical Association*, 115 (1990), 240–57.

NEWCOMB, ANTHONY, 'Once More "Between Absolute and Program Music": Schumann's Second Symphony', *19th Century Music*, 7 (1983–4), 233–50.

NEWLIN, DIKA, *Bruckner, Mahler, Schoenberg* (New York, 1947).

NEWMAN, WILLIAM S., *The Sonata since Beethoven* (New York and London, 1972²).

—— *The Sonata in the Classic Era* (New York and London, 1983³).

O'LOUGHLIN, NIALL, 'Shostakovich's String Quartets', *Tempo*, 87 (1968–9), 9–16.

POZNANSKY, ALEXANDER, *Tchaikovsky's Last Days: A Documentary Study* (Oxford, 1996).

PROUT, EBENEZER, *Applied Forms* (London, 1895).

QUANTZ, JOHANN JOACHIM, *Versuch einer Anweisung, die Flöte traversière zu spielen* (Berlin, 1789³).

RATNER, LEONARD G., *Classic Music: Expression, Form, and Style* (New York, 1980).

RINGER, ALEXANDER, 'Clementi and the *Eroica*', *Musical Quarterly*, 47 (1961), 464–8.

ROSEN, CHARLES, *The Classical Style: Haydn, Mozart, Beethoven* (London, 1971).

—— *Sonata Forms* (New York, 1988²).

SAID, EDWARD W., *Beginnings: Intention and Method* (London, 1997³).

SANDERS, ERNEST H., 'Form and Content in the Finale of Beethoven's Ninth Symphony', *Musical Quarterly*, 50 (1964), 59–76.

SEIDEL, WILHELM, 'Schnell–Langsam–Schnell: Zur klassischen Theorie des instrumentalen Zyklus', *Musiktheorie*, 1 (1986), 205–16.

SIMPSON, ROBERT, *Carl Nielsen: Symphonist* (New York, 1979²).

SISMAN, ELAINE R., *Haydn and the Classical Variation* (Cambridge, Mass., 1993).

—— *Mozart: The Jupiter Symphony* (Cambridge, 1993).

SMITH, BARBARA HERRNSTEIN, *Poetic Closure: A Study of How Poems End* (Chicago, 1968).

SOLOMON, MAYNARD, 'Schubert's "Unfinished" Symphony', *19th Century Music*, 21 (1997–8), 111–33.

SOMFAI, LÁSZLÓ, 'Vom Barock zur Klassik: Umgestaltung der Proportionen und des Gleichgewichts in zyklischen Werken Joseph Haydns', in Gerda Mraz *et al.* (eds.), *Joseph Haydn und seine Zeit* ( Jahrbuch für Österreichische Kulturgeschichte, 2; Eisenstadt, 1972), 64–72.

SPONHEUER, BERND, 'Haydns Arbeit am Finalproblem', *Archiv für Musikwissenschaft*, 34 (1977), 199–224.

STRACHAN, IAIN, 'Shostakovich's "DSCH" Signature in the String Quartets', *DSCH Journal*, 10 (Winter 1998), 48–9.

STRAVINSKY, IGOR, *Poetics of Music in the Form of Six Lessons*, trans. Arthur Knodel and Ingolf Dahl (Cambridge, Mass., and London, 1970).

STROHM, REINHARD, *Dramma per musica: Italian Opera Seria of the Eighteenth Century* (New Haven and London, 1997).

TALBOT, MICHAEL, 'Modal Shifts in the Sonatas of Domenico Scarlatti', *Chigiana*, 40, NS 20 (1985), 25–43.

—— *Tomaso Albinoni: The Venetian Composer and his World* (Oxford, 1990).

—— 'The *Taiheg*, the *Pira* and Other Curiosities of Benedetto Vinaccesi's *Suonate da camera a tre*, Op. 1', *Music and Letters*, 75 (1994), 344–64.

—— 'The Work-Concept and Composer-Centredness', in Michael Talbot (ed.), *The Musical Work: Reality or Invention?* (Liverpool, 2000), 168–86.

—— 'Vivaldi's *Quadro*? The Case of RV Anh. 66 Reconsidered', *Analecta musicologica*, forthcoming.

TARASTI, EERO, *A Theory of Musical Semiotics* (Bloomington, Ind.,1994).

TARUSKIN, RICHARD, 'Public Lies and Unspeakable Truth: Interpreting Shostakovich's Fifth Symphony', in David Fanning (ed.), *Shostakovich Studies* (Cambridge, 1995), 17–56.

TILMOUTH, MICHAEL, 'Finale', in *The New Grove Dictionary of Music and Musicians*, ed. Stanley Sadie (London, 1980), vi. 558.

Tobel, Rudolf von, *Die Formenwelt der klassischen Instrumentalmusik* (Bern and Leipzig, 1935).

Tovey, Donald F., *Essays in Musical Analysis* (London, 1935–9).

Treitler, Leo, 'History, Criticism, and Beethoven's Ninth Symphony', *19th Century Music*, 3 (1979–80), 193–210.

Vickers, Brian, 'Figures of Rhetoric/Figures of Music?', *Rhetorica*, 2 (1984), 1–44.

Volkov, Solomon, *Testimony: The Memoirs of Shostakovich* (London, 1979).

Wagner, Cosima, *Die Tagebücher*, 2 vols. (Munich, 1977).

Warrack, John, *Carl Maria von Weber* (London, 1968).

Webster, James, *Haydn's Farewell Symphony and the Idea of Classical Style: Through-Composition and Cyclic Integration in his Instrumental Music* (Cambridge, 1991).

—— 'The Form of the Finale of Beethoven's Ninth Symphony', *Beethoven Forum*, 1 (1992), 25–62.

Wheelock, Gretchen A., *Haydn's Ingenious Jesting with Art: Contexts of Musical Wit and Humor* (New York, 1992).

White, Chappell, *From Vivaldi to Viotti: A History of the Early Classical Violin Concerto* (Philadelphia, 1992).

Whittall, Arnold, 'Two of a Kind? Brahms's Op. 51 Finales', in Michael Musgrave (ed.), *Brahms 2: Biographical, Documentary and Analytical Studies* (Cambridge, 1987), 145–64.

Wilson, Elizabeth, *Shostakovich: A Life Remembered* (London, 1994).

Wörner, Karl H., *Das Zeitalter der thematischen Prozesse in der Geschichte der Musik* (Regensburg, 1969).

Zaslaw, Neal, *Mozart's Symphonies: Context, Performance Practice, Reception* (Oxford, 1989).

Zilkens, Udo, *Beethovens Finalsätze in den Klaviersonaten: Allgemeine Strukturen und individuelle Gestaltung* (Rodenkirchen, 1994).

# INDEX TO MUSICAL WORKS

Pages containing musical examples are shown in *italics*.

# GENERAL INDEX

Where headings or subheadings are followed by an asterisk, reference is selective. Sequences of pages are shown in **bold** if the subject appears in them intermittently (i.e. not as a continuous argument and not necessarily on each intervening page).

Abraham, Gerald 135 n 8
Accademia della Crusca 16
'accompanied' sonata 155
Adagio, popular in the 20th c. 118
Adams, John 55, 180
Aeolian scale 124
Agawu, V. Kofi 4, 65 n 35, 198 n 1
Albinoni, Tomaso 64, 118, 173–4, 228
Algarotti, Francesco 163
Alkan, (Charles-)Valentin 7 n 12, 28, 67, 90, 107 n 2, 111–12, 179
allemande (*allemanda*)* 46, 128, 143, 144
Altman, Yevgeni 200 n 4
Apel, Willi 26
arch form 62 n 29, 162, 218
Arensky, Anton 147 n 14

Bach, Carl Philipp Emanuel 62 n 24, 165
Bach, Johann Christian 58
Bach, Johann Sebastian 5 n 8, 14, **19–34**, 37 n 2, 45, 46, 47, **55–67**, 94 n 27, 96 n 30, 100, 102, 104 n 38, 124, 126, **141–51**, **173–80**, 184–5, 198, 202, 205, 225
Bach revival 147
Balakirev, Mily 166
Baldini, Giuseppe 143 n 9
balletto:
  as dance 46
  synonymous with suite 21, 143
banquet, as metaphor for a multimovement work 106
bar form 37
Barber, Samuel 118, 127, 155, 180
Bargiel, Woldemar 147
Barthélemon, François 175 n 50
Bartók, Béla 14, 74, 107 n 2, 121, 126, 148, 154, 162, 180, 203, 214, 216, 224
Bauer-Lechner, Natalie 7 n 13
Becker, Dietrich 144
Beethoven, Ludwig van **1–13**, 20, **27–34**, **52–79**, **82–104**, **111–26**, 127–8, 131, 133, **145–79**, **183–96**, 197, **205–26**
Beethoven Quartet 199, 200, 223, 224, 225
beginnings, character of 4–5
Bekker, Paul 13, 45 n 8, 47, 96, 116
  his views on the evolution of the symphony 13, 96, 169–71
Bennett, William Sterndale 147

Berg, Alban 29, 89 n 20, 142 n 4, 175, 180, 203
Beria, Lavrenti 221
Berlioz, Hector 7 n 12, 17, 29, 62, 83, 88, 90, 101, 122, 169, 186, 193 n 17
Berwald, Franz 72, 162
Biber, Heinrich 100
bifocal close 19, 97 n 31
bifocal recapitulation 19
binary form* 57, 61, 65–7, 73, 151
  mimics ritornello form 66, 173
binary variant 59, 66
biography, as a basis for music 88, 90, 133
Bishop, John 1 n 1
Bizet, Georges 55, 96, 148
Blake, William 186
Boccherini, Luigi 150, 155 n 24, 165
Boismortier, Joseph Bodin de 157
Bonds, Mark Evan 19, 89
Bonporti, Francesco Antonio 145
Borisovsky, Vadim 199, 200, 224
Borodin, Alexander 118, 166, 205
Boulez, Pierre 89 n 20
bourrée 144
Brahms, Johannes 12, 15, 29, 31–3, 50, 68–9, 72 n 55, 75 n 62, 80, 98–9, 108, 116, 119, 127, 155 n 23, **162–79**, 198
Braun, Joachim 204 n 14, 207 n 21
breakthrough (*Durchbruch*) 131 n 3, 138
Britten, Benjamin 107 n 2, 125 n 23
Brossard, Sébastien de 16
Broyles, Michael 89
Bruckner, Anton 7, 12, 13, 45 n 8, 65, 79, 90, 99–102, 113–14, 118 n 18, 166, 169, 170, 171, 197
Brumel, Antoine 40–1
Buhler, James 135, 136, 137
Burney, Charles 58
Burrows, David 26
Busoni, Ferruccio 179
Byrd, William 21 n 10

'café-Hungarian' style 131, 221
Cage, John 202
Cahn, Peter 185 n 10
calculated inconclusiveness 121
cantata, for solo voice 149
Carner, Mosco 135
Castello, Dario 21–5, 219

Said, Edward W. 4
Saint-Saëns, Camille 147–8
Samson, Jim 66 n 38
Sanders, Ernest H. 168 n 38
sarabande (*sarabanda*) 46, 143, 144, 150
*Satz*, its meaning 17
Scarlatti, Alessandro 163
Scarlatti, Domenico 66, 73, 149, 152
Schein, Johann Hermann 46–7, 106
scherzo, its position in the cycle 52, 107,
    165–6, 228
Schiller, Friedrich 94, 169
Schlegel, August Wilhelm 89
Schoenberg, Arnold 8, 29, 89, 122, 142, 148,
    223
Schubert, Franz 12, 13, 59, 62 n 26, **65–79**, 97,
    98, 112–14, 119, 133, 145, 156, 169–70, 171,
    172, 179, 197, 201, 208 n 25
Schulhoff, Erwin 168, 172
Schumann, Clara 133
Schumann, Robert 12, 29–30, 32, 33, 62,
    75 n 63, 96–8, 109, 132–5, 136 n 11, 139,
    142, 155 n 23, 165, 170, 171, 178, 184 n 6,
    217
Schütz, Heinrich 99, 220
score, as carrier of a work's identity 28, 34
Sechter, Simon 65
Seidel, Wilhelm 55, 107–8, 198
Selfridge-Field, Eleanor 22, 24
sensuous vagueness 99, 101
serenade 29, 140
*Seufzer* figure 207
sewing-machine rhythms 124
Shebalin, Vissarion 199
Shirinsky, Sergei 199, 200, 225
Shirinsky, Vasili 199, 220, 223
Shostakovich, Dmitri 12, 14, 29, 30, 51, 65,
    68–9, 107 n 2, 121, 123, 124 n 21, 154, 163,
    166, 172, 198–228
  his bass lines 205
  favours inter-movement links 204–5
  favours moderate tempi 204–5
  favours thin textures 202
  fond of intensive development 205
  influenced by Bach 205
  influenced by Beethoven 205
  influenced by Jewish music 30, 204, 207,
    209, 211–12, 221
  'late-period' manner 199, 205
  his musical monogram DSCH 200 n 3, 203,
    208, 212, 213, 217, 218, 225
  octatonic elements in his music 203
  uses few supplementary markings 203
Shostakovich, Irina 199
Shostakovich, Nina 199
Sibelius, Jean 29, 103–5, 124, 148, 172, 208
Simpson, Robert 12
Simrock, publishing house 33
Sisman, Elaine R. 48 n 11, 63, 65 n 35

Skryabin, Alexander 7 n 16, 28–9, 114–15, 118,
    155, 200, 201
slow introductions, distinguished from slow
    movements 20
Smetana, Bedřich 90, 162, 194
Smith, Barbara Herrnstein 7, 71–2, 108, 186
social realism 201
socialist realism 83, 199, 201, 202
Solie, Ruth A. 193 n 18
Solomon, Maynard 112, 113
Somfai, László 57 n 7
Somis, Giovanni Battista 149
sonata* 1–2, 7, 140, 149–55
  associated with female performers 151–2
  forms used in* 2, 64
  name for any kind of instrumental
    movement 143 n 7
  its structure 21–27, 48, 56, 126, **149–55**
  see also *Finalsonate*
*sonata a quattro* 157
sonata form* **57–62**
sonata-rondo form* 61, 151, 154–5
  converges with sonata form 61–2, 154–5
sonatina form 59
Spohr, Louis 167, 179
Sponheuer, Bernd 13, 47, 91
Stalin, Josef 200, 201, 204, 211
Steibelt, Daniel 1
Stevenson, Ronald 31
Strachan, Iain 200 n 3
Stradella, Alessandro 48–9
Strauss, Richard 29, 87, 138, 170, 206
Stravinsky, Igor 84, 163, 172, 180, 202
string quartet* 2, 7
  its evolution 156–7
  its structure 155–63
Strohm, Reinhard 163, 164
strophic variations 225
subdominant emphasis 75, 96, 174 n 48, 188,
    189, 190
suite (*seguita*, sett)* 29, 140–8, 222, 226
  its alternative names 143
  'antique' type 145, 147
  avoids run-on relationships 141
  avoids slow movements 142
  'characteristic' type 145
  its entertainment function 147
  its evolution 21, 141–7
  'extract' type 145, 147
  its retrospective character, in the 20th
    c. 148
  its revival 145–8
  its structure 46–8
  as title 141
summative transformation 136
symmetry and asymmetry, in instrumental
    cycles 108
symphonic concerto 179
symphony* 1 2, 7, 140, 163–72